Lives of
POOR BOYS
who became
FAMOUS

By Sarah K. Bolton

FAMOUS MEN OF SCIENCE

LIVES OF POOR BOYS WHO BECAME FAMOUS

LIVES OF GIRLS WHO BECAME FAMOUS

FAMOUS AMERICAN AUTHORS

Lives of

POOR BOYS

who became

FAMOUS

Sarah K. Bolton

Illustrated by
CONSTANCE JOAN NAAR

THOMAS Y. CROWELL COMPANY
New York

PRINTED IN THE UNITED STATES OF AMERICA
ISBN 0-690-50301-6

Contents

Benjamin Franklin

Among the many great figures of American history, there are few more interesting or versatile personalities than Benjamin Franklin. For, in the course of his long life, this many sided man achieved worldwide fame as a newspaperman, philosopher, statesman, scientist, diplomat and humanitarian; and there is scarcely a field of human endeavor to which he did not make some valuable contribution. He was one of America's first citizens of the world.

Benjamin Franklin was born in Boston, January 17, 1706, the son of Josiah Franklin, a soap and candle maker who was hard pressed to support his large family of seventeen children. Benjamin was the fifteenth child, and, when he was only ten years old, his parents decided somewhat reluctantly that he must choose a trade. The idea of being apprenticed did not appeal to the boy, for he had a quick and eager mind and had already discovered the magic world of books which he wished to explore. His mother would have liked to encourage her studious son, and because of his fondness for books, suggested that he might like to become a preacher. But a story told at this time makes it quite clear that young Franklin was not of a religious turn of mind. One day, it is said, the boy and his father were down in the cellar packing a barrel of meat, when he asked: "Father, why don't you say a blessing over this whole barrel of meat right here? It would save wasting so much time and breath at the table!"

Soon after this revealing incident, Josiah Franklin took his young son and went about with him among the various tradesmen of Boston. They visited the shops of carpenters, bricklayers, coopers, shoemakers, and blacksmiths. But the boy found none of these trades to his liking. Finally his father said to him kindly enough, for he could not help loving the bright and even-tempered lad, "Very well, you shall be my apprentice until you decide what you wish to do." So for a time Benjamin ladled grease, measured wicks, and dipped candles in his father's workshop. He hated the work and soon began to think of running away to sea, as one of his elder brothers had done. Fortunately for him, however, his father was a discerning man who did not wish to lose another of his sons to the sea, and who therefore began to look about him for some other more congenial trade for the boy. After

CJ NAAR

3

the matter had been put to him seriously, young Benjamin decided that he would really like to be a printer. His eldest brother, James, was a printer and he could learn the trade with him. James Franklin needed a boy just at this time, so the papers were signed and Benjamin was bound over to his brother for nine years. He would then be of age and a full-fledged printer.

The boy began his apprenticeship with high hopes. In those days, the profession of printing was one of considerable importance in the community. People referred to the printer as "Mr. Printer" or "Mr. Editor," and took off their hats to him when they met him on the street. This was a pleasant prospect, but the lad found that the lot of a printer's "devil" was anything but an easy one. His brother, James, was bad-tempered and exacting and often cuffed him about from one job to another. Despite the manner in which he was treated, Benjamin learned the printing business from beginning to end. He ran errands, tied up bundles, cleaned presses and washed type. When his brother was out, he tried his hand at the case and before long he could set type and handle the press as proficiently as any man in the shop. He was soon promoted for his diligence, but the promotion did not help him much for he was still treated unkindly.

Doubtless the boy would not have put up with

this sort of treatment except for the fact that he had developed a real liking for printing and a desire to learn everything there was to know about the trade. He was now beginning to find himself and even to branch out a little. For some time, his evenings had been spent in studying and writing, and it occurred to him that he could write copy that was every bit as good as that which he set up on the press every day. So one evening he wrote an article in his very best style, and in the morning slipped it under the door of his brother's office. James Franklin was publisher of the *New England Courant,* one of the three papers printed in America, and, in spite of his unpleasant manners, he had excellent judgment in literary matters. He was delighted with Benjamin's article, and he published it under the impression that it was the work of some distinguished person who did not wish to sign it. Young Franklin kept up his little deception and his brother published many of the anonymous articles of his own apprentice. In addition to his articles, it is also said that the boy wrote some very good verse at this time. But his father happened to hear of it and hastened down to the *Courant* office to persuade his son to give up such a frivolous pursuit, for so it seemed to him.

Not long after this, there began for young Franklin a period that was to change the course of his life. The tensions of the *Courant* office and his brother's continued ill-temper made the boy restless and eager to break away. One day he decided to run away to New York. He had very little money and no knowledge of anything but printing, and he found the city inhospitable. At the only newspaper office he was curtly told that there was no place for him. Discouraged, he thought once more of the sea, but again the idea of his father's distress restrained him. He decided to try his luck in Philadelphia.

The journey there was a hard one. He had to walk a good part of the way. More than once he was held up as a runaway servant. Finally he found a boat going to the city and managed to get aboard by offering to work out his passage at the pumps. His arrival in the city which was to be his home for the rest of his life was hardly auspicious. He was tired, ragged and ravenously hungry. At the first bakery near the wharf, he stopped to buy three pennyworth of bread. To his astonishment he received three large rolls. His pockets were bulging with his little store of extra clothing, so he tucked a roll under each arm and walked along munching the third. Just then a pretty young girl came to the door of her home, and she laughed merrily as she watched the odd looking boy passing by. She was Deborah Read, and seven years later she became Franklin's wife.

Benjamin Franklin soon made a place for himself in Philadelphia. He worked and studied hard, often going without food in order to buy books. When he was still in his early twenties, he was owner and publisher of the Philadelphia *Gazette,* said to be one of the best papers in the colonies. The success of Franklin's paper was very largely due to the innovations he had made in newspaper publishing. He would have none of the single sheet of rather dull items which was the usual newspaper of those days. Instead, his paper contained bright, well-written articles on timely subjects, and was enlivened by the use of "ads," a great novelty at the time.

In addition to the newspaper, the Franklin press turned out a great many pamphlets or leaflets. To a great extent, these leaflets took the place of books as we know them, for in colonial days book publishing was a slow and expensive business with a limited market. Most of the leaflets were about politics and the rights of the colonies, subjects which were very dear to the freedom loving Americans of colonial times.

Franklin also ventured into the field of popular literature with great success. He knew that with the exception of the Bible the almanac was almost the only book in many colonial homes, and he determined to put out an almanac that would be readable, entertaining and worthwhile. He called it "Poor Richard's Almanac," and for twenty-five years the wise and witty sayings of "Poor Richard" delighted and amused the people of the colonies. At last, in the final issue, Franklin gathered together all his sayings throughout the years and put them into an address called "The Speech of Father Abraham." This wonderful speech, the talk of a wise old man to people who have come to a public sale, has been translated into ten different languages and is still famous throughout the world.

With his boundless energy, Franklin found time to take a very lively and practical interest in civic affairs in Philadelphia. He and his friends formed a club, the Junto or Leather Apron, for discussion and study. It was the habit of the members to bring what books they could to the club room, and then to borrow them from each other. From this beginning came the idea of a public library and a new way of learning was opened to the people. Next Franklin formed a Union Fire Company, the first of its kind in America, and a Fire Insurance Company. He observed the inefficiency of the old city watchman system and soon he had a movement on foot which grew into the modern police force of today. Largely at his instigation, the streets of Philadelphia were paved and lighted. He started a society for the study of science, and was a leader in founding a High School which later grew into the University of Pennsylvania. He also helped to start the first public hospital in America.

In 1737, Franklin was made Postmaster of Philadelphia, and later was made Postmaster General of the colonies. Here again his genius for practical organization demonstrated itself. When he took over, the mails were carried by post riders who traveled thirty miles a day on horseback. There were never more than three mails a week even between the largest cities; and the service, inadequate as it was, was a great financial drain on the colonies. Franklin improved the service immeasurably and introduced the idea of the penny stamp which was eventually to make the mails self-supporting and to lay the foundation for the wonderfully efficient postal service of today.

As Franklin grew older his interests constantly broadened. There was nothing in the least stuffy or preachy about him, but he did wonder a good deal about the qualities of mind and heart which go to make up the character of a really good man. With an engaging earnestness, he wrote out for himself a set of rules on order, simple living, truthfulness and justice which he tried to follow. When a Quaker friend told him that he thought too much of his own opinion, Franklin thanked him and, in a wry humor, made out another set of rules on meekness of spirit.

All his life long Franklin was hungry for knowledge, not because of personal ambition, but because he loved life and people and wanted to know all that he could about the world in which he lived. So much of his time was spent in reading and studying. He taught himself French, Italian, Spanish and Latin that he might enjoy the great literatures of the world. Like his father he loved music and could play the harp, the violin and the guitar. A good game of chess he regarded as a fine challenge to wit and skill. And he loved to talk—much to the delight of his listeners. For Franklin, with his keen mind and his wide knowledge, was one of the great wits of his time, and as a story-teller he charmed his audiences—whether they were his fellow workmen of the Philadelphia Junto, or the lords and ladies of the court of France.

While he was still a young man, Franklin found that his publishing business did not require all his attention, so he turned the active management over to a partner and prepared to devote more of his time to study and experiment in the field of science. He was one of the first to pioneer in sci-

entific farming, and much to the astonishment of
the neighboring farmers, he succeeded in producing a fine crop in a field that had always been barren and unproductive. All nature delighted him
and when, by chance, he came upon a colony of
ants he spent hours watching and studying their
habits. The result of his observations was a little
pamphlet on ants, written with such skill and accuracy that it aroused the interest of many leading
scientists.

Everyone is familiar with the story of how
Franklin drew electricity from the sky with only
a silk kite, a hemp string, and his own door key.
As simply as this did Franklin demonstrate that
lightning and thunder were caused by electric cur-
rents of air. It was too early for this knowledge to
be put to practical use, but Franklin's great discovery assured him of a permanent place in scientific history. Did he, perhaps, foresee in some way
how electricity would in time change the course of
the world by means of telephones, the telegraph,
electric lights, and radio?

It was natural that in days of stress the people of
the American colonies should turn for advice to a
man of Franklin's wisdom and broad experience.
Certainly no man in the colonies gave more of his
time and his devotion than Franklin did, for he
loved freedom as he loved his life. One of the most

troublesome problems confronting the colonies was that of securing some means of unified action. It was Franklin who drew up the famous Albany Plan of Union. The plan was not adopted because it was felt that it gave too much power to England, but it did provide a blueprint upon which later plans for unity of action were based.

When the difficulties between the colonies and the mother country became more serious, Franklin was sent to England to plead the case of a better understanding of colonial problems. There could have been no better choice. During his ten years in England, he worked with dogged patience to show the English people what America was really like. He made an enormous number of friends for himself and for his country, and he won over to the American cause many of the ablest and most respected men in English public life. But against the stubbornness of King George III and his little group of advisers he could not prevail. All his life Franklin had had a deeply rooted hatred of war, but now, when he saw that war between England and the colonies was inevitable, he returned to Philadelphia determined to help in whatever way he could.

Franklin was now sixty-nine years old, and he had earned a rest. However, scarcely had he landed when he was made a member of the Second Continental Congress; and to him went the tremendous job of helping to organize the Army and Navy and raising money. Undoubtedly, his arduous task was made a little easier for him by the fact that George Washington had been appointed Commander-in-Chief of the Army. For although Franklin was twenty-six years older than Washington, the two men were firm friends and had great faith in one another.

Franklin, along with Thomas Jefferson, John Adams, Roger Sherman and Robert R. Livingston, was appointed a member of the committee chosen to draw up the Declaration of Independence; and he played no small part in determining what that great document was to say. When the Declaration was read to the delegates, an appeal was made to all those present to sign it. "Aye," said Franklin quickly, "We must all hang together, or certainly we shall all hang separately." He knew the prime value of unity.

At first the war did not go well for the colonies and Franklin was asked to go to France and attempt to get help. Aged though he was, he did not refuse; for the people of the colonies knew his talents for persuasion and they had insisted that he be their envoy. They knew he was a born diplomat and they knew of old his knack for getting whatever was needed. Had he not, they asked, solved the dilemma of the Quakers who were eager to support the colonies, but could not do so because of their religion? Ingeniously, Franklin had substituted the word, "grain" for gunpowder and "fire-engines" for cannon, and had thus enabled the Quakers to vote money for the support of the war and to do it with a clear conscience.

The French were delighted when they heard that Franklin was to be the American Minister. And the indefatigable Franklin, with his charm, his resourcefulness, and his deep faith in the American cause got everything he asked for. The French sent soldiers and supplies to the colonies, lent them money, and arranged for the transfer of prisoners of war.

The war ended in 1783 and Franklin was one of the signers of the peace treaty. Two years later Jefferson was sent to France and Franklin was at last permitted to come home. Someone asked Jefferson if he had come to take Franklin's place. "No," he said. "No one could do that. I am just his successor."

Franklin had only five years to live in the United States, his own country, to which he had devoted so large a part of his life. After his return from France, his health suddenly failed and his last years were marred by illness and pain. On April 17, 1790, he died at the home of his daughter in

Philadelphia, aged eighty-four years and three months.

It is said that one of his last public acts was to write a letter to Congress, asking them to do away with slavery. Benjamin Franklin with his great vision and his wisdom was always ahead of his time.

Samuel Johnson

SAMUEL JOHNSON spent the better part of his life in an obscurity and a misery that would have crushed the talents of a lesser man. Yet, secure in the knowledge of his genius, this great man of English letters lived on to hear himself called the brightest ornament of the eighteenth century —a century studded with brilliant names.

He was born in Lichfield, England, in 1709, literally in the midst of books; for his father was a learned, if improvident, bookseller. The boy had access to all the books in his father's shop, and here, in long hours of browsing among the classics, he acquired much of that vast store of learning that was to astonish all who knew him in later years.

As they watched their son growing up, young Samuel's parents may well have had some misgivings about what the future held for him. He was an ungainly, awkward lad, afflicted with scrofula, a disfiguring disease that scarred his face and left him blind in one eye. It was one of the superstitions of the eighteenth century that the touch of the reigning monarch would cure this dreadful disease. The child's mother early seized upon this feeble hope and, when he was barely three, she bundled him up and took him to the court at London that he might receive the touch of Queen Anne. Of course no good came of this; but all his life Samuel Johnson cherished a little silver cup and spoon that his mother had bought for him as a memento of this trip.

But the boy's brilliance more than made up for his disfigured body. His memory was prodigious. When he was still in short dresses, his mother gave him the Prayer Book one day, and, pointing to the Collect, said, "You must get this by heart." She went upstairs, but no sooner had she reached the second floor than she heard him following. He could repeat the Collect perfectly, after having glanced over it but twice. He was often a lazy scholar so that sometimes his Latin had to be caned into him, but no schoolmaster ever forgot the brilliant lad. In fact, when he was grown and

CJ NAAR

about to leave for college, the mistress of the little dame school at which he first learned his letters appeared with a gift of gingerbread for him to take on his journey, saying that he was the best student she ever had.

By the time he was sixteen, the boy could learn nothing more in the local schools. He went to work in his father's shop and, in betweentimes, read everything within reach.

A friend of his family enabled young Johnson to enter Pembroke College at Oxford. His stay at college was anything but happy. His poverty, his ungainly appearance, and his inordinate pride placed the young man always on the defensive. He grew gruff; he rebuffed those who wished to help him; and he developed eccentricities of speech and manner that marked him all his life. He left Pembroke without a degree and cast about for employment.

Johnson knew better than anyone that he was not cut out to be a teacher, but for a time he worked as an usher in a grammar school, until he could stand the boys' gibes at him no longer. He left the school; and then, unpredictably, the penniless youth married. The marriage which seemed so foolhardy proved one of the great blessings of Johnson's life. His wife was a widow more than twice his age, and, by all accounts, neither very attractive, nor especially gifted. Yet Johnson found in her all the companionship and the understanding that he needed in his lonely, embittered life.

In 1737, Johnson went to London. He had decided to become a writer, but he had no illusions about what lay ahead of him. In the early eighteenth century, the profession of writing was at its lowest ebb, and an author was lucky if he kept himself out of debtor's prison. One publisher to whom Johnson applied for work advised him to get a job as a porter at which he could at least earn enough to keep himself in food. For years in London, Samuel Johnson labored at the most onerous and distasteful task of literary hackwork, but in whatever spare moments he had, he kept on at his own writing. When he was forty years old, he at last succeeded in publishing a long rhetorical poem, entitled *Vanity of Human Wishes*. This poem done in the best Classical manner is said by competent critics to be the most impressive thing of its kind in the English language. It brought the struggling author the recognition he deserved.

After several years spent in writing for periodicals of the day, the *Rambler* and the *Idler,* Johnson was commissioned to undertake a work for which he was pre-eminently suited, his great *Dictionary of the English Language*. His publisher paid him eight thousand dollars; but the work required

seven years and much clerical assistance. When
the *Dictionary* appeared in 1755, the author was
famous but practically penniless.

The publication of Johnson's *Dictionary* was
the occasion for one of the most famous literary re-
buffs in history. Almost a decade before, when he
had first begun the work, the obscure author had
waited upon the Earl of Chesterfield, a well-
known patron of the arts, from whom he hoped to
obtain assistance. He was turned away from the
great man's drawing room. By the time the *Dictionary* was ready, Johnson's fame had grown.
Lord Chesterfield thought that he would like to
be known as the patron of so distinguished a work;
he made discreet inquiries which reached Johnson's ears. In the morning, his Lordship received a
letter; with consummate dignity, the aging lexi-
cographer wrote: "The notice which you have been
pleased to take of my labors, had it been early, had
been kind; but it has been delayed till I am indifferent and cannot enjoy it; till I am solitary, and
cannot impart it; till I am known, and do not
want it. I hope it is no very cynical asperity not to
confess obligations where no benefit has been received, or to be unwilling that the Public should
consider me as owing that to a Patron, which
Providence has enabled me to do for myself."

The authoritative *Dictionary,* the first of its

kind, in which Johnson traced the strong roots of
the English language, established him as the ar-
biter of eighteenth-century letters. The role became him. Unquestionably, the learned man
ranked higher as a critic and a molder of literary
trends than he did as a creative writer. His best
work, a series of biographies of the English poets,
showed the analytical quality of his mind, and his
extraordinary critical gifts.

In 1762, Johnson was pensioned by the King for
his notable contributions to English letters. Free
from want for the first time in his life, he became
a familiar figure in the drawing rooms of London.
He was a famous talker, and loved to hold forth
at his Club where such men as Sir Joshua Rey-
nolds, Edmund Burke, and Oliver Goldsmith met
the lively challenge of his wit. Here, too, was his
ubiquitous biographer, James Boswell, who sat at
his feet and recorded for posterity all that the great
man had to say.

Early in his life Johnson acquired a reputation
for a satirical and biting tongue. Yet toward those
less fortunate than himself he was more than kind.
To the end of his days he maintained what can
only be called a household full of freaks. In this remarkable establishment there was a doddering
quack doctor named Levitt; a Miss Carmichael
whose antecedents no one knew; a tyrannical Mrs.

Desmoulins, and her aging daughter. None of these people had the remotest claim on Johnson and their combined eccentricities must have made a shambles of his home; yet he supported them without question because they had nowhere else to go.

The good Dr. Johnson died in 1784 and was buried in Westminster Abbey, not very far from the place to which he had been taken as a sick and ailing child to receive the Queen's touch.

James Watt

SOMETIMES it happens that a single great invention can change the lives of men the world over and set in motion a whole new era of human progress. One such invention was the printing press. Another was the steam engine without which our modern industrial society with all the benefits it has brought to mankind could never have developed.

James Watt, the inventor of the first practical steam engine, was born in the little town of Greenock, Scotland, on January 19, 1736. As a small child

he was very delicate and so he was not sent to school, but was taught at home. His mother taught him to read and his father taught him a little writing and arithmetic. The little boy was an apt student and, very early, he began to show his extraordinary talent for mechanics. When he was barely six, he would amuse himself for hours by drawing all kinds of mechanical lines and circles on the hearth with a colored piece of chalk. Another of his favorite games was to take apart his toy carpenter tools and to refashion them into different ones.

Despite the family's poverty and the ill health of their only son, life in the Watt home was very pleasant. Mrs. Watt was a gay and wise woman who loved young James for his cheerful, amiable disposition, and often relied on him to settle the small quarrels that arose among the children. "Let James speak," she would say, "from him I always hear the truth." His mother found, too, that her son had a quick and vivid imagination. Once when he was about fourteen, she sent him to visit friends in Glasgow. After a few days the friends wrote to her, asking that she take the boy home at once. He had been telling the family so many interesting stories each evening that he kept them all up until very late at night, and they could not get their work done the next day.

This gift for story telling was but one phase of the boy's eager mind. His curiosity about all scientific matters was endless, and his interest in the phenomenon of steam began in his early boyhood. His aunt once described how the boy would sit "for an hour taking off the lid of the teakettle, and putting it on, holding now a cup and now a silver spoon over the steam, watching how it rises from the spout, and catching and condensing the drops of hot water it falls into." Before the lad was fifteen, he had read a natural philosophy twice through as well as every other book he could lay his hands on. He had made an electrical machine, and sometimes startled his young friends by giving them unexpected shocks. He had a bench for his special use and a forge, where he made small cranes, pulleys, pumps, and repaired instruments used on ships. He was fond of astronomy and would lie on his back on the ground for hours, looking at the stars.

Much though he loved to read and study, and to tinker about at his workbench, the time soon came when James had to earn his living, for his family was very poor. When he was eighteen he started off for Glasgow to learn the trade of making mathematical instruments. He carried meager equipment. In his small trunk were some carpenter tools, his leather apron, and his best clothes, consisting of a ruffled shirt, a velvet waistcoat, and silk stockings. In Glasgow he found a position with a man who sold and mended spectacles, repaired fiddles and made fishing nets and rods. Before long the young workman found that he could not learn much in this shop, and when a friend of his family, an old sea captain, suggested that he might have better luck in London, he thought it a fine idea. Even in London, however, he had difficulty in obtaining work, but at last he came upon a place where he could at least learn the trade he had chosen for himself. This was in the shop of Mr. John Morgan, and he was required to pay a hundred dollars for a year's teaching. The boy's father could not help him so he had to earn most of his tuition by getting up very early in the morning and working at odd jobs before his employer's shop was open. Then, once the doors opened, he had to work through until nine o'clock at night. It is scarcely surprising that this rigorous life soon began to affect his health.

In spite of these hardships, the young man did learn his trade, and at the end of the year, he returned to Glasgow eager to set up his own shop. But the powerful city guilds in Glasgow looked with distrust at any craftsman who had not served a full apprenticeship, and they refused to allow James Watt to rent a shop. Just when it seemed that there was no place for him in Glasgow, he was befriended by one of the professors at Glasgow University who had heard of the young mechanic's skill and who now offered him a room at the university where he might work. The little university shop did not prosper for there was small demand for the instruments that Watt made. So he began to take on other types of work, particularly the making and repairing of musical instruments. One day a customer commissioned him to build an organ. This required that Watt learn something of the theory of music of which he had no previous knowledge. This Watt did in a very short time, and, when the organ was completed, not only was it a remarkably good one for those times, but Watt had added several clever inventions of his own.

The professor who gave Watt his little place at the university probably did far more for the young man than he realized. For at the university the young inventor, brimful of ideas and eager to experiment, found a congenial group of friends who shared his intellectual interests. A good deal of their talk centered about the possibilities of the steam carriage. The idea of using steam as a source of power was not new. Hero, a Greek physician who lived at Alexandria a century before the Christian era tells how the ancients used it. In

Watt's time, some crude engines had already been made. The best of these was that of Thomas Newcomen which was called an atmospheric engine. The Newcomen engine was essentially a steam pump and had been used in an attempt to pump water out of the coal mines. The engine proved not very practical, however, for it was slow and cumbersome, and extremely wasteful in its operation.

In 1764, Watt had an opportunity to repair one of the Newcomen engines which was being used as a model at the university. From then on he began to study the principle of steam power in earnest. He saw no reason why the steam engine could not be made efficient or why it could not be adapted to driving all kinds of machinery. So limited was his equipment that at first he experimented with common vials for steam-reservoirs and canes hollowed out for steam pipes. For months he worked night and day, trying new plans and testing the varied powers of steam. At last the basic principles of the steam engine seemed to become clear in his mind. His excitement over his discovery mounted and he wrote to a friend: "My whole thoughts are bent on this machine. I can think of nothing else." He hired an old cellar and for two more months he worked to perfect his model. Luck was against him. His tools were poor, the foreman of the shop died just when he was most needed, and the Watt engine, when it was completed, leaked in every part. Now the inventor scarcely knew what to do. He was sure that he had discovered the right principle, but he could not afford to spend more of his time in unrewarding research. His business at the shop had fallen away during his long absence; he was in debt; he had no money to continue his experiments; and his family was in dire need.

Watt was thoroughly discouraged and, for the moment, it seemed to him that inventing was a very foolish way in which to spend one's time. He might have given up his work for good had it not been for his wife, Margaret Miller, whom he had married soon after he set up shop at the university. She refused to let him give way to despair, and kept him from abandoning his work.

Watt's genius was too apparent to go unrecognized for long, and after a time friends induced Dr. John Roebuck, founder of the Carron iron-works to help the young inventor. He agreed to become Watt's partner, to pay his debts which amounted to five thousand dollars, and to take out a patent on the engine. Jubilantly, Watt set off for London, but his enthusiasm was soon dampened.

The patent officials there were very indifferent and
the impatient young man found himself wasting
endless hours trying to get their attention.

This was one of the most difficult periods in
all Watt's life. When his business in London was
finished, he returned home and went to work once
more on his engine. Again he had no luck. The
cylinder had been badly cast and was almost
worthless; the piston, although it was wrapped in
cork, oiled rags and even an old hat, let the air in
and the steam out. The new model was a dismal
failure. Watt almost gave up hope. "Today," he
said, "I enter the thirty-fifth year of my life, and I
think I have hardly yet done thirty-five pence
worth of good in the world."

To add to the inventor's troubles, Dr. Roebuck
had fallen into debt and could not help him as he
had promised. Then his wife died and he was left
alone to care for his children. Watt now had no
choice but to go back to surveying as a means of
earning his living. Although this meant the tem-
porary abandonment of his chosen work, Watt
gained a considerable reputation as a civil engineer. He made numerous surveys for canals and
harbors throughout Scotland, and invented a
simple micrometer for measuring distances.

A turning point was soon to come. In Birmingham lived Matthew Boulton, a rich manufacturer,

eight years older than Watt. He had a hardware establishment and employed over a thousand men in making clocks and reproducing rare vases. He was much interested in the possibilities of the steam engine and had corresponded with Benjamin Franklin about it. Through Dr. Roebuck he had learned of Watt and his inventions. It took Boulton a long time to make up his mind, three years in fact, but he was finally induced to engage in the manufacture of steam engines and to give Watt one third of the profits. The first engine constructed at Boulton's factory by skilled workmen under good conditions was a complete success. Orders began to pour in, for the condition of the coal mines in England had been growing steadily worse, and there was almost a desperate need for a machine that would pump out the water effectively. The firm of Boulton and Watt prospered, and Watt's reputation spread beyond his native land. He was invited to work for the Russian Government which had become interested in his experiments, and was offered the sum of five thousand dollars for his services. This was a very large amount by the standards of the day.

Watt had to refuse this offer because he could not be spared from the growing firm. He was also influenced by the fact that he had just remarried. His second wife, Anne MacGregor of Scotland, was an excellent housekeeper and made a pleasant, although a rather strict home for him and his children.

No sooner was the firm well established than trouble arose from other quarters. Infringement of the patents became a commonplace, for it was not difficult to bribe an unscrupulous workman to disclose the principles upon which the Watt engine was based. Even from the miners themselves there came complaints. Several of the new steam engines had been installed in the Cornwall mines which bore the quaint names of "Ale and Cakes," "Cook's Kitchen," and "Wheat Fanny." When the miners found that the engines did a thorough job of clearing the mines of water, they opposed the granting of a patent, apparently in the belief that it would give the owners a monopoly on a machine which was sorely needed in the mines.

During all this period of turmoil, Watt was continually working on new inventions. He made a letter copying press which, however, met with little success because people feared that its use would result in the forgery of names and letters. Boulton asked him repeatedly to try his hand at inventing a rotary engine. Eventually this was done not by Watt but by the head workman of the firm, William Murdock. Murdock was an inventor of great talent who deserves far more recognition than he is usually accorded. He developed the use of lighting by gas, and made the first model of a locomotive that frightened the townspeople nearly out of their wits as it came puffing down the street. A staunch friend of Watt, Murdock remained in the employ of the firm of Boulton and Watt to the end of his days, although his friends thought that he was treated very shabbily by the two partners for he was never made a member of the firm. But he seems to have been much more interested in pure research than in any gains for himself. An amusing story is told about how he went up to London to make known his discovery of the fact that fish skins could be successfully used to replace isinglass. He went to board at a fine house and guilelessly continued his experiments in his room. He was quite astonished at his landlady's anger when she found the walls of his room decked out with a fine array of fish skins hung up to dry.

When the rotary engine was finished, Watt and Boulton attempted to obtain a charter for its manufacture. Once again they encountered difficulties. The millers and mealmen feared that, if flour were ground by steam, the wind and water mills would be forced out of business, and the workmen thrown out of work. There were demonstrations against the new machine. In one town a large mill was burned down with a loss of over fifty thousand dollars. Finally the unrest died down as the millers began to realize their mistake. For they now saw that, if their theory were carried to its logical conclusion, it would be necessary to abolish all machinery and to go back to the grinding of corn by hand.

So again the firm of Boulton and Watt weathered the hard days. The firm's stake in the success of the new machine was enormous, for it had cost well over two hundred thousand dollars to develop. About this time Watt invented his "parallel motion" and the governor for regulating the speed of the engine. These added greatly to its effectiveness and orders for the new engine came in rapidly from America and all over the world.

In 1800, Watt retired from the firm and turned over his share to his sons, James and Gregory. James continued the business for many years, but Gregory who was his father's favorite died in 1804.

Watt spent many long years in the exacting service of science, but this did not make him a man of narrow interests or keep him from enjoying the good things of life. At Heathfield, not far from Birmingham, he built himself a lovely home in the midst of forty acres of trees, flowers, and shaded walks. He had a real gift for friendship and, at his hospitable home, he gathered around him men of science and literature from all over England, among them Dr. Priestley, the discoverer of oxygen, Dr. Darwin, and Josiah Wedgwood. But, to the end of his days, he was always the scientist and the searcher for new ideas. In the garret of his home he maintained a workshop, not very different from the original little shop in which he had tracked down so many great scientific principles. Here, in leather apron and with soiled hands, he kept working on new experiments, just as zealous and just as eager as when he had first pondered the properties of steam.

James Watt died in 1819 in his eighty-third year and was buried in the parish church of Handsworth near his home. There are statues of the great inventor at Handsworth and at Westminster. But a far greater tribute lies in the words of William Wordsworth, the English poet. He was only expressing the opinion of his countrymen when he said of Watt that considering both the magnitude and universality of his genius he was perhaps the most extraordinary man that England had ever produced.

Wolfgang Amadeus Mozart

At the foot of the Mönchberg in southern Austria nestles the little city of Salzburg. Each summer its usually placid streets hum with activity, and the air is filled with music from the annual festival. Thousands of travelers make the pilgrimage to Salzburg to hear the music, to stare at a bronze statue in the square of St. Michael, and to visit a plain two-story dwelling of stucco which is now a public museum. For these are relics of the man whose genius dominates the festival: the composer Mozart.

Wolfgang Amadeus Mozart was born in Salzburg on January 27, 1756. At an early age the child manifested a sensitive, deeply affectionate nature. He was especially devoted to his older sister, Marianne, whom the family called Nannerl, and to his wise and kindly father. Leopold Mozart's family before him had been bookbinders by trade. But Leopold had broken the tradition by becoming a musician. An excellent organist and violinist, he obtained an appointment as court musician, and

later as court composer and conductor to the archbishop of the diocese. The positions brought honor,
but small financial reward. A prolific composer,
the elder Mozart turned out scores of symphonies,
serenades, concertos, oratorios, masses and all
forms of music.

When Nannerl was seven, her father began to
instruct her on the harpsichord. Her three-year-old
brother Wolfgang would listen intently as the lesson progressed. He moved his playthings from one
room to another to the sound of the violin. Soon
he began to amuse himself by picking out simple
chords. At four his own lessons began, and before
long he was composing little pieces which astonished his father.

In 1762 Leopold Mozart took his talented children on a three weeks' concert tour to Vienna.
They traveled by boat up the Danube, and on arriving at port, Wolfgang so charmed the customs'
officers by a violin minuet that the family was ex-
empted from paying the usual customs fee. When
the children appeared by command before the im-
perial court at Schönbrunn, so delighted was the
Empress Maria Theresa with the boy's playing
that she held him in her arms and kissed him
soundly. One day as he was walking with two
daughters of the Empress, he slipped on the polished floor and fell. Marie Antoinette, afterward

Empress of France, lifted Wolfgang up. "You are
very kind. When I grow up, I will marry you," the
boy told her gravely. His father was alarmed at this
childish audacity, but the pretty princess only
kissed the little musician.

The following year Leopold Mozart was made
vice-kapellmeister, and shortly afterward he set
out with his family on a tour which was to last
three and a half years. In Paris the seven-year-old
Wolfgang composed two sets of sonatas which
were published, dedicated to Marie Antoinette.
With his sister Nannerl, he performed for the
French Court. The two children were allowed to
sit at the royal table. Poems were written about
them, and everywhere they aroused wonder and
admiration. But Wolfgang remained a modest
child.

Their tour next took the Mozart family to London. Here his concerts were well received, and he
composed six sonatas dedicated to Queen Char-
lotte. He emerged triumphantly from sight and
improvisation tests given him by a Fellow of the
Royal Society. In London the boy met Johann
Christian Bach, a son of the great composer. Bach
took the little musician on his knees, and alter-
nately they played at sight the works of Sebastian
Bach and those of Handel. Throughout the wearying tour the Mozart children won considerable

fame, but fortune proved elusive. Royalty gave them "enough gold snuffboxes to set up a shop," their disillusioned father wrote home, "but in money I am poor."

After fifteen months in England, Leopold Mozart crossed the channel to Calais with his children, on the way to The Hague, where they had been invited by a Dutch princess. At Lille, however, Wolfgang, always a frail child, became seriously ill. At The Hague, too, he took to his bed with a raging fever. Even then he could not give up his music. A board was laid across the bed, and on this he wrote out his compositions. Resuming the tour, the boy gave two concerts at Amsterdam.

At last, his ardor dampened by their lack of financial success, although many honors had been bestowed on them, Leopold Mozart took his family back to Salzburg. They returned via Paris and Dijon, later traveling through Switzerland. Everywhere they aroused admiring attention.

The following year a second tour to Vienna was undertaken in order to be present at the marriage of the Archduchess Maria Josepha. Shortly after their arrival, however, the bride contracted smallpox and died. Wolfgang also took the disease, and for nine days the boy was blind. When he had recovered sufficiently to perform, other obstacles to success arose. The new emperor, Francis Joseph, was not generously inclined, and although Maria Theresa treated the Mozarts kindly, they gained no substantial rewards. The nobility were indifferent to music. And the envious court musicians were determined not to be outdone by a boy of twelve, who was equally at home in German or Italian opera. They made a concerted attempt to disparage whatever he composed. Throughout his life, Mozart was to be troubled by the intrigues of established musicians. Saddened and disappointed, once again the Mozarts went back to their old home.

A period of study and composition followed. Then an opera which Wolfgang had written in Vienna was performed with success at Salzburg. The Archbishop appointed the boy concert-meister, at a salary of about five dollars monthly. At last the elder Mozart decided that Wolfgang must go to Italy to study. They gathered together the money with difficulty and the two set off for Italy. At concerts given in the principal cities, the boy astonished his audiences by his musicianship. The Mozarts found themselves in Rome during Passion Week. On the first day father and son went to the Sistine Chapel to hear the famous "Miserere" of Allegri. So sacred was this music considered that the musicians were forbidden to take home any part of it, or copy it out of chapel, under pain of excommunication. Immediately upon returning to his lodgings, however, Wolfgang wrote the music out from memory. All Rome was amazed at this remarkable feat of a boy of fourteen.

So great was the art he displayed at a concert in Naples that the audience declared there was witchcraft in a ring which he wore on his left hand, and he was obliged to remove it. At Milan, when Wolfgang was nearly fifteen, he composed the opera "Mithridate." This he conducted personally for twenty nights in succession before enthusiastic audiences. Requests poured in for operas from Maria Theresa in Vienna, from Munich, and from other cities. The young composer was busy every moment. He often became ill from overwork. The needs for funds to meet heavy expenses, however, made constant work a necessity. In the midst of this activity, he found time to write warm letters home to his mother and sister. "Kiss Mamma's hand for me a thousand billion times," wrote the tired and homesick boy on one occasion. Although his childhood had been spent largely away from home, he maintained his tenderness and affection for his family all his life.

They returned to Salzburg in 1771. Five uneventful years passed for Wolfgang. He traveled here and there, to Milan, to Florence, to Vienna, seeking patronage or producing operas, from which efforts he won no permanent gain. Leopold Mozart, whose salary as vice-kapellmeister had been withheld during his absence from Salzburg, now failed to receive a desired promotion to the position of kapellmeister. He began to cast about for a new means of subsistence. Now sixty years of age, he resolved to earn a pittance for the family by giving music lessons, while Frau Mozart accompanied Wolfgang to Paris.

The separation was a hard one for the devoted father, and for Nannerl, who wept the whole day long. Mozart, now twenty-one, enjoyed considerable fame, and looked forward to his adult career with an optimistic faith in Providence. "I have God always before me," he wrote. "Whatever is according to His will is also according to mine. There I cannot fail to be happy and contented."

At Munich, Augsburg and Mannheim, the young musician gave concerts, for which he received applause but very little profit. Stopping for a while in Mannheim, he attempted to secure the position of tutor to the children of the elector, but was unsuccessful. While in Mannheim, he met Aloysia Weber, a pretty girl of fifteen, whose father was a prompter at the National Theatre. Aloysia had a fine voice, and Mozart promptly fell in love with her. The girl was ambitious for a ca-

reer on the stage, and the young composer asked
nothing better than to write operas in which she
might be the star. When he learned of the affair,
Leopold Mozart, who had spent his entire life
helping his son to achieve fame, was greatly distressed. Affectionately but firmly he wrote to his
son, admonishing him: "Off with you to Paris.
Get the great on your side. *Aut Caesar, aut nihil.*
From Paris, the name and fame of a man of great
talent goes through the whole world."

In obedience to his motto, "God first, and then
Father," the young man reluctantly set off for
Paris and Versailles. To his disappointment he
found that scores of applicants waited for every
position, and he did not meet with the expected
success, earning only a few louis d'or. Then he received news of the death of his mother, and the
young musician journeyed back toward Salzburg.

Having received his father's consent, he stopped
at Mannheim to see the Webers. Learning that
Aloysia had gone upon the stage in Munich, he
hurried to that city to pay her a visit. She had been
offered a good salary. Mozart had, unfortunately,
won no new laurels at Paris. The girl who had
wept at his departure a few months before now
professed scarcely to recognize her unprepossessing
and penniless suitor. The proud and sensitive Mozart, wounded deeply by Aloysia's coolness, left

Mannheim without delay and hurried on to Salzburg. Aloysia married a comedian, with whom she had a very unhappy life. She gained a degree of fame, however, singing the music which Mozart wrote for her.

The young composer remained at home for a year and a half, until called to Munich to write the opera "Idomeneo." Then Vienna beckoned, and here he met the Webers once again. The elder Weber had died, and Mozart boarded with the family, who were in difficult circumstances. He gave music lessons to Constance Weber, a younger sister of Aloysia. She was a plain, kind-hearted girl, somewhat indolent, but with a great appreciation of her gifted teacher. Before long Mozart had fallen in love with his pupil, and despite the protests of his aged father, married Constance when she was eighteen and he twenty-six.

"The moment we were made one," Mozart wrote, "my wife as well as myself began to weep, which touched everyone, even the priest, and they all cried when they witnessed how our hearts were moved." Little could Mozart and his Constance foresee how prophetic were those tears. Unsteady employment, a rapidly increasing family, and a wife who was ill most of the time, made the struggle for existence ten times more difficult than before his marriage.

Struggling to fulfill his responsibilities to his own family, he could do nothing now to aid his aged father or his sister Nannerl. Once when he had prepared to visit his father for the first time after his marriage, having waited months to accumulate the necessary funds, he was arrested for a debt of fifteen dollars, just as he was stepping into the carriage.

The Emperor Francis Joseph inquired of him one day, "Why did you not marry a rich wife?" With dignity Mozart replied, "Sire, I trust that my talent will always enable me to support the woman I love." Unfortunately, this was not the case. From the time of his marriage until his death nine years later, he labored incessantly in his vain effort to make ends meet for his wife and numerous children. An astonishing number of compositions poured from his pen; among them six quartets dedicated to his beloved friend Joseph Haydn; the opera "Figaro" written when he was twenty-nine, and which enjoyed the greatest popularity; "Don Giovanni" written at thirty-one; and the "Flauto Magico" which he wrote without recompense, for the benefit of a theater director who was in want. The two latter compositions were hailed with delight by music lovers. Of "Don Giovanni," Goethe later wrote to Schiller, "That piece stands entirely alone; and Mozart's death has rendered all hope of anything like it vain."

Whenever Mozart appeared at the theater, the audience all over the house clamored for him to appear on the stage. Despite his widespread popularity, he could not earn enough to live. "Don Giovanni" brought only one hundred dollars, and the other great compositions even less. The composer gave lessons every hour he could spare, conducted concerts in the open air, borrowed from his friends, denied himself his necessities, in order to send money to his sick wife at Baden. He pawned his silver plate to make one more unsuccessful journey to seek the patronage of indifferent princes. Often he fainted at his tasks after midnight. Still he wrote to "the best and dearest wife of my heart," "If I only had a letter from you, everything would be all right," and promised her to redouble his efforts in order to earn their livelihood.

Mozart was a faithful and devoted husband. If he left home in the morning before Constance awakened, he would leave a note for her: "Good morning, my dear wife. I shall be at home at —— o'clock precisely." Once he was composing beside Constance as she slept. Suddenly a noisy messenger entered. Alarmed lest his wife, who had been ill for eight months, should be disturbed, Mozart rose hastily, allowing the penknife in his hand to fall and bury itself in his foot. Without a word or a groan, he left the room. A surgeon was called to treat his injured foot, and the composer was lame for some time. Constance, however, was never told of the incident.

His compositions found few purchasers, for they were not written in a popular style. Publishers threatened to close their doors to him unless he produced something for the average taste. "Then I can make no more by my pen," he complained bitterly, "and I had better starve and go to destruction at once." Indeed, in such straits did he live that he was unable to buy fuel, and a friend calling on Mozart and his wife found them waltzing in order to keep warm.

One day a sepulchral-looking man visited Mozart to ask that he write a "Requiem" on the death of the wife of an Austrian nobleman. The nobleman, later revealed as Count von Walsegg of Stappuch, was to be acknowledged as the author. Mozart consulted with his wife, as was his custom. Constance endorsed the project, and the composer accepted the commission for fifty dollars. Burdened with more work than he could do, harassed by debts he could not pay, hurt by the jealousies and intrigues of several musicians, and disappointed at the reception of his new opera at Prague, his hopeful outlook deserted him at last, and he told Constance that the "Requiem" would be written for himself.

At this low ebb in their fortunes, their sixth child was born. Forgetting her own burdens in her anxiety concerning her husband, Constance prevailed upon him to give up work for a time. Mozart's active mind could not rest, however, and even as he lay on his sickbed, ill with a malarial fever, he composed. The day before his death, he requested his friends to gather around his bedside and sing a portion of the "Requiem." He joined them in the alto, then burst into tears, crying, "Did I not say that I was writing the 'Requiem' for myself?"

A messenger arrived now to tell him that he was appointed organist at St. Stephen's Cathedral. For years he had longed for the position, but now his good fortune came too late. After a brief lifetime of toil and anxiety, he was dying, but death was unwelcome. "Now I must go," he lamented, "just as I should be able to live in peace. I must leave my family, my poor children, at the very instant in which I should have been able to provide for their welfare." Shortly after he sank into a delirium, and early on the morning of December 5, 1791, the thirty-five-year-old composer died. Prostrated with grief, Constance was too ill even to attend the funeral.

Mozart's body was laid beside his harpsichord. Then, in a driving rain, he was given a third-class funeral, the plainest possible. Baron von Swieten and a few mourners accompanied the procession to the cemetery, but because of the bad weather only the keepers attended the burial itself. Weeks afterward, when Constance was able to visit the spot, she found a new grave digger who was unable to tell her where her husband was buried. Mozart was the composer of fourteen Italian operas, seventeen symphonies, and dozens of cantatas and serenades —about eight hundred compositions in all—but his body rests in an unknown grave.

The Emperor Leopold aided Mozart's widow in a concert to raise fifteen hundred dollars to pay her husband's debts and ease her own straits. Eighteen years later she married the Danish councillor, Baron von Nissen, who educated her children.

It was half a century before Mozart's native city of Salzburg erected the statue in St. Michael's Square. Seventy years after his death, Vienna too built a monument in the Cemetery of St. Mark, dedicated to the man who spent much of his life in need and distress, but filled the world with music.

Michael Faraday

Most men of genius seem to have some deep-rooted foreknowledge of their destiny. So perhaps it was not so foolhardy as it seemed for young Michael Faraday to dream of becoming a scientist. But there was little enough in his favor. Born in 1791, he was the son of a London blacksmith who was so poor that the only home he could provide for his family was a hovel over a livery stable. The four Faraday children often went cold and hungry. Sometimes their only food for days was a loaf of bread carefully apportioned out among them.

Michael's schooling came to an end with a year or two at a village board school where he learned the rudiments of reading, writing and arithmetic. From then on he had to earn his way. His first employment was as an errand boy for a bookseller who maintained a newspaper library. Every morning it was the small boy's task to carry a newspaper around to various customers and to wait while they read it through. Then they paid him his penny and he trudged wearily on to the next house on his

route. This did not last long, however, for the bookseller liked his neat, clever little errand boy, and
within a year took him on as an apprentice to learn
the trade of bookbinding. In any case this was a big
step forward, but to Michael Faraday it proved to
be much more than that. It was an open sesame to
all the riches of knowledge. To his intense delight,
he found that sometimes books on science were
brought to the shop to be bound. Not one left the
shop until young Michael had read it from cover to
cover. He pored over Marcet's *Conversations on
Science;* and when he found an article on electricity in the *Encyclopaedia Britannica* he thought it a
treasure trove. Soon he scraped together a few pen-
nies in savings; and with his new-found knowledge
he began to construct an electrical machine, at first
using only a glass vial, later a real cylinder. Thus, at
thirteen he felt himself an independent scientist
with the whole world before him to explore.

One evening as he was going home from work,
he noticed in a window a small sign, announcing
that a Mr. Tatum was to give a series of lectures on
natural science. To the bookseller's apprentice, the
price was staggering—twenty-five cents a lecture.
With a tremor of disappointment in his voice, Michael confided the wonderful news to his brother.
Robert was three years older than he and employed
as a blacksmith. Touched by the little fellow's ear-

CJNaar

nestness and not a little proud that anyone in his
family should have such high aspirations, Robert
produced the money. And then to prove that good
things come in threes, Michael's employer gave him
some time off from his work, and a fellow lodger at
the bookseller's home gave him a few lessons in
drawing that he might illustrate his notes. The next
week Michael attended every one of the lectures
and took careful, precise notes in a clear hand. Then
he bound the notes with all his best skill in four
volumes and dedicated them to his employer.

The next event, although a minor one, was to
prove decisive in Michael's scientific career. A
kindly customer at the book shop noticed the boy's
enthusiasm for anything having to do with science,
and he took him to hear four lectures by the celebrated Sir Humphry Davy at the Royal Institution.
Faraday was spellbound. Now he knew that science
alone must be his career. So great was his desire that
he became daring. He sat down and wrote a long
letter to Sir Humphry in which he poured out his
heart. He told him what the lectures had meant to
him; he spoke of his own dream of becoming a scientist. He asked if there were not some humble post
in which he might serve at the Royal Institution.
He hardly expected an answer; but in a few days
one did come, for Sir Humphry had been a poor
boy and he could not help but sympathize. His an-

swer, however, was very non-committal. Science, he said, was a harsh mistress and offered small hope of reward. He, himself, was going abroad for an extended visit, but when he got back he would see if anything could be done for the boy.

With only this faint hope before him, Faraday set to making crude galvanic experiments of his own. He wrote eagerly of his experiment to a friend, adding somewhat ruefully, "Time is all that I require."

But time was the one thing he did not have. His father had died and his mother was now wholly dependent upon him for support. His apprenticeship came to an end, and he had to seek work at the only trade he knew—bookbinding. He found what seemed a good opportunity in the shop of a French bookbinder in London. This man was childless, and he promised young Faraday that he would inherit the business if he would agree to stay with him for the rest of his life. But before many weeks had gone by, the young man was miserable. Not only was he unable to carry on his experiments, but his new employer proved to have an ungovernable temper. Then one day like a bolt from the blue came a summons from no less a person than Sir Humphry Davy. He wished to see Michael Faraday at the Royal Institution the next morning.

Faraday spent a sleepless night and as early as he

could in the morning he hastened off to the interview that was to change his entire life. The result was more than he had dared to hope for. He was to be employed as a laboratory assistant, which in those days meant that he was to sweep the floor, clean the instruments, and make himself generally useful. In return he was to have the use of two rooms at the top of the house, and he was to be paid six dollars a week. Had the young man been offered the presidency of the Royal Society he could hardly have been happier, for here at last was his chance to work in the environment he loved.

Sir Humphry was not slow to recognize the extraordinary gifts of his young assistant. More and more he accepted him as a partner and entrusted him with important parts of the experiments carried on in his laboratory. Under Sir Humphry's guidance, the student scientist extracted sugar from beet root and treated chloride of nitrogen. Often their experiments were dangerous. On one bad day there was an explosion that tore a deep gash in Faraday's hand and spattered Sir Humphry with flying glass.

Some months later, Sir Humphry decided to go abroad once more, and he asked Faraday to come along as his assistant. Nothing in the young man's imagination could compare with the actual experience. Sir Humphry's trip lasted a year and a half, and in that time Faraday crowded the education of a lifetime. Sir Humphry traveled in the grand manner, and as a member of his staff, Faraday visited all the great cities of Europe and found himself welcomed as an honored guest into the homes of world famous scientists all over the continent. To the student who had never before been more than a stone's throw from London, all Europe was a dazzling kaleidoscope, and he stored every detail of its richness and its beauty in his mind. He haunted the art galleries; he lingered before the great cathedrals; he stood awed at the splendor of the Alps.

However much he delighted in his travels, nothing could make Michael Faraday forget his home or his family. From abroad he wrote his mother: "The first and last thing in my mind is England, home and friends." Then he added somewhat plaintively: "I have several times been more than half decided to return hastily home: I am only restrained by the wish of improvement."

When at last Sir Humphry turned homeward, Faraday was very well pleased. At the Royal Institution, he found a promotion and a raise in salary awaiting him. He was now to earn the princely sum of five hundred dollars a year. He plunged into his work and once more became completely absorbed in it. Day by day he perfected his technique and made many independent experiments of his own. Then he tried his hand at lecturing, for it seemed to him that a scientist ought to be able to present his discoveries to the world at large in clear, lucid terms. Before the City Philosophical Society, a group of young men interested in science, he gave a series of lectures on chemical affinity. Sir Humphry spoke approvingly of the lectures; and thus encouraged, Faraday published his first paper, an article on caustic lime which appeared in the *Quarterly Journal of Science*. In the next year, he wrote six papers for the *Quarterly,* outlining his experiments with gases and minerals; and he gave a second series of lectures.

No longer was the young man an apprentice in science. Soon a wealth of brilliant and original work began to pour out of his laboratory at the Royal Institution. Within a year or two, he had published thirty-seven papers; had written a book on the alloys of steel; and had presented a paper before the Royal Society itself on two new compounds of chlorine and carbon, and a new compound of iodine, carbon, and hydrogen. But all at once his thoughts turned to something very different and he began to behave in a very unscientific fashion.

For he had fallen in love with Sarah Bernard, the pretty and attractive daughter of a silversmith.

While she hesitated about marrying him, Faraday was on tenter hooks. He wrote letters, he wrote poems, he implored in every way he knew. At last the story had a happy ending, and Sarah Bernard and Michael Faraday were married on June 12, 1821. Sarah Faraday was probably the ideal wife for a struggling young scientist. She was content with a very simple, quiet life; and she found her happiness only in furthering her husband's career and his well being.

After his marriage, Faraday returned to his work with renewed zeal. There now came twenty years of brilliant scientific research that made him the wonder of his age. Elected a Fellow of the Royal Society, he began at once twelve lectures on chemical manipulation before the London Institution; six on chemical philosophy before the Royal Society; published six papers on electro-magnetism; and started a course of lectures for children which he continued for nineteen years. Faraday's delight in working with children reveals a very different side of his character from that of the austere scientist working alone in his laboratory. For, along with his logical, analytical mind, he had a warm, vibrant personality; he loved children and he enjoyed their eager questioning. Just as much care and precision went into the preparation of his lectures for children as into those given before the most learned men of Europe. Once when **Faraday** was asked at what age he thought science should be taught to the young, he replied, with a smile, that he had never found a child too young to understand him.

Michael Faraday was approaching the climax of his career. He was already famous throughout Europe. All London, from the Court down, flocked to his brilliant and stimulating lectures. He might, had he so chosen, have had any number of important university posts, but he refused them all, preferring the comparative obscurity of his laboratory at the Royal Institution with its opportunity for pure research. In his youth, Sir Humphry Davy had told him that science was a harsh mistress, offering small hope of reward. He found this not altogether true, for each new experiment he undertook filled him with a sense of high excitement and expectancy. He seemed always on the verge of some new wonder. And the only reward he asked was that he might add a little to the sum of human knowledge. Despite all the pressing demands upon his time, he produced one hundred and fifty-eight scientific essays and thirty series of *Experimental Researches in Electricity,* which form, as Dr. Gladstone said, one of the most marvelous monuments of intellectual work with which the world has ever been enriched.

Working on in his beloved laboratory, Faraday became the greatest experimental scientist of his time. Much of his earlier work had been in chemistry; but more and more he became engrossed in the study of magnetism and electricity. He began an intensive study of all the work that had been done. He spent more than eighteen years at it, experimenting endlessly and checking the discoveries of such men as Galvani who had found that the legs of a dead frog contract under an electric current; of Volta and his voltaic pile; and of Ampère and Arago who had proved that electricity will produce magnets. During this period, Faraday worked day and night; he was like a man beset by a dazzling vision. Yet month after month he had to report, discouragingly, that in his own work there were no affirmative results.

At last, however, all the zeal and patience that had gone into his work were rewarded. Faraday made his own great discovery of electro-magnetism, that magnets will produce electricity, and the age of electrical machines was ushered in. In quick succession there followed two other discoveries that were to further revolutionize the world. Faraday proved the principle of electric induction, upon which our modern telephone system is based; and he was able to demonstrate the identity of various kinds of electricity.

Faraday was now forty-nine and the strain of his years of intense labor began to tell upon his health. His tired brain lost its vigor and its ability to reach out into the unknown to solve some new riddle of the universe. It seemed as though his life's work was at an end. But Faraday did what was for him a very hard thing to do. Yielding to the entreaties of his wife, he left London and his laboratory, and took what was to be a five year vacation from all scientific work. He traveled abroad; he rested in the country, enjoying the companionship of plain people; and at last he regained his health, and the great powers of his mind came flowing back.

Back in his laboratory once more, Faraday began to ponder the relationship between electricity and light. He started a new series of long and difficult experiments. The Italian scientist, Morichini, had demonstrated the magnetizing power of solar rays. After almost innumerable trials, Faraday was able in a final experiment, "high, beautiful and alone," to magnetize a ray of light. This crowning discovery of Faraday's career set in motion a long train of events which ended, many years later, in Thomas Edison's production of the incandescent lamp that made electric lighting a practical reality.

The remaining years of Faraday's life were quiet ones. Honors came to him from all over the world, but he cared little for them. He worked tirelessly on in his laboratory, until his memory began to fail. Then he retired to his lovely home at Hampton Court which had been presented to him by the Queen. Here on August 25, 1867, he died in his study. The people of England wanted their great scientist to be buried in Westminster Abbey with all the honors due his genius; but he had requested, shortly before his death, that he be buried in some simple, quiet place with only a plain marble slab to mark it. So his grave is a simple one in Highgate Cemetery. To the end of his life, he wished to be "plain Michael Faraday."

David Glasgow Farragut

Many people associate the name of David Glasgow Farragut only with a single fighting phrase. But to navy men the name Farragut recalls one of the most glowing chapters in American naval history.

He was born in 1801 near Knoxville, Tennessee, in a region very close to the American frontier. One of his earliest recollections was of his mother, armed with an ax, fending off an Indian attack while her children huddled in the garret for safety. When David was seven years old, the family moved to New Orleans, and here, during the first long, hot summer, David's mother died of yellow fever. This tragedy meant that the Farragut home had to be broken up and the five children distributed about among relatives and friends. It fell to David's lot to be adopted by a Captain Porter, a friend of his father's, and an old line navy man. The little boy greatly admired Captain Porter's resplendent uniform and he was sure he would like the Navy just as well.

From that moment on, David Farragut's boyhood became a series of colorful adventures. By the robust standards of the day, a boy of eleven was not considered too young for active duty. So the War of 1812 found David on his first cruise along the Atlantic coast. He was aboard the *Essex,* Captain Porter's ship which had captured the British *Alert* and was crowded with prisoners. One night as the boy lay apparently asleep, the coxswain of the *Alert* came to his hammock, pistol in hand. David lay motionless until the man passed on. Then he crept noiselessly to the Captain's cabin. As he heard the lad's story, Captain Porter sprang from his cot and shouted: "Fire! Fire!" Immediately the seamen were on deck, and had the mutineers in irons before they had recovered from their amazement.

CJ NAAR

On his second voyage, this time in the Pacific, David again showed his mettle. Incredibly enough, at twelve years of age, he had received orders to take a prize vessel to Valparaiso. The captain of the captured ship was required to navigate her under the young midshipman's direction, but when David commanded that the "maintopsail be filled away," the captain defied any man aboard to carry out the order. Then he went below for his pistols. David took the situation calmly enough. He called one of the sailors, repeated his order, and saw that it was carried out. This done, he sent word to the enraged captain not to come back up on deck on penalty of being cast overboard. From that time on, the boy was undisputed master of the vessel and was respected and admired by all the crew.

All too soon, David was to experience the tragic side of war. In 1814, the *Essex* cruising off Chile, was attacked by two British ships, the *Phoebe* and the *Cherub*. Hour after hour the battle raged, the outclassed *Essex* heroically fighting on. Graphically, Farragut, himself, has described the terrible scene:

"I shall never forget," he said, "the horrible impression made upon me at the sight of the first man I had ever seen killed. It staggered and sickened me at first, but they soon began to fall so fast that it all appeared like a dream. . . . Soon after this some gun primers were wanted and I was sent after them. Just as I climbed down the wardroom ladder, the gunner opposite the hatchway was struck full in the face by an eighteen pound shot and fell back on me. We tumbled down the hatch together. I lay stunned for a moment by the blow, but soon recovered consciousness enough to rush up on deck. The captain, seeing that I was covered with blood, asked if I was wounded. 'I believe not, sir,' I replied. 'Then,' said he, 'where are the primers?' This brought me completely to my senses and I ran below again and carried the primers on deck." Thus did the boy learn his first lesson in military discipline.

At last, after a desperate battle, the *Essex* was forced to surrender. David went below to help the ship's surgeon in dressing wounds. The sick men lay quietly as they awaited their turns at the first aid station, but, in the next few hours, the boy learned all he ever needed to know of the courage and fortitude of the American seaman. He saw one young lieutenant, badly wounded, give up his place in line so that another might be cared for first. And, long afterward, he remembered the cry of a dying Scotsman: "I left my own country and adopted the United States to fight for her. I hope I have this day proved myself worthy of the country of my adoption."

But even capture had its lighter side. When David was taken aboard the *Phoebe* as a prisoner of war, he could not keep back his tears of shame. "Never mind, my little fellow," said the captain, "it will be your turn next, perhaps."

"I hope so," answered the boy resolutely.

Soon David's pet pig, "Murphy," was brought on board and he immediately claimed it.

"But," said an English sailor, "you are a prisoner and your pig too."

"We always respect private property," the lad replied, seizing hold of "Murphy." This vigorous retort clinched the argument, and the pet was restored to its irate young owner.

After his release, David returned to Captain Porter's home in Chester, Pennsylvania, and was sent to a school there for the summer. His schoolmaster was a remarkable man, a former member of Napoleon's Guard. The old soldier did not believe in teaching by books, but by practice and example. He took the boys on field trips and taught them much useful lore about plants and minerals as well as how to swim and climb. But David's days ashore were brief. In the fall he was off to sea again on a Mediterranean cruise. The ship stopped at Naples and at Pompeii, and the lad had his first glimpse of the wonders of the Old World.

In 1817, the chaplain of young Farragut's ship

was appointed consul at Tunis. The chaplain, Mr. Folsom, had grown fond of the promising youth, and he asked that David be allowed to stay with him for a time. For David, this was an excellent opportunity to further his education. Now a handsome robust boy of sixteen, he remained at the consulate for more than nine months. Under the chaplain's tutelage, he studied French, Italian, English literature, and mathematics. The consul was an excellent teacher, and in these gracious, cultivated surroundings, David Farragut acquired a good deal of the broad knowledge and the poise for which he was noted in later years.

Although he loved the sea, the young man returned to his duties aboard ship almost reluctantly. During his long months at Tunis, a strong and lasting bond of affection had sprung up between the orphan lad and the wise and kindly chaplain. Their friendship was a life long one. Nearly forty years later, when he was famous throughout the world, Admiral Farragut sent his greetings to his old friend as a token of his respect and regard for him.

The next years were eventful ones. Farragut, newly appointed a lieutenant, was placed in charge of a squadron to destroy the bands of pirates that preyed upon coastal shipping off the West Indies and in the Gulf of Mexico. On this mission, he cruised about in the Gulf for more than two years.

Often he and his men had to organize landing parties and pursue the pirates far inland over trackless country to hidden strongholds where they sometimes found whole cargoes of stolen goods. It was an exciting, dangerous life, but a wearing one. "For years," Farragut wrote in his memoirs, "I never had a bed, but lay down to rest wherever I could find a place."

At last it could be reported that the Navy's job was done, and that the pirate gangs were broken up, never again to be a threat to American merchant vessels. Although he was unaware of it at the time, these years of roving through southern waters had given Farragut knowledge and training which was to be invaluable in his later exploits. For the present, however, he was tired of his wandering life, and wished to re-establish some contact with his family. So the young man, not yet twenty, but already an accomplished naval officer, went back to New Orleans. There, he found that his father was dead and that his sister scarcely recognized him. He felt no sense of kinship and, disappointed and lonely, was glad when he was recalled to duty.

Two years later, in Norfolk, Virginia, he met and married Susan Marchant. Unfortunately for their happiness, Susan Farragut became ill soon after her marriage. She never recovered, but remained an invalid until her death sixteen years later. During these years, Farragut's chief concern was for his wife's welfare—even to the sacrifice of his career. When she required treatment by a specialist in New Haven, he went there and conducted a school on a receiving ship so that he might be near her. His tender care of his wife and his constant anxiety for her revealed much of the richness and depth of Farragut's character. For, as a friend of the family once remarked, only a really great man has both a brave and gentle heart.

At the time of his wife's death, David Farragut was nearly forty. Still his star had not yet risen, and he spent the next twelve years in relatively routine duties, partly in Norfolk where he was a lecturer in gunnery, and partly on the Pacific Coast where he established a Navy Yard. At the beginning of the Mexican War, he offered his services to the government, but he was not called to action. He felt no bitterness about this, for as he said when he was asked to express a preference for a post, "I have no volition in this matter; your duty is to give me orders, mine to obey. I have made it the rule of my life to ask no official favors, but to await orders and then obey them." But whatever he was called upon to do, Farragut did well; and everyone who came into contact with him knew him for what he was: a brilliant naval officer with an extraordinary knowledge of naval techniques and a genius for winning the loyalty and devotion of his men.

April 17, 1860 was the turning point in David Farragut's life. On that day, Virginia by a vote of eighty-eight to fifty-five, seceded from the United States. The next morning, Farragut who was then at Norfolk expressed his disapproval of this action, and said bluntly that President Lincoln would be justified in calling for troops to defend the Union. He was soon informed that persons with those sentiments could not live in Norfolk.

Farragut's second wife, Virginia, was like himself a Southerner by birth and inclination. Now, he hurried to her and told her of his decision to remain loyal to the Union. He did not minimize the hardships ahead. "This act of mine may cause years of separation from your family," he pointed out, "you must decide quickly whether you will go North or remain here."

There was no hesitation on Mrs. Farragut's part. Quickly she packed and set out with her husband for Baltimore. They found the city in confusion with Federal troops fighting a riotous mob, but they succeeded in securing passage for New York on a canal boat. David Farragut loved the South and did not wish to fight against her, but he knew now that he had no other course. In New York he offered his services to the Federal Government. Then he rented a little cottage at Hastings-on-Hudson and quietly awaited his orders.

In Washington, the military experts gathered to map out the campaign against the South. To their minds, one project—the capture of the city of New Orleans—seemed paramount. New Orleans, the richest city of the South, receiving each year millions of dollars' worth of sugar and cotton for shipment, lay at the mouth of the Mississippi, the great artery of transportation for the Confederacy. If the city could be captured, the very life blood of the South would be cut off. But to seize the city would not be easy, for it was exceptionally well guarded. At the mouth of the Mississippi were two almost impregnable forts, Jackson and St. Philip, which mounted one hundred and fifteen guns and were garrisoned by fifteen hundred men. Above the forts were fifteen vessels of the Confederate fleet, including the ironclad ram, *Manassas*. Below the forts, passage up the river was blocked by a heavy iron chain in which were bound scores of cypress logs, forming a huge obstruction.

Their chief difficulty, the military strategists found, was in selecting a man capable of performing so formidable an undertaking as the capture of this stronghold. Finally Gideon Welles, Secretary of the Navy, announced with quick decision: "Farragut is the man." The orders which Farragut received in his cottage at Hastings-on-Hudson were explicit: "The certain capture of the city of New Orleans. The Department and the country require of you success. . . . If successful, you open the way to the sea for the Great West, never again to be closed. The rebellion will be riven in the center, and the flag to which you have been so faithful will recover its supremacy in every State."

David Farragut was no longer a young man, but in his heart he was confident of his ability to carry out his mission, and he was deeply grateful for the honor which had come to him. He started out at once, saying: "If I die in the attempt, it will be only what every officer has to expect. He who dies in doing his duty to his country, and at peace with his God, has played the drama of life to the best advantage."

Farragut's fleet consisted of forty-eight vessels, carrying over two hundred guns. His flagship was the sloop-of-war, *Hartford,* of nineteen tons burden and two hundred twenty-five feet long. Five other sloops-of-war, sixteen gunboats, twenty-one schooners, and five small ships made up the flotilla. On April 18, 1862, the ships had all reached their positions and were ready for the attack. For six days and nights their mortars kept up a constant fire on Fort Jackson, throwing nearly six thousand shells.

Still the fort did not yield. Meanwhile Farragut's entire fleet was endangered by Confederate fire rafts—small, flat boats loaded with dry wood, smeared with tar and turpentine—which were sent down the river aflame in an attempt to fire the Union ships.

Farragut saw now that the forts could not be battered into submission by mortar fire. He made up his mind to by-pass the forts. This was a dangerous and heroic step. If he won, New Orleans must fall; if he failed—but he must not fail. Two gunboats were sent out to cut the chain which stretched across the river. All night long, Farragut watched and waited anxiously for the return of the gunboats. At last they came, having succeeded in the face of a galling fire in cutting the chain and making a passage for the fleet.

At half past three on the morning of April 24th, the fleet was ready to start. The *Cayuga* led off the first division of eight vessels. Both forts opened fire. In ten minutes she had passed beyond St. Philip only to be surrounded by eleven Confederate gunboats. The *Varuna* came to her relief, but was rammed by two Southern boats and sunk in fifteen minutes. The *Mississippi* encountered the enemy's ram, *Manassas* riddled her with shot and set her on fire so that she drifted below the forts and blew up.

Then the center division led by the *Hartford*

passed into the terrific fire. First she grounded in avoiding a fire raft; then a Confederate ram pushed a raft against her, setting her on fire; but Farragut gave his orders calmly as though there were no danger at all. The flames were put out and the ship steamed on, doing terrible destruction with her shells. Then came the last division, led by the *Sciota* and Commander Porter's gunboats. In the darkness, lighted only by the flashes of its guns, the fleet had cut its way to victory.

"Thus," says Farragut's son in his admirable biography, "was accomplished a feat in naval warfare which had no precedent, and which is still without a parallel except the one furnished by Farragut himself, two years later, at Mobile. Starting with seventeen wooden vessels, he had passed with all but three of them, against the swift current of a river, but half a mile wide, between two powerful earthworks which had long been prepared for him, his course impeded by blazing rafts, and immediately thereafter had met the enemy's fleet of fifteen vessels, ten of them ironclads, and either captured or destroyed every one of them. And all this with a loss of but one ship from his squadron."

The next day, at eleven o'clock in the morning, Farragut called the officers and men of his fleet into assembly that they might "return thanks to Almighty God for His great goodness and mercy in permitting us to pass through the events of the last two days with so little loss of life and blood."

On April 29, a battalion of two hundred and fifty marines and two howitzers manned by sailors from the *Hartford* entered the city of New Orleans. They marched to the city hall where they raised the Union flag, and remained in possession of the city until the arrival of General Butler with his troops on May 1st. With the fall of the city, Fort Jackson and Fort St. Philip were cut off and immediately surrendered.

From here, Farragut went to Vicksburg with sixteen vessels, the *Hartford* in the lead, "like an old hen," says Farragut, "taking care of her chickens." They passed the batteries there with a loss of fifteen men killed and thirty wounded. Three months later, he received a Congressional citation for the gallant services of himself and his men, and was made a rear admiral. He remained on the Mississippi and the Gulf for some months, doing effective work in sustaining the blockade and destroying the salt-works along the coast. When the famous passage of the batteries at Fort Hudson was made, Farragut's adored son, Loyall, stood beside him on the deck. The ship's surgeon urged that the boy be sent below, but Farragut would not hear of it. "We will trust in Providence," he said simply. Neither would the boy himself heed the surgeon's plea, for he wanted to be stationed on deck where he could see the fight.

Every day was full of exciting little incidents which bore witness to the courage of the men of the fleet. On one occasion, Admiral Farragut needed someone to carry a dispatch down the river to General Butler who was then in command at New Orleans. His secretary volunteered immediately. A small dugout was covered with twigs and, thus camouflaged, looked like a floating tree in the water. That night, the yeoman lay down in his little craft, with paddle and pistol by his side, and drifted with the current. Once along the way, a Confederate boat pulled out into the stream to have a look at the somewhat large tree. "Only a log," it reported on its return to shore. Without further mishap, the little boat sped down the river, and the young man delivered his message to the General. When the messenger returned to his ship, he was amazed at the praise and admiration with which he was greeted. To him, there seemed to be nothing spectacular about his exploit.

Admiral Farragut now returned to New York for a short time. Here, everyone wanted to meet the hero of New Orleans and to see the historic *Hartford* which had received two hunded and forty direct hits in her nineteen months of service. The city gave the gallant admiral a wonderful ovation, and the Union League Club presented him with a beautiful sword, its scabbard of gold and silver and its hilt set in precious stones.

But Farragut did not linger long in the city. He had another job to do. His next point of attack was to be Mobile Bay. Here, under the protection of the forts, Morgan, Gaines and Powell, Confederate ships had succeeded in breaking through the Union blockade. An amusing story is told of the capture of one of these blockade runners. The ship's captain was brought before Farragut, and turned out to be an old acquaintance who claimed that he was bound for Matamoras on the Rio Grande. Farragut, who had a keen sense of humor, expressed amazement that he should be three hundred miles off his course, and said good-naturedly, "I am sorry for you; but we shall have to hold you for your thundering bad navigation."

On August 4th, 1864, Farragut wrote to his devoted wife, "I am going into Mobile Bay in the morning, if God is my leader, as I hope He is, and in Him I place my trust." On August 5th, there occurred the most brilliant battle of his career.

Farragut's course was a hazardous one. Because the Bay was mined, the ships had to pass close to Fort Morgan. But at half past five on the morning of August 5th, Farragut's fourteen boats and four monitors moved into action. The column was led by the monitor, *Brooklyn,* which had special mine-sweeping equipment. Very soon the monitor *Tecumseh* almost abreast of the *Brooklyn,* struck a mine and went down with every man aboard. At this, the *Brooklyn* stopped, became confused, and began to back.

"What's the trouble?" came the call from the admiral's deck.

"Torpedoes."

"Damn the torpedoes!" Farragut shouted. "Go ahead." And the ship swept over the torpedoes to the head of the fleet, where she became the special target of the enemy. Her timbers crashed and her "wounded came pouring down—cries never to be forgotten." Throughout the battle, no place was too dangerous for the brave old Admiral as he gave his commands and directed his men. Twice his sailors had to lash him to the rigging, so precarious was his perch. At last Farragut gained the day, but with a tragic loss of three hundred and thirty-five men. As he looked upon the dead laid out on the port side of his ship, he wept like a child. But the battle of Mobile Bay was decisive. The forts fell one by one; more than one thousand four hundred prisoners were taken; and it was now clear that the Confederacy could not hold out much longer against this final blow.

On Farragut's next visit to New York, the city

could not restrain itself. Crowds surged to the Battery to greet him; a great public reception in his honor was held at the Custom House; and fifty thousand dollars was subscribed to buy him a home in New York. Congress made him a Vice-Admiral and there was talk that he might become a candidate for the presidency. But he soon scotched these rumors, saying: "I have no ambition for anything but what I am—an admiral. I have worked hard for three years, have been in eleven fights, and am willing to fight eleven more if necessary, but when I go home I desire peace and comfort." At his home in Hastings-on-Hudson, the streets were arched with banners bearing the eloquent words: "Mobile," "Jackson," "St. Philip," and "Mobile Bay." On July 25, 1866, the rank of admiral was created by Congress and Farragut was appointed a full admiral in recognition of his distinguished services to his country.

The next year Farragut was placed in command of a European squadron. With his wife who accompanied him by special permission of the President, he visited most of the major countries of Europe. He was received with ceremonial pomp by Queen Victoria at Osborne House; Napoleon III welcomed him to the Tuileries; and the Grand Duke of Russia and Victor Emmanuel made him their guest.

But David Farragut's great achievements had come late in life. He was an old man now and had not many years left in which to enjoy the homage which was his due. He died on August 14, 1870, in Portsmouth, New Hampshire. His best monument is the famous statue which stands in Farragut Square in Washington, inscribed with the fighting words of a gallant officer who embodies in his life the best traditions of the United States Navy.

William Lloyd Garrison

THE year 1805 saw in the United States a strange anomaly. In a land dedicated to freedom, there were close to one million slaves. Ever since colonial days, many strong voices had spoken out against the terrible shame of slavery. Wise men such as Benjamin Franklin and Alexander Hamilton had warned of the dangers that slavery held for the young republic. Here and there attempts were made to outlaw the evil system. Vermont, in 1777, forbade slavery within its borders; other Northern states followed suit. In 1780, the Quakers decreed that no member of their sect might hold a slave. But

CJ NAAR

these things were not enough. All along the Atlantic seaboard from Baltimore to New Orleans the slave trade grew and flourished.

It remained for William Lloyd Garrison, fiery, New England born reformer, to devote his whole life to a relentless crusade against the system he despised.

The harsh conditions of Garrison's boyhood prepared him well for his long struggle. Born in Newburyport, Massachusetts, in 1805, he was the son of a sea captain who set out one day on a voyage and never returned. The boy's mother, a nurse by profession, tried her best to support herself and her son. But her work kept her away from home much of the time, and, when the child was not yet ten, she was forced to apprentice him—first to a shoemaker, then to a cabinetmaker. Quick-witted young William found both these trades intolerable. In a short time, his masters willingly returned his indenture papers to him with something like relief.

The boy tried again. He was set to learn the printer's trade in the shop of Ephraim Allen, proprietor of the Newburyport *Herald*. This was a stroke of luck. The printer's office was Garrison's only school, and it proved a good one. The young apprentice read the articles he set in type. Quietly studious, he assimilated much of what he read; he learned to use words, to reason, and to debate. At sixteen, the fledgling editor was writing articles of his own, some on political subjects, under strange pseudonyms such as "An Old Bachelor," and "Timothy Pickering."

When Garrison was twenty-one, he undertook, with the optimism of youth, to start a paper of his own. *Free Press,* as it was called, was too radical for local consumption and soon closed its doors.

From Newburyport, Garrison went to Boston where he encountered Benjamin Lundy whose influence upon his life was to be decisive. Lundy, a Virginia born Quaker, was a thoughtful, compassionate man of thirty-nine, who hated the injustices he saw all about him. In spite of his galling poverty, he managed single-handed to publish a monthly paper, *Genius of Universal Emancipation,* in which he conducted a determined campaign against slavery. Lundy's views on the subject, while just, were moderate. He favored gradual emancipation of the slaves and recolonization in Africa. Garrison's approach was much more vigorous. He demanded immediate emancipation for all slaves, and equal rights for every human being, regardless of his color.

Nevertheless, Garrison decided to throw in his lot with Lundy. Together the two men went to Baltimore and joined in the editorship of the *Genius.* Baltimore, with its auction blocks and its open slave pens, inflamed Garrison to fever pitch. Soon the *Genius* was blasting away at slavery in fiery editorials in which Garrison denounced the slave trade between Baltimore and New Orleans as "domestic piracy." This was strong language; but the young editor was no coward. He took a daring step. He began to name names. One long list of slave dealers carried the name of a prominent ship owner of Newburyport, Garrison's home town. The slave traders became alarmed at the tone of the *Genius*. They singled out the Newburyport ship owner and urged him to bring formal charges. Almost at once Garrison was arrested for "gross and malicious libel." A prejudiced court found him guilty and fined him fifty dollars. He could not pay and was taken off to prison. At twenty-four, he was imprisoned for exercising his right of free speech.

Undaunted, Garrison employed his prison hours in writing four lectures on slavery which he proposed to give immediately upon his release. The release was not long in coming. In the North, men of liberal views, John Greenleaf Whittier and Henry Clay, were incensed when they heard the story of how the young man had been thrown into jail in order to suppress his writing. They rallied to his aid; and his fine was paid by Arthur Tappen of New York.

Intent upon his lectures, Garrison hurried forth

from prison to find his ideas labeled "fanatical," and doors slammed resoundingly in his face. In Boston, then the center of liberal opinion in America, only one small hall was offered for his use. Here in October, 1830, he gave three lectures, outlining his principles and his plans.

In January, 1831, Garrison's famous paper, the *Liberator,* made its appearance. Determined to publish the paper as long as he and his partner could subsist on bread and water, Garrison made a stirring address to the public as the first issue of the *Liberator* came off the press. "I will be as harsh as truth and as uncompromising as justice. On this subject I do not wish to speak or write with moderation. I am in earnest, I will not equivocate; I will not excuse; I will not retreat a single inch—*and I will be heard.*"

But on one important fact Garrison had failed to count. The economy of the North was as hopelessly entangled in the system of slavery as that of the South. The textile mills of New England grew rich upon the products of slave labor. Hostility against the young firebrand who was so vehement in his denunciation of slavery mounted by leaps and bounds. A concerted witch hunt began. The Vigilance Association of South Carolina offered a reward of $1500 for the apprehension of anyone found distributing the *Liberator.* In Raleigh,

North Carolina, a grand jury indicted the young editor, hoping that he might be brought to trial there. The state of Georgia promised $5000 to any person responsible for the capture and conviction of the editor of the now notorious paper.

Against all these threats, Garrison pursued his way resolutely. In his book, *Garrison and His Times,* Oliver Johnson gives a graphic description of the besieged office of the *Liberator:* "The small windows bespattered with printer's ink; the press standing in one corner; the long editorial and mailing table covered with newspapers; the bed of the editor and the publisher on the floor—all these make a picture never to be forgotten."

Nevertheless, the leaven of abolition was beginning to work. In 1832, one stormy night, twelve "fanatics" gathered in the basement of a church in Boston and organized the New England Anti-Slavery Society.

The following year, the directors of the American Colonization Society, a group which advocated recolonization of the slaves in Africa, sent a representative abroad to test out public opinion there. Thereupon, the Anti-Slavery Society decided to send Garrison to England to point out to the friends of abolition how cruel and unjust the recolonization plan was. Garrison was enthusiastically received by such distinguished Englishmen as Lord Brougham, Bishop Wilberforce, and Sir Thomas Lowell Buxton. When his new English friends expressed surprise that he was not a Negro, Garrison said this was the greatest compliment of his life, for it showed how earnestly he had labored for the slave.

Upon his return to America, Garrison found the American Anti-Slavery Society in the process of formation. Its first meeting was held in Philadelphia on December 4, 1833, with delegates present from eleven states. John Greenleaf Whittier was chosen secretary of the Society. Years afterward, the distinguished poet often said that he felt more pride in seeing his name among the signers of the Declaration of Principles adopted at that first meeting than he did in seeing it on the title page of his books.

Along the Atlantic seaboard, the tension over the slavery question grew sharper and sharper. People began to choose their side. At Canterbury, Connecticut, a young Quaker schoolmistress admitted several Negro girls to her school. Before long her well was choked with refuse, her house was stoned, and sullen storekeepers refused to sell their goods to the brave little schoolteacher. In New York, vandals broke into a Presbyterian church where anti-slavery lectures had been held and desecrated it. To the south in Philadelphia, there were race riots that lasted three or four days.

In Boston where Garrison was fighting on, a mob broke into his office shouting: "We must have Garrison! Out with him! Lynch him!" The young man was seized and dragged into the street with a rope coiled about his body. He seemed doomed, until a voice cried out: "He shall not be hurt. He is an American!" So the daring Abolitionist escaped lynching, but the Mayor of Boston placed him under "protective custody." Once more Garrison found himself in prison, and on the walls of his cell he scrawled: "William Lloyd Garrison was put into this cell on Wednesday afternoon, October 21, 1835, to save him from the violence of a respectable and influential mob, who sought to destroy him for preaching the abominable and dangerous doctrine that all men are created equal and that all oppression is odious in the sight of God. Confine me as a prisoner, but bind me not as a slave. Punish me as a criminal, but hold me not as a chattel. Torture me as a man, but drive me not like a beast. Doubt my sanity, but acknowledge my immortality."

The attack on Garrison served him better than he knew. From then on, his fame and that of his paper spread throughout the country. Many famous men and women became converts to the cause of abolition. In Faneuil Hall in Boston a mass meeting was held to protest the murder of Elijah Lovejoy, a young Illinois preacher, by a pro-slavery mob. One speaker made a disparaging remark. Then out onto the rostrum stepped aristocratic, debonair young Wendell Phillips. With his deep conviction, his moral passion, Phillips magnetized his audience. The young orator of Boston had found a cause worthy of his talents.

The conflict between small groups of pro- and anti-slavery forces pointed the way for the major struggle that was to develop. The year 1854 saw the repeal of the Missouri Compromise of 1820 which had prohibited slavery north of latitude 36° 30', the southern boundary of Kansas. Kansas now became a battleground. From Missouri armed men crossed over the border, determined to establish slavery in this new area. Equally determined men came from the North resolved to prevent the spread of slavery. The Fugitive Slave Law which enabled slave owners to search for their slaves in northern states caused a wave of bitterness and resentment to sweep over the land. The hanging of John Brown at Harper's Ferry gave the Abolitionist cause its first national martyr.

On April 12, 1861, Fort Sumter was fired upon; and the long dreaded Civil War was at last a stark reality. Nearly two years later on January 1, 1863,

President Lincoln issued his Emancipation Proclamation which set four million human beings free. In that moment, Garrison saw the accomplishment of all that he had fought for, all that he had lived for. When the stars and stripes were raised once more at Fort Sumter, Garrison was invited by President Lincoln to be a guest at the ceremony. All Charleston went wild as he arrived in the city. Children sang; and men and women crowded about his carriage. Garrison spoke simply to those who hailed him as their liberator: "Thank God, this day, that you are free. And be resolved that, once free, you will be free forever. Liberty or death, but never slavery!"

In 1865, the *Liberator* appeared for the last time. With his own hands, Garrison set the type and on the first page printed the official ratification of the Thirteenth Amendment to the Constitution, prohibiting slavery in the United States forever. Then his work well done, the great Crusader retired from public life. He had seen a dark era in American history pass; and he knew that his beloved country was now safe. In his mind's eye, he saw her future as a nation, strong, united and dedicated once again to the freedom of all men.

Giuseppe Garibaldi

G IUSEPPE GARIBALDI, the Italian whose name is outstanding among those who have fought for freedom, was born to the sea and to adventure. His birthplace was Nice in southern France in the year 1807; and here little Giuseppe, one of the many sons of a poor Italian sailor, learned early to fend for himself. Along the sunny Riviera coast he picked up the lore of the fishermen; often he went with his father on voyages far out into the Mediterranean; he climbed the lonely mountain passes near his home. When he was only twelve he set out on his first voyage of discovery in a borrowed skiff with a crew of small playfellows. All went well until Nemesis overtook the young mariners in the form of the senior Garibaldi who commandeered ship and crew alike and headed straight for home.

Little by little, the boy grew in skill and daring and his love of adventure became a passion. But he had gentler gifts as well. He loved books, delighted in mathematics and had a fine instinct for languages. His mother, seeing these things, hoped with all her devout heart that he might become a priest. Yet she did not complain when her fiery, quick-tempered son told her that he would choose the sea. Perhaps it was best, she thought, and she offered a prayer for his safety.

The lad found the life of a sailor much to his liking and at twenty-one he was second in command on the brig *Cortese* bound for the Black Sea. This was a disastrous voyage. Three times the ship was attacked by pirates who stripped the vessel of everything that could be carried away—sails, charts, instruments—and left the sailors to perish without food or clothing. But somehow the *Cortese* managed to reach Constantinople where the crew found refuge. Here Garibaldi fell dangerously ill and would undoubtedly have died but for some Italian exiles who took him in and cared for him. In return for their kindness, Garibaldi stayed among them for a time and taught in one of their schools. Then, recovered at last, he returned to the sea to enter the Sardinian navy.

A captain at twenty-seven, Garibaldi had already seen much of the world; and he burned with anger at the poverty and oppression that he saw rampant in his native land. As a child he had visited Rome, the Eternal City, whose very stones recalled her ancient glories. As a young man he remembered that visit and he dreamed of a strong, united, demo-

cratic Italy where free men might live. That dream, he felt, must be realized within his own lifetime. Yet for a time all thoughts of a republic seemed hopeless. For years Italy had been the battleground of Europe. Now the Congress of Vienna was parceling out the country—virtually as spoils to the victors. Lombardy and Venice went to Austria; Parma and Lucca to Marie Louise; and the two Sicilies to Ferdinand II. For those who objected to these high-handed proceedings there were prisons, where a man could die silently and unnoted.

Nevertheless, revolt was brewing among the silent, suffering Italian people. Garibaldi learned of a young lawyer of Genoa, Giuseppe Mazzini, who had organized a society called "Young Italy." Its adherents were pledged to the cause of an Italian republic. He hastened to join them. Mazzini and his followers made daring plans. While Garibaldi held the strategic arsenal of Genoa, Mazzini was to seize Piedmont for the republic. But just as the conspirators were poised to carry out their brilliant scheme, they were betrayed by one of their own number. All who were implicated in the plot were immediately sentenced to death, but Garibaldi, in the dress of a peasant, escaped over the mountain passes to Nice, where he found a friendly ship willing to take him to South America.

The talents of the young revolutionist found fertile soil in South America. Exiled and penniless, he arrived at Rio de Janeiro; but to his delight he found a little band of his countrymen already there. With their help, he managed to buy a vessel and begin trading along the coast. Soon, however, came his chance to fight again for freedom. The Republic of Rio Grande revolted against Brazil, and Garibaldi at once pledged himself and his companions to the service of the new republic. They manned a small vessel which they named the *Mazzini* and went gallantly into action. In a brilliant first engagement, the *Mazzini* captured a large ship loaded with precious copper. Its second encounter was less fortunate. Garibaldi was badly wounded and he and his men taken prisoners. Imprisoned for many months, the Italian patriot was often cruelly tortured, but it was apparent that no amount of suffering could force him to betray his adopted country. Eventually, his release was secured through the good offices of a Senora Alemon, and he returned to Rio Grande to re-enter the war.

In all his adventurous life, Garibaldi had had very little time in which to think of marriage and a home. Besides, he asked himself, what woman would be willing to share the dangers of his life? But here in Rio Grande he found a woman to whom these dangers were nothing. Beautiful, imperious, well-born, Anita Garibaldi was surely one of the most remarkable women of her time. Fearlessly devoted to the cause of liberty, she stood beside her husband in every battle and shared every hardship with him. The tales of her courage are legendary. When a soldier fell dead at her feet, she seized his carbine and kept up a constant fire. In another battle, she became separated from her husband and was taken prisoner. She crept out of the camp in the night, leaped on a horse, and without food or protection plunged into a dark and treacherous forest. Only after eight days of wandering did she find her husband.

A year or so later when his first son, Menotti, was born, Garibaldi set out on a long trek across the marshes to buy some clothing for the child. While he was away, the little republican camp was attacked by Imperialists and Anita was forced to flee into the woods with her twelve-day-old baby. For months the courageous young mother kept her child alive only by warming him with her own breath as she carried him tied in a scarf about her neck through the dismal swamp lands.

After six years of service for the South American republic, Garibaldi determined to settle down with his little family to a quieter life. He bought a house in Montevideo and began to teach school, as he had done once before when he was exiled from home. But he might have known that it was hope-

less. Soon Uruguay began a struggle for her independence and Garibaldi was unable to resist her
call to arms. The exploits of Garibaldi and his Italian Legion made their name famous throughout
the world, and assured the victory of the little Uru-
guayan republic. Still, at the close of the war, when
the grateful people conferred the title of General
on Garibaldi and offered a large tract of land to the
Italian Legion, the great soldier declined the gift in
simple, stirring words. "In obedience to the cause
of liberty alone," he said, "did the Italians of Montevideo take up arms and not with any views of gain
or advancement."

Fourteen years had gone by since Garibaldi had
left Italy under sentence of death. He was forty-one,
in the prime of his life and vigor, and now he heard
wonderful news from across the sea. Italy, he was
told, was ripe for revolution. Charles Albert, King
of Sardinia, had declared himself ready to give con-
stitutional liberty to his people, and to help throw
off the Austrian yoke. Garibaldi believed that his
hour had come and that at last he might free his
beloved country. He chose fifty-six men from his
Italian Legion and sailed for Nice in the ship
Esperanza. On the long voyage home, Anita
Garibaldi made a Sardinian flag from a counter-
pane, a red shirt, and a bit of an old green uniform;
and the men talked of the great deeds they hoped

to do under this banner of freedom. Garibaldi, dressed in a white cloak lined with scarlet, was a brave figure as he presented himself to the Sardinian king and offered his services. In fact, he was too brave a figure, for the timid Charles Albert remembered Garibaldi's republican sentiments and declined his aid. Once more the patriot's hopes were dashed.

However, Garibaldi did not have long to wait. Rome declared herself a republic and on April 28, 1849, Garibaldi and his troops entered the city prepared to defend her. It was his hope that France and England would remain neutral while Rome fought for her independence, but Louis Napoleon sent French troops to support the Papal party. For three months the people of Rome fought from street to street, armed with any weapons they could lay their hands on. At last, the struggle against the superior forces of France and Austria proved too uneven. The republican supporters were crushed and Pius IX re-entered the city.

Garibaldi alone refused to yield. He called his soldiers together, and, leaping on horseback, shouted, "Venice and Garibaldi do not surrender. Whoever will, let him follow me! Italy is not yet dead." Across dangerous mountain passes, he made his way with Anita and about two hundred of his troops to a place on the Adriatic coast where thirteen boats were waiting to carry them to Venice. Nine of the boats were captured by the Austrians, and the rest driven into hiding. Garibaldi and his wife succeeded in escaping onto dry land, but the long strain of battle had been too much for Anita. In a little while she died in a peasant cottage to which she had been carried. The loss of his gallant wife was a crushing blow to Garibaldi; he seemed numb and completely indifferent to his own fate. But at last his friends made him understand that his great work of liberation must go on at any cost, and he sought refuge in the rocky island of Caprera.

From his hiding place on Caprera, Garibaldi went to America where he quietly bided his time, sure that another chance to free Italy would come to him. For a year and a half he lived in a little cottage on Staten Island in New York and earned his living as a humble candlemaker. Then, for a time, he became captain of a vessel plying between China and Peru. True to the great principle of freedom for which he fought, Captain Garibaldi refused to allow his ship to be used in slave-trading although this was common practice in those days.

After four years in America, Garibaldi was forced by circumstances to return to Italy. His mother had died and there was no one left to look after his three children. With the little money he had saved, he bought part of the little island of Caprera, off the coast of Sardinia, and settled there with his family. Again he waited.

His homecoming was opportune. In 1859, Napoleon III declared war on Austria; and Cavour, the great Italian statesman, decided that now was the moment for Italy to free herself from Austria. Quickly, he called Garibaldi from Caprera, made him Major General of the Alps, and placed him in command of the Italian forces in the war against Austria. At once the people of Italy rallied around. Lombardy sprang to arms. The red blouse and the white cloak of the Liberator seemed to inspire men with confidence; and there began a series of battles, which, for bravery and dash and skill, made the name of Garibaldi the terror of Austria, and the hope and pride of Italy. Tuscany, Modena, Parma and Lucca declared their allegiance to the Italian king, Victor Emmanuel. Austria was humbled at the great battles of Magenta and Solferino and she gladly gave up Lombardy.

At last it seemed as though all Italy were to be united. Garibaldi started with his famous "Mille" or thousand men, to free the two Sicilies from the despotic rule of Francis, the son of Ferdinand II. The first battle was fought at Palermo. After four hours of hard fighting Garibaldi defeated a picked regiment of Neapolitan soldiers who outnumbered his own troops by four to one. At that the Sicilians arose almost as one man to acknowledge their liberator. Peasants flocked in from the mountains; women dressed themselves in red and wore red feathers in their hats in honor of their hero. As the troops moved from town to town they were greeted by cheering throngs. To the Sicilians Garibaldi was a saviour. Among the French legend had it that Garibaldi was invulnerable, that no bullet would pierce his body.

Had he chosen to do so, Garibaldi might have set himself up as the dictator of all Italy. But he was too great a man for that. As soon as the war was over, he resigned his authority, gave the two Sicilies into the care of his sovereign, and retired penniless to his island home at Caprera.

Still there remained for Garibaldi one unfinished task. Rome was not yet the capital of Italy and, until it was, he could not rest. At length he grew tired of waiting for the king to take action, and with three thousand troops he started to march on Rome. But Victor Emmanuel, always fearful of what action France might take if Rome were molested, sent royal troops against Garibaldi and he was captured and imprisoned on the Gulf of Spezzia. The king could scarcely have done anything more unpopular. The people of Italy were outraged at the imprisonment of their national hero. They crowded into the prison to visit him; they brought him gifts and messages from all Italy, and finally they prevailed upon the government to release him.

Garibaldi remained at his Capreran home until 1864, when he visited England. Everywhere in that country he met with a tremendous ovation. Rich and poor alike outdid themselves in paying honor to the man who had fought so hard and so long for the freedom of his native land. He was given the keys to the city of London; ladies wore his colors; crowds thronged after him in the streets; he was feted by the Duke of Sutherland and by Tennyson at his beautiful home on the Isle of Wight. English sympathizers made up a purse for him for they knew of his poverty, but this he refused with characteristic pride.

After his triumphant trip abroad, Garibaldi went back to Caprera to await another opportunity to march on Rome, for he was more than ever determined to free that city. He made a second attempt in 1867, but was promptly arrested and again imprisoned. However, his dream was soon to be realized. For when Napoleon III fell at Sedan, the French troops were withdrawn from Rome and Victor Emmanuel entered the city without a struggle and claimed it in the name of Italy.

The crowning achievement of Garibaldi's long and turbulent life came in 1874 when he was elected to Parliament. As he entered the city of Rome, a wildly cheering populace greeted him and escorted his carriage in triumph through the streets. The scene in the Senate House as the aged Garibaldi took his oath of office was a touching one. He still wore the cloak and the red shirt of his revolutionary days, but he was old now; he leaned heavily on the arm of his son, Menotti; and his voice, when he spoke, was tremulous with emotion. The House rose to its feet to acclaim the old man who had spent his life in the service of his country.

During the last years of his life, Garibaldi lived happily at Caprera with his second wife, Francesca and the two children of his second marriage, Manlio and Clelia. The Italian government granted him a pension of ten thousand dollars a year, and his home was made beautiful with gifts from all over the world. And now that his work was done, Garibaldi was truly content. He spent his time in gardening, and in writing the memoirs of the great days of liberation. Often as the old patriot sat by a window looking out over the sea, he was heard to murmur: "Quanti o allegro!"—"How joyful it is!" He died peacefully on June 2, 1882, and was buried near his home amid the surroundings he loved so much.

Ezra Cornell

I~N THE~ winter of 1819, two emigrant wagons made their way slowly along the road that led from New Jersey to the little village of De Ruyter in upstate New York. The wagons were heavily laden; in the first were Elijah Cornell, his wife and six children, in the second were all the worldly possessions of the little family. The journey of two hundred and fifty miles was a long, tedious one through a sparsely settled region over almost impassable roads. At night, even in the cold, the family had to make camp by the roadside. Yet for the young Quaker, Elijah Cornell, the time passed swiftly enough. He was dreaming of the home he meant to set up for his family in these new western lands.

For more than twenty years, the Cornells made their home in De Ruyter. Skilled and industrious as he was, Elijah Cornell tilled his farm and worked in his pottery shop, and thus managed to make a modest living for his large brood of eleven children. He taught his sons his own skill in pottery

CJNAAR

that they might have a trade, and more than that he instilled in them, in true Quaker fashion, high ideals of honesty and independence. In this whole-some environment, Ezra Cornell, the oldest of the Cornell children, grew into boyhood—tall, mus-cular, and as resourceful as he was eager to make his way in the world. When, at sixteen, he wanted more than anything else to have a final year at the village school, he and his brother earned their way —by clearing four acres of beech and maple wood-land, plowing the tract and planting it with corn. Adept and nimble witted, young Ezra next learned carpentry in a matter of months. His father had a new pottery built and the boy had helped in the work. Once the pottery was finished, Ezra and his brother turned to, cut timber and built a two story house for the family. The house proved to be one of the finest in town, and, according to the neigh-bors, no master carpenter could have done a better job.

It was evident that the quiet town of De Ruyter could not satisfy the eager boy for long, and at eighteen he left home. Although he had already mastered several trades, the young man worked for a time at anything that came his way—thus gain-ing new experience and new skills. For two years he shipped timber down the canal from Syracuse to New York. Next he found work in a shop that made wool-carding machinery. Then he heard that there were good opportunities for steady work in Ithaca, a thriving little town some forty miles distant. He walked most of the way there for he had no money for his fare, and soon found employment as a repair man in a cotton mill. His work there was so outstanding that within a year Colonel Beebe, the proprietor of a very successful plaster mill, had learned of the young man and decided that he would like to have him in his employ. This proved to be a happy arrangement on both sides. Young Cornell remained with Colonel Beebe for twelve years, starting as a mechanic in the mill and rising to the position of general manager. More than once in those years was the young man called upon to use all the ingenuity he had acquired as a jack-of-all trades. On one occasion, he drew up plans and superintended the work of tunneling water from Fall Creek to the mill, all without previous experience in engineering.

The years in Ithaca were happy ones for Ezra Cornell. His work prospered and he bought a few acres of land near the mill and built a simple, but comfortable home for himself and his young bride. In this house his nine children were born and, as he watched them growing up in comfort and security, he thought that life was indeed good to him.

Abruptly the picture changed. Depression crept

across the nation; business stagnated; and the once prosperous plaster mill of Colonel Beebe was forced to close its doors. So at thirty-six, Ezra Cornell found himself with a large family to support, no job, and very meager prospects. But not for nothing did he come of pioneer stock. Since there was very little chance of obtaining work, he set out to try to sell the patent right for a new type of plow recently invented. He walked from Maine to Georgia, trying everywhere to interest people in his patent, but he met with little success. On all his long journey, the only person who had seemed genuinely interested in the patent was F. O. J. Smith, a member of Congress and the enterprising editor of the *Maine Farmer*. Before he returned home, Cornell decided to pay another call on Mr. Smith.

When he entered the office of the *Maine Farmer*, Cornell found his friend Smith on his knees in the middle of the floor with the mould board of a plow lying beside him and a rough diagram sketched in chalk on the floor before him. Smith arose hastily and exclaimed to his visitor: "Cornell, you are the very man I want to see. I have been trying to explain a machine I want made, to my neighbor, Robertson, but I cannot make him understand it. I want a kind of scraper for digging a ditch for laying a telegraph pipe underground." He then went on to explain that Congress had appropriated

thirty thousand dollars to enable Professor Morse
to test the practicability of his telegraph on a line
between Washington and Baltimore, and that he
had undertaken the contract for laying the pipe.

At once, Cornell grasped the idea and made a
drawing of the type of machine he thought would
be necessary. Smith seemed a little skeptical at first,
but urged him to construct a machine such as the
one he had outlined and offered to pay all the expenses involved. By now Cornell was full of enthusiasm. In a nearby machine shop he hurriedly made
the patterns for the necessary castings and then the
woodwork for the frame. On its very first trial at
Smith's homestead, the machine was a success. The
strange-looking plow, drawn by four oxen, cut a
furrow two and one-half feet deep and one and one-
fourth inches wide, and at the same time laid the
pipe along the bottom.

When Cornell was asked to take charge of laying the pipe for the Washington and Baltimore
telegraph line, he needed no further urging. The
vast potentialities of the telegraph had captured his
imagination. He saw what it would mean to a
young and growing nation, and he knew that he
had at last found his life's work. The immediate
work of laying the pipe began well. It had been
decided to lay the pipe between the double tracks of
the Baltimore and Ohio railroad and, with an eight

mule team, nearly a mile of pipe was laid each day. Soon, however, an obstacle came from an unexpected source. No less a person than Professor Morse himself came hurriedly to ask if the work could not be stopped for a few days without the newspapers learning of it. He was not sure, he said, that this method was the best one; he needed more time to experiment. In spite of all the hard work he had put into the machine, Cornell agreed at once to do what the Professor asked. He stepped back to his plow and called out to his men: "Whip up your mules, boys, we must lay another length of pipe before we quit tonight." Then deliberately he drove the machine against a sharply jutting rock, thus wrecking it beyond repair. No one could say that it had not been just an unfortunate accident.

Now, at Professor Morse's own request, Cornell began to experiment in the basement of the Patent Office at Washington, meanwhile studying every book on electrical science that he could lay his hands upon. Before long it became evident that better results could be obtained if the telegraph wires were put upon poles, as Cooke and Wheatstone had done in England. For many months more, the two men worked incessantly, often with the crudest equipment; but when the telegraph line between Washington and Baltimore was completed, it justified all their hopes. Their next problem was to popularize the new invention and gain public support for it.

This was a heartbreaking task. The government refused to back the invention any further; private capital was afraid to touch it; and the public remained stolidly apathetic. In Boston where a second line was built for demonstration purposes, the public came, stared awhile at the interesting new curiosity and then moved on to the next exhibit. In New York, where Cornell made his next effort, the newspapers gave cordial notices of the new line that had been erected on lower Broadway opposite Trinity Church, but they continued to be unimpressed. In fact, the *Herald* stated bluntly that it was opposed to the telegraph. Under present conditions, the *Herald* went on, it could obtain news ahead of its competitors by means of its special courier service; but were the telegraph to come into general use this advantage would be swallowed up, since all the papers could get the news at the same time.

However discouraging this sort of nonsensical talk was to Ezra Cornell, it could not stop the progress of the telegraph once it had proved workable. After many months, Cornell succeeded in forming the Magnetic Telegraph Company which was to erect a telegraph line connecting New York, Philadelphia, Baltimore and Washington. He was made manager of the company at the munificent salary of one thousand dollars a year, yet even on that pittance he subscribed to five hundred dollars' worth of company stock, so sure was he of its eventual success.

Next Cornell carried his venture westward. He built a line from New York to Albany and soon had it running on a modestly profitable basis. In Chicago he organized the Erie and Michigan Telegraph Company, but he found the western city completely uninterested in subscribing to the stock. But now, by a curious quirk of fortune, the telegraph became suddenly popular in the East. New companies burgeoned out overnight; the public caught the fever and hastened to invest its money in what now seemed a highly profitable enterprise.

Cornell was disturbed by this new turn of events. Wisely, he saw that if small, ill-organized companies were to spring up everywhere, the whole future of the telegraph industry would be jeopardized. To stave off this danger, he worked to consolidate the little companies into one strong, powerful company that would assure the orderly growth of the infant industry. This became the Western Union Telegraph Company, in which for fifteen years Ezra Cornell was the largest stockholder.

With the establishment of Western Union, Ezra Cornell's pioneer work in the development of the telegraph came to an end. For more than a decade, he had spent all his time and energy in traveling about the country endeavoring to make the American people understand the tremendous significance of Professor Morse's great invention. Now he could retire, if he chose, secure in the knowledge that he had accomplished all that he had set out to do. But a life of ease had no appeal for him. Instead, he returned to Ithaca where he had spent so many happy years and bought a three hundred acre tract of land. Here he developed a model farm, planted with rich orchards, and stocked with the finest cattle. Soon his neighbors recognized him as a leader in agricultural matters. He was elected president of the County Agricultural Society; and in 1862 he was asked to represent the New York State Agricultural Society at the International Exposition in London. This trip to England and the Continent gave Ezra Cornell and his wife the first vacation that they had had in thirty years. Upon his return, he was again called upon for public service, this time in the State Legislature where he served for six years, and where his quiet wisdom earned the respect of all who knew him.

Even in the midst of all these activities, much of Cornell's interest was still centered in Ithaca itself. He encouraged the manufacture of glass, for which this region is now famous. He gave generous support to the churches, and he built the Cornell library, the first of many contributions to the city's cultural life.

But these things were not enough for Ezra Cornell. To one of his Quaker background, it was unthinkable that a man should amass a large personal fortune, unless it were used for some constructive purpose. But what specific purpose? All his experience had taught Ezra Cornell that education is the brightest weapon of an enlightened democracy. He thought of his own boyhood and of how he had cleared four acres of land to pay for a few more months at the village school. He determined to build an institution where anyone might find instruction in any subject. At once he allotted two hundred acres of his cherished farm to the university, and set aside five hundred thousand dollars for the initial expenses. In 1868, Cornell University with Andrew D. White as its first president opened its doors to some four hundred students from twenty-seven states. From that day on, Ezra Cornell's devotion to the welfare of the university never faltered; at the time of his death it was estimated that his contributions in money alone amounted to more than three million dollars.

Today, beautiful Cornell University, built high on the hills of Ithaca overlooking Lake Cayuga, is recognized as one of the world's leading educational institutions; and year by year hundreds of young graduates go out to serve wherever educated men and women are needed. It is a monument of which any man might be proud; and James Froude, the English historian with all his unique ability for estimating the true quality of a man, wrote well of Ezra Cornell when he said: "There is something I admire even more than the university, and that is the quiet, unpretending man by whom the university was founded. . . . Mr. Cornell has sought for immortality and the perpetuity of his name among the people of a free nation. There stands his great university, built upon a rock, built of stone as solid as a rock, to endure while the American nation endures."

Abraham Lincoln

IN THE year 1816, a little family of four left their cabin in Hardin County, Kentucky, and set out on horseback with their scanty possessions for the wilderness to the northwest. They were Thomas Lincoln, his wife Nancy Hanks, and their children, Sarah, a girl of nine, and Abe, a tall, awkward boy of seven. Cutting their trail through the wilderness with an ax, and living off the game Thomas Lincoln brought down with his rifle, they made their way to the settlement of Gentryville, Indiana, where they built the new cabin that was to be their home.

The cabin, constructed of logs, without doors or windowpanes, had a sod floor. A bed of dried leaves, a stool or two, a log table, and a single book, the Bible, were the only furniture. From this book, Mrs. Lincoln, a pale-faced, gentle woman, taught her children daily. Thomas Lincoln could neither read nor write. But his son, Abe, had studied for two or three months in a makeshift school such as the frontier country afforded, and had learned to read. His quick mind and retentive memory soon enabled him to learn the Bible almost by heart. Studying under his mother's guidance, the boy became devoted to her as the embodiment of kindliness and steadfastness.

But the hardships of pioneer life were too much for frail Nancy Hanks. When Abe was ten years old, his mother died of consumption and was buried in a plain box under the trees near the cabin. For the boy, who was to lose his sister at twenty, the loss was profound. Day after day he sat on the grave and wept. Months afterward, still disconsolate, he wrote a letter to Parson Elkins, a minister the Lincolns had known in Kentucky, asking him to come

CJ NAAR

119

and preach a funeral sermon. The minister came, riding on horseback over one hundred miles, and in the presence of neighbors who had gathered one Sunday morning in carts and on horseback, Parson Elkins conducted the funeral service for Nancy Hanks Lincoln. Thus the lad bade farewell to the best friend of his early childhood.

In the months that followed, the lonely boy began to wonder what lay beyond the cleared patch where he planted his corn. He sought in books the answers to his questions. Borrowing a copy of Bunyan's *Pilgrim's Progress,* he read and re-read it until he could repeat much of it from memory. Eagerly he pored over *Æsop's Fables* and *Robinson Crusoe,* which someone had lent him. His curiosity was stirred by the thought of the great world beyond Kentucky and Indiana, that he hoped to see one day.

In due time Thomas Lincoln remarried. The new Mrs. Lincoln was a widow, an old friend of Nancy Hanks. She and her three children came to live in the Lincoln cabin. With them they brought a bureau, some chairs, a table and bedding. For the first time Abe, who had slept heretofore in the cabin loft on a sack filled with corn-husks, was to lie in a real bed. The Lincoln children welcomed their new mother to their desolate home. She was to prove a good mother to them, instilling fresh energy into the easy-going Thomas Lincoln, making the cabin more comfortable and attractive. Abe she encouraged to delve more and more into the world of books, teaching him the principle of thoroughness, and planting in him the desire to explore the new horizons that lay beyond the log settlement and the wilderness that fringed it. And she provided the boy with an object for the deep devotion of which he was capable. Years later, when he governed thirty million people, Lincoln thought of his childhood and said, "All that I am or hope to be, I owe to my angel mother. Blessings on her memory." And it is not known whether he referred to Nancy Hanks, or to Sarah Bush Lincoln, for he owed much to both.

A dog-eared copy of Weems' *Life of Washington* fell into Abe's hands, and the barefoot lad in scanty buckskin breeches dreamed for hours over the story of the revolutionary leader. Evidently it made a vivid impression. A few days later a woman, rebuking him for creating a boyish disturbance with some of his companions, remarked chidingly, "Now, Abe, what on earth will ye ever be if ye keep a-goin' on in this way?" Abe studied the question thoughtfully, replying in his slow drawl, "Well, I reckon I'm goin' to be President of the United States one of these days."

The treasured *Life of Washington* came to grief.

One stormy night the rain beat between the logs of the cabin and soaked the volume as it lay on a board upheld by two pegs. Reluctantly Abe took it back to the owner, and by working three days at twenty-five cents a day, paid out the damages and made the book his own.

Already the few months of schooling which were to make up his formal education had drawn to an end. He was "living out" now, hoeing, planting and chopping wood for neighboring farmers, giving the wages to his parents. In the evenings he warmed his lanky body at the friendly fire of his employer for the moment, reading Plutarch's *Lives* and the *Life of Benjamin Franklin,* tending the baby, telling stories or making an impromptu speech, reciting poetry, even improvising rhymes himself. Occasionally he engaged in games of strength, for he could wrestle and jump with the best.

At eighteen Abe found a position in a small store. But his head was too busy with dreams of Washington and Franklin to allow him to be satisfied with standing behind a counter. Fifteen miles from Gentryville courts were held at certain seasons of the year. When Abe could find a spare day, he trudged over in the morning to listen to the cases, returning at night. Meantime he had managed to borrow what seemed a strange book for a country store clerk—*The Revised Statutes of Indiana.*

One day he was in court when an able lawyer, John A. Breckenridge, defended a man on trial for murder. Abe listened intently as the attorney made his plea to the jury. Never had he heard anything so eloquent. When the court adjourned, the tall, homely boy, overcome with admiration for the great man, pressed forward to shake his hand. But the lawyer passed on indifferently, without speaking. Thirty years later the two met in Washington, when Abraham Lincoln was the President of the United States. He thanked Breckenridge then for his stirring speech in Indiana.

In March, 1828, came the long-awaited opportunity to see the world beyond Gentryville. Abe was asked to take a flat-boat down the Mississippi River to New Orleans, by a man who had faith in his honesty and diligence. The pay was two dollars a week and rations. Since a flat-boat could not make the return trip upriver, it was sold for lumber at the journey's end, and Abe returned to Gentryville on a river steamer. On this trip to New Orleans Lincoln, now a broad-shouldered youth of six feet four, saw things that made an indelible impression on his mind: the spectacle of brown men and women in chains, being sold like sheep in the southern slave markets. It may well have been this voyage that aroused the unyielding conviction that slavery was wrong which years later was to culminate in the Emancipation Proclamation.

Two years later Abe helped the family of his father, Thomas Lincoln, move to Illinois. Over muddy roads and through creeks he drove the four yoke of oxen which drew the household goods to their destination. Then he helped his adopted brothers to build a log house, plowed fifteen acres of prairie land for corn, and split rails to fence it in. Once more he began "living out," working for neighboring farmers. Now that he had become of age, his scanty wages no longer belonged legally to his father, but to himself. He did not always receive money for his labor, however. Once he needed a new pair of trousers. For every yard of brown jeans, dyed with white walnut bark, necessary to make them, he split four hundred rails.

Since he had no trade and no funds, he was forced to perform whatever labor offered itself. For a year he worked first for one farmer and then another. At last he and his half-brother were hired by a Mr. Offutt to build a flat-boat and take it down-river to New Orleans. Abe carried out his responsibilities well, and so pleased was the owner that on Lincoln's return he was immediately placed in charge of a mill and store at New Salem. He proved unfailingly fair in his dealings with his customers. Once, having sold a housewife goods amounting to two dollars and six and a quarter cents, he found that in adding the items he had overcharged her six and a quarter cents. Although night had already fallen, he locked the store, and walking two or three miles, returned the money to his astonished customer. On another occasion, a woman bought half a pound of tea. Discovering afterward that he had used a four-ounce weight on the scales, he immediately set out on the long walk to his customer's home, to deliver the four additional ounces due her. These incidents won for Lincoln the nickname "Honest Abe," which clung to him all his life.

Courtesy to womenfolk was a fundamental quality of his character. One day as he waited upon his customers, one of the men present began to use profanity. The young clerk leaned over the counter and asked him to desist. After the ladies had departed, the man had angry words with Lincoln, and challenged him to fight. "Well, if you must be whipped," Abe replied, "I suppose I may as well do it as any other man." The broad-shouldered Lincoln emerged victorious over his foe, who later became a life-long friend.

The young store-keeper was anxious to improve his speech. Hearing that a grammar could be purchased six miles away, he made the long trip by foot to obtain one. Evenings he spent poring over the book, and since candles were too costly, he burned one shaving after another as he scanned the pages. Eager to keep abreast with the politics of the day, he subscribed to the *Louisville Journal*. Other books that came to his hands were devoured by Lincoln, who made careful notes from each of them.

After a short time, Lincoln's employer, Mr. Offutt, failed, and once again the young man was adrift, without job or funds. War had begun with Blackhawk, chief of the Sacs tribe, and the Governor of Illinois was calling for volunteers. A company was formed in New Salem, and "Honest Abe" was chosen captain. In the campaign that followed, Lincoln earned the affection of his men by his thoughtfulness of them rather than himself, and learned valuable lessons in military strategy. Now his friends asked him to become a candidate for the State Legislature. He hesitated to run, fearing that his friends were ridiculing him and that his being comparatively unknown would defeat him. But James Rutledge, president of their debating club, counseled: "They'll know you better after you've stumped the country. Anyhow, it'll do you good to try."

The twenty-three-year-old Lincoln entered the race. He made some earnest stump speeches, and although he was defeated, his personal popularity brought him two hundred seventy-seven votes out of the two hundred eighty cast in New Salem. It was a common saying that "Lincoln had nothing, only plenty of friends."

The County-Surveyor now found that he needed an assistant. He paid a visit to Lincoln, bringing along a book for the young man to study, if he wished to prepare himself for the job. For six weeks Lincoln studied the book, reciting to a teacher. Whenever he had an hour's leisure, however, he could be found immersed in his law books, for by this time he had fully decided to become a lawyer.

Lincoln was boarding now at the home of a friend, Mr. Rutledge. The daughter of the family, Ann, was a charming girl, and Lincoln became deeply attached to her. She, however, was engaged to another man, and their marriage was imminent. Shortly before the wedding, the young man of Ann's choice was obliged to visit New York on business. He wrote back of his father's illness and death. Then his letters ceased.

After many months had elapsed, the young lawyer began paying court to Ann Rutledge. At first she could not forget the young man she had promised to marry. But the following year, won by Lincoln's devotion, she agreed to be his wife. Lincoln was now completely happy. He plunged into his studies with renewed vigor. He had been elected to the Legislature, and borrowing some money in order to buy a new suit of clothes, he made the hundred-mile trip to the State Capitol on foot. Although he did not take an active part in the speeches and debates, he worked faithfully on committees and carefully studied the needs of the state.

As the summer days of 1836 passed swiftly by, the health of Ann Rutledge began to fail. She grew rapidly weaker, and in the latter part of August sent for Lincoln to come to her bedside. What happened at that last farewell has never been known. On the twenty-fifth of August, Ann Rutledge died.

"The love and death of that girl shattered Lincoln's purposes and tendencies," Mr. Herndon, his law partner, commented in later life. "He threw off his infinite sorrow only by leaping wildly into the political arena." The following year, when Lincoln was twenty-eight, he was admitted to the bar. Moving from New Salem to the larger town of Springfield, he formed a partnership with J. P. Stuart, from whom he had borrowed his lawbooks. Still too poor to pay for lodgings, he slept on a narrow lounge in his law office. Once again he was elected to the Legislature; and, in the Harrison presidential campaign, was chosen one of the electors, and wielded his vote for the Whig Party.

On November 4, 1839, four years after the death

of Ann Rutledge, Lincoln married Mary Todd. A bright, witty and rather handsome girl, she came of a good Kentucky family. She admired and had faith in Lincoln's ability, and her ambition spurred him on in his political career. From this union were born three sons: Robert, Willie, and Tad (Thomas). Until his death, Lincoln remained a devoted husband and father.

He was forging steadily ahead now, gaining a reputation as an honest and able lawyer who would never accept a case unless he were convinced of the rightness of his client's cause. In 1846 he was elected to Congress by an unusually large majority. Opposed to the war with Mexico and to the extension of slavery, he expressed his convictions fearlessly. Despite the efforts of the growing anti-slavery bloc, the compromise measures of 1850 were passed. As a result of this legislation, California was admitted as a free state and slave trade was abolished in the District of Columbia, but the Fugitive Slave Law gave slave-owners the right to recapture their slaves in any free state and return them to bondage. Lincoln commented gloomily to Herndon, "How hard, oh how hard it is to die and leave one's country no better than if one had never lived for it!"

In 1854, through the efforts of Stephen A. Douglas, senator from Illinois, the Kansas-Nebraska Act was passed. Under this act, those states were allowed to decide for themselves whether or not slavery would be permitted. But the Missouri Compromise of 1820 had expressly stated that slavery should be prohibited forever in this locality. Feeling ran high in the entire North. When Douglas returned to his home in Chicago, his constituents refused to hear him speak without refutation. Abolitionists in Illinois called upon Abe Lincoln to answer the arguments of Douglas.

At the State Fair at Springfield, in October of that year, a great crowd gathered to hear the debate. Douglas made his stand with ability and eloquence. The following day Lincoln spoke. It was a three-hour-long speech, charged with deep conviction. A complete hush settled over the audience. When the speaker had concluded, an uproar of applause broke out. Men shouted and women waved their handkerchiefs, cheering the triumph of Lincoln. After this debate, the two men spoke to immense crowds in all the large towns of the state. The results of the Kansas-Nebraska bill were as anticipated. The blood of pro-slavery men and abolitionists flowed in the streets, newspaper offices were razed by angry mobs, and Douglas' hopes of attaining the Presidency were shattered.

When the newly formed Republican Party held its second convention in Philadelphia, June 17,

1856, Abraham Lincoln received one hundred and ten votes for Vice-President.

About this time an incident occurred which added to Lincoln's fame. A man was murdered at a camp meeting, and two young men were arrested. One was a penniless youth whose mother, Hannah Armstrong, had befriended Lincoln in the early years. Believing her son to be innocent, she wrote to Lincoln, now a prominent lawyer, asking his aid. When the trial opened, the spectators clamored for Armstrong to be hanged. The principal witness testified that by the aid of the bright moonlight he had seen the prisoner inflict the death-blow. Careful cross-examination by Lincoln, who introduced the almanac showing that no moon was visible on the night in question, showed the perjury of the witness. The sympathy of the jury was won by his stirring appeal, and even Lincoln was moved to tears as the youth was acquitted. He refused to accept a penny from the grateful mother for his part in restoring her son to liberty.

The following year Lincoln was invited to deliver a lecture at the Cooper Union Institute in New York. He was not very well known in the East. His home in Springfield was an unostentatious two-story frame house. When seen at all by people, except in his public appearances, he was usually pulling one of his children in a wagon in front of his home, hatless and in shirt-sleeves, deeply absorbed in thought. When the crowd gathered at the Cooper Union, they were prepared to hear a fund of stories and the usual stump speech. They heard instead a masterly review of the history of slavery in the United States, and a prophecy concerning its future. The breadth and eloquence of the speech astonished them. The New York *Tribune* commented, "No man ever before made such an impression on his first appeal to a New York audience."

After the Cooper Union address, Lincoln spoke in various cities to crowded houses. A Yale professor took notes and gave a lecture to his students on the New York speech. Surprised at his success among men of learning, Lincoln once asked a prominent professor why his speeches were received with such interest. "The clearness of your statements," came the reply, "the unanswerable style of your reasoning, and your illustrations, which were romance, and pathos, and fun, and logic, all welded together."

Concluding his addresses in the East, Lincoln visited his son Robert at Harvard College, and then returned home. When the Republican State Convention met on May 9, 1860, at Springfield, Illinois, Lincoln was invited to sit on the platform. The throng was so dense that he had to be carried over the heads of the people. Ten days later at the National Convention in Chicago, Lincoln won the nomination over William H. Seward of New York, a leading candidate. Springfield went wild with joy. When the news of his victory was brought to him, he observed quietly, "Well, gentlemen, there's a little woman at our house who is probably more interested in this dispatch than I am; and if you will excuse me, I will take it up and let her see it."

The resulting campaign was one of the bitterest in the history of the United States. The South believed that war would result if Lincoln were elected. The North was clamoring for decisive action in the slavery question. When the votes were counted, the total for Lincoln amounted to 1,857,-610, while his opponent, Stephen A. Douglas, received 1,291,574. A fever of excitement swept the country. The South prepared for war by seizing the forts. By the date of the inauguration, most of the southern states had already seceded.

Lincoln said goodbye to many friends, and left Springfield for Washington. Of his law partner, with whom he had practiced for twenty years, he requested that his name be left on the old sign until he returned from Washington. Herndon, moved to tears, replied, "I will never have any other partner while you live." He remained faithful to his word. Hannah Armstrong had an intimation that she would never see Lincoln again. His enemies would assassinate him, she warned. Smiling, he replied, "Hannah, if they do kill me, I shall never die another death."

Once in Washington, Lincoln found an empty treasury, and a country drifting steadily into war. The lines etched deeper on his face, and his eyes grew more clouded with concern. In his inaugural address, he declared: "In your hands, my dissatisfied countrymen, and not in mine, is the momentous issue of civil war. The government will not assail you. You can have no conflict without being yourselves the aggressors. . . . Physically speaking, we cannot separate."

On April 12, 1861, the Confederate troops fired on Fort Sumter. The dreaded conflict had begun. Quickly President Lincoln called for 75,000 volunteers. Thousands of young men left their colleges and places of business to respond. "The Union must and shall be preserved!" was the rallying cry. Then came the call for 42,000 men for three years.

Lincoln began to study the science of war in earnest. He pored over military books and sought out on maps every creek, hill and valley in Confederate territory, denying himself the time to eat or sleep. On May 24th the young Colonel Elsworth had been shot at Alexandria because he had pulled

down the secession flag. His funeral was conducted
from the East Room of the White House. This incident aroused the North more deeply than ever.
The press clamored for battle. On July 21, 1861,
the Union Army under General McDowell attacked the Confederates at Bull Run, and was defeated. The South was jubilant, and in the North
people realized that the war was to be a long and
bloody one. At the request of the President, Congress voted five hundred thousand men and five
hundred million dollars to carry on the war.

A vast undertaking faced President Lincoln. The
southern ports had to be blockaded and traffic on
the Mississippi halted. A large and valiant army of
Confederate soldiers, fighting on their own familiar soil, had to be defeated, if the nation were to remain intact. The burdens of the President were
made heavier by the criticism to which his policies
were subjected. One school of thought declared that
the President was going too far. Others complained
that he moved too slowly and with too much le-
niency toward the slave states. England, to whom
the southern states were bound in close trade ties,
sided with the Confederacy. Only careful leadership averted a war with that country.

In the summer of 1862 bitter battles were fought
in Virginia: Fair Oaks, Mechanicsville, Malvern
Hill, and others. General McClellan campaigned

with varying success, losing thousands of men in the Chickahominy swamps. Following the battle of Antietam, September 17th, in which each side lost over ten thousand men, he was relieved of his command and succeeded by General Burnside. Although the Union Army had met with some successes in the West under Grant, at Fort Donelson and Shiloh, and in the South under Farragut, the outlook was grim.

That the thousands who were risking their lives in battle were to Lincoln not merely ciphers presented in the operational rooms of the General Staff, but human beings for whose individual lives he felt a deep personal responsibility as a fellow man, is indicated by numerous incidents. The tall, gaunt man who had paced the floor beside the deathbed of his own son Willie in February, muttering "This is the hardest trial of my life," refused to uphold the sentence of death for a young sentinel who had slept at his post. "I could not think of going into eternity with the blood of the poor young man on my skirts," Lincoln said. "It is not to be wondered at that a boy raised on a farm, probably in the habit of going to bed at dark, should, when required to watch, fall asleep, and I cannot consent to shoot him for such an act." The lad was pardoned and returned to his ranks. When found among the dead at Fredericksburg, he wore next to his heart a photograph of the President, with the words, "God bless President Lincoln."

An Army officer once traveled to Washington to see about the execution of twenty-four deserters who had been court-martialed and sentenced to be shot. "Mr. President," he argued, "unless these men are made an example of, the Army itself is in danger. Mercy to the few is cruelty to the many." "Mr. General," came the reply, "there are already too many weeping widows in the United States. For God's sake, don't ask me to add to the number, for I won't do it." On another such occasion, he declared, "Well, I think the boy can do us more good above ground than under."

In faded, shabby clothing, a mother of three soldiers, whose husband had fallen in battle, visited the President and asked that her eldest son be released to care for her. Lincoln quickly consented. Before he could be discharged, however, the boy died of wounds in a hospital. Lincoln then released the second son, declaring to the mother, "Now you have one, and I one of the other two left: that is no more than right." "The Lord bless you, Mr. President," she replied gratefully, "may you live a thousand years and always be at the head of this nation!"

The war was now six months old, and the crucial issue of slavery still undecided. General McClellan had advised caution, declaring, "A declaration of radical views, especially upon slavery, will rapidly disintegrate our present armies." And so Lincoln had bided his time, awaiting the opportune moment. In the fall of 1862 he decided to act. "I have promised my God that I will do it," he told his Cabinet on September 22nd, issuing the Emancipation Proclamation by which four million slaves would gain their freedom on January 1, 1863. He was aware of the historic import of his action, for two years later he commented, "It is the great event of the nineteenth century."

The following year, 1863, saw even graver events. In July the passage of the Draft Act, by which men were to be conscripted into the Army according to a lottery of names, caused a riot in New York City. Many lives were lost. Vicksburg fell to General Grant on July 4th; and Meade was victorious in the terrible three-day battle of Gettysburg, July 1–2, in which more than twenty thousand perished on each side. Announcing the victory at Gettysburg, Lincoln expressed the desire that the Fourth of July be observed as a day of prayer. His sturdy faith had been a constant source of guidance in the heavy responsibilities that were his.

On November 19th of that year, solemn ceremonies were held at Gettysburg to dedicate the field as a national cemetery. In brief but impassioned words, Lincoln consecrated the nation to the vast undertaking ahead: "The world will little note, nor long remember, what we say here; but it can never forget what they did here. It is for us, the living, rather, to be dedicated here to the unfinished work which they who fought here have thus far so nobly advanced. It is, rather, for us to be here dedicated to the great task remaining for us, that from these honored dead we take increased devotion to the cause for which they gave the last full measure of devotion; that we here highly resolve that these dead shall not have died in vain; that this nation, under God, shall have a new birth of freedom, and that the government of the people, by the people, and for the people, shall not perish from the earth."

The following year Grant, the hero of Vicksburg, assumed command of the Army. For the first time since the start of hostilities, Lincoln experienced some relief from his burdens. "Wherever Grant is," he observed, "things move." He now called for five hundred thousand more men. The beginning of the end was in sight. Sherman swept through the Confederate states to the sea. Grant had begun the siege of Richmond, declaring, "I propose to fight it out on this line if it takes all summer."

Lincoln had been elected to the Presidency for a

second time. In his second inaugural address, fore-seeing the end of the conflict, he urged the people: "With malice toward none, with charity for all, with firmness in the right, as God gives us to see the right, let us strive on to finish the work we are in; to bind up the nation's wounds; to care for him who shall have borne the battle, and for his widow and orphans; to do all which may achieve and cher-ish a just and lasting peace among ourselves and with all nations." On April 9, 1865, the long-awaited surrender came, when Lee gave up his sword to Grant at Appomattox Court House. Everywhere people gathered in their churches, of-fering their thanks that the war between the states was over. At a terrible cost, the Union had been pre-served, and four million slaves restored to freedom and given citizenship. Henceforth the nation was to know that no matter what thorny problems arose, they could not be solved by secession, for the pact of federation was inviolable. They could only be solved, as Lincoln had pleaded in his second inaugural address, by working together harmo-niously and without rancor.

The leadership of the gaunt, sad-eyed man whose belief in the union and in human equality had guided the nation through the dark years of the war was needed more than ever for the difficult period of reconstruction ahead. But the nation was to be deprived prematurely of his guidance. Five days after the surrender of General Lee, Lincoln attended a performance at Ford's Theater. During the war years he had worked night and day, without stopping to rest, explaining, "The tired part of me is inside and out of reach. . . . I feel a presentiment that I shall not outlast the rebellion. When it is over, my work will be done." His words were prophetic, for while he was enjoying the play, a half-crazed actor, John Wilkes Booth, crept into the box behind the President and fired a bullet into his brain. Then springing down upon the stage, he shouted, "Sic semper tyrannis! The South is avenged!" Lincoln scarcely stirred in his chair. Removed unconscious to a nearby house, he died April 15, 1865. His assassin was captured twelve days later, and shot while trying to escape.

Lincoln was gone, but his wisdom and courage were written indelibly into the history of the United States which he struggled so well to preserve in the first major crisis of its nationhood. The citizen who came from a humble Kentucky cabin to the White House had led the way toward "a new birth of freedom."

Ole Bull

No TRAVELER who has ever visited Bergen, Norway, can ever forget that picturesque old town with its quaint houses, its strange narrow streets, and its warm-hearted people in their colorful native costumes. Here on February 5, 1810, was born Ole Bornemann Bull, destined to become the greatest violin virtuoso of his time. His father was a chemist by profession, but the entire family was musical, and often the relatives from the surrounding countryside gathered at Ole's home for an evening of music. On these occasions, the small boy would creep under a table or a sofa and listen enraptured for hours, or until he was discovered or carried off to bed.

From his infancy, the imaginative child lived in a world of music. He seemed to feel it everywhere about him; in the spring, as he played in the fields, he fancied he heard the thousand little melodies that nature makes, in the songs of birds, the sound of waterfalls, and in the stirring of the meadow grasses swayed by the wind.

One of the happiest days in young Ole's life came

CJNAAR

in his fourth year, when his uncle gave him a small violin. The child was enchanted with the precious instrument, and learned his notes at the same time as he learned his primer. He was forbidden his music until his lessons were finished, but more often than not he disobeyed and had to be punished.

Ole's mother was a woman of high intelligence and rare cultivation, and she soon recognized the extraordinary talents of her son. When the child was eight years old, she prevailed upon his father to provide him with a music teacher and to buy him a new red violin, one of the best to be had. Long years afterward, Ole Bull told the story of the little red violin with tears of nostalgia in his eyes at the scene it recalled: So excited was the young musician by his beautiful gift, that he could not sleep on the first night it was in the house. At midnight, he stole out in his night clothes to take one more look at it. Soon he was fingering the little instrument, raising the bow, and trying it gently across the strings. Then, abandoning all caution, the boy broke into a capriccio of which he was especially fond, and the music swelled louder and louder. Just as he reached the climax of his impromptu performance, Ole felt himself seized by his irate father; the treasured violin slipped from his grasp, fell to the floor and was broken beyond repair.

Despite the disaster of the red violin, Ole continued his music lessons, and within two years he far outstripped his teacher in skill and technique. He began to compose melodies of his own, and would sometimes hide in caves or in clumps of bushes while he tried out his own improvisations. When he could not make his violin do as he wished, he would fling it away impetuously, and not touch it again for a long time. At other times, he would play for days and nights on end, scarcely taking time to eat or sleep. At fourteen, he first heard of Paganini, the great master, and begged for some of his music to play—a difficult feat for a boy of his age.

Ole's mastery of the violin went further than his ability to play. One day an old miser, of whom the Bergen boys were afraid, called Ole into his home as he was passing, and said, "Are you the boy who plays the fiddle?"

"Yes, sir."

"Then come with me. I have a fiddle I bought in England that I want to show you."

The fiddle needed a bridge and a sounding post, and these the boy gladly whittled out. Then he played for the old man his favorite air, "God Save the King." The lad thought no more of the matter until the next afternoon, when to his surprise he received four pairs of doves, one of which wore a blue ribbon around its neck with a card attached bearing the name of Ole Bull. This simple gift, expressing the gratitude of an old man, meant far more to Ole Bull than all the diamonds he received in later years from European royalty.

Ole's preoccupation with music did not keep him from growing into a strong, vigorous boy with a deep sense of justice. His father had engaged a private tutor, Musaeus by name, for his sons. The tutor was a stern man whom the boys heartily detested. He took a perverse pleasure in caning the boys as frequently as possible; and he soon decided that Ole's music interfered with his other studies and forbade his playing the violin. At last, Ole and his brothers could bear it no longer. One morning at half past four, as the teacher was dragging the youngest boy out of bed, Ole sprang upon him and gave him a sound beating. The smaller boys put their heads out from under the bed clothes and cried out, "Don't give up, Ole! Give it to him!" The whole household soon appeared on the scene and though little was said, the feeling seemed to be that justice had been done.

When Ole was eighteen, he was sent to the University of Oslo to study for the ministry. His father asked that he give up his music for a time and concentrate upon the classical studies needed for the profession he wished to enter. Ole had every intention of following his father's dictum, but before many days had passed some Bergen students asked him to play for a charitable association.

"But," said Ole, "my father has forbidden me to play."

"Would your father object to your doing an act of charity?"

"Well, of course that alters the case a little."

So Ole played nearly the whole night through at the home of one of the professors. He kept telling himself that his father would be pleased if the faculty and his fellow students liked him, but the next morning he failed in his Latin examination. The worried young student confided his plight to the professor at whose home he had played, and was secretly delighted when the professor replied:

"My boy, this is the very best thing that could have happened to you. Do you honestly think yourself fitted for a curacy in Finland or a mission among the Lapps? You are first and last a musician, and you should devote all your energies to music alone."

Then the good man told him that old professor Thrane of the music department was seriously ill, and that the position of director of the University's Philharmonic Society was now vacant. Ole could have the appointment for the asking, he continued. Thus Ole Bull's musical career began.

The young man grew restless at Oslo. He was filled with doubt and wondered whether or not he had real talent. He determined to go to Cassell and to consult Louis Spohr. But the great Louis Spohr, at the height of his fame as a musician, had no time or patience for the unknown student who had traveled five hundred miles to see him. He brushed him aside, saying that he was leaving immediately for Nordhausen where he was to play at a musical festival.

Ole followed the master to Nordhausen, and his doubts grew deeper as he listened to the music and realized how different Spohr's methods and interpretations were from his own. Then and there he resolved to go to Paris. Three weeks went by during which he gave three concerts at Trondhjeim and Bergen, earned five hundred dollars, and set out for the Wonder City.

To the untraveled young musician from Norway, Paris was a city of light and song. Here he might mingle with the great of the musical world. At the Grand Opera there were gallery seats to be had where he could listen night after night to the wonderful voice of the celebrated Madame Malibran. There were innumerable concerts at which he could revel in the music of Berlioz and other famed composers.

For a while, it did not matter to Ole that no one

in Paris paid any attention to him. And he was too bemused to notice that his money was dwindling fast. The situation became desperate when a chance acquaintance stole all his clothes and what little money he had left. He was now penniless.

Strangely enough, an epidemic of cholera restored his fortunes. That summer, Paris was swept by the dreadful plague, and Ole Bull, half ill and feverish, was forced to seek new lodgings. He wandered aimlessly about the city until, almost exhausted, he came to a house with a "furnished room to let" sign in a window.

An elderly woman opened the door and was about to tell him there were no vacant rooms, when her pretty granddaughter, Alexandrine Felicie, called out, "Look at him, grandmamma." Putting on her glasses, the old lady saw that the young man bore a striking resemblance to her son who had died. The next day found him established at the Villeminots' house, but very ill of brain fever. For many weeks Madame Villeminot and her granddaughter nursed him back to health. When he recovered, the Musical Lyceum of Oslo, having heard of his misfortunes, sent eight hundred dollars to aid the career of this talented countryman.

A brave experiment brought Ole Bull his initial musical success. A friend of his, a certain Monsieur Lacour, thought he had discovered that a new type of varnish would increase the sweetness of tone in a violin. He persuaded Ole to use one of his instruments at a soiree given by a Duke of the Italian Legation. As the musician began to play before the fashionable assembly, the heat of the room brought out a strong odor of asafoetida in the varnish. The young man became embarrassed and then excited and played as though beside himself. The audience acclaimed this unorthodox new player, and on the next day he was invited to give a concert for the Duke of Montebello.

With the confidence of his first success, Ole Bull set out on a concert tour through Switzerland and Italy. Unlike most young artists, he had the rare facility of being able to accept criticism and of turning it to his advantage. In Milan, one of the music journals said of him, "He is not master of himself; he has no style; he is an untrained musician. If he be a diamond, he is certainly in the rough and unpolished."

Ole Bull went at once to the publisher and asked who had written the article. "If you want the responsible person," said the editor, "I am he."

"No," said the artist, "I have not come to call the writer to account, but to thank him. The man who wrote that article understands music; but it is not enough to tell me my faults; he must teach me how to rid myself of them."

That same evening, the editor of the journal took Ole Bull to call upon the critic who had written the article. Ole talked long and earnestly with him, and decided at once to devote six months to study under able masters before again appearing in public.

When the violinist emerged from his self–imposed exile, he was warmly received at Venice. But it was at Bologna that he won the acclaim that was to continue for the rest of his life. Madame Malibran had been engaged to sing in two concerts, but on the afternoon of her first performance she quarreled with her manager, Senor Zampieri, and refused to appear. The manager was distraught. Meanwhile, in a poor quarter of the city, Ole Bull was practicing by an open window, unaware that he was being overheard by Madame Rossini, a member of the opera company. She hastened to the manager and told him of the wonderful playing she had heard. On the night of the concert, Zampieri burst into Ole's bedroom and asked him to improvise. He listened for a few minutes, then hurried the young artist off to the theater.

The audience was, of course, cold and unreceptive when they learned that Madame Malibran was not to appear. Then Ole Bull began to play, and people seemed to hold their breath. When the curtain fell, the house shook with applause; flowers were showered down upon the artist; he was immediately engaged for a series of concerts. Outside the theater, an admiring throng drew his carriage to his hotel, while a procession with torchlights acted as a guard of honor.

Almost overnight, a new artist had become the idol of two continents. Ole Bull continued on his triumphant way to Florence and to Rome. At Rome he composed his celebrated "Polacca Guerriera" in a single night. The idea for this wonderful piece of music had come to him long ago in Naples as he stood alone at midnight, watching Mt. Vesuvius flame.

Next he returned to Paris where he was to give his first concert at the Grand Opera. Flushed with joy at the fulfillment of his boyhood dream, the violinist began to play and then—to his horror—the a-string of his instrument snapped. For a moment he turned pale; then with scarcely a tremor he transposed the entire piece and finished it on three strings. Musicians in the audience marveled at the stupendous feat, and could hardly believe that the string had broken.

Ole Bull was now twenty-six and at the height of his fame. But he had never forgotten the pretty little Felicie Villeminot who had cared for him when he was ill and unknown. In the summer of 1836, Ole married little Felicie, and was a devoted husband to the day of her death twenty-six years later. In many of his letters from abroad, he often said, "the word *home* has above all others the greatest charm for me."

There seemed no end to the demands made upon the young artist, once his fame was established. In sixteen months, he gave two hundred and seventy-four concerts in the British Isles alone. In London, the *Times* said of him, "His command of the instrument, from the top to the bottom of the scale—and he has a scale of his own of three complete octaves on each string—is absolutely perfect." In Liverpool, he played before unbelievably large audiences and on one occasion fell victim to the physical hazards of his profession. So intense was his playing of the "Polacca" with an exceptionally strong orchestra, that he ruptured a blood vessel and had to have his coat cut from him.

On his return to Scandinavia, he gave five concerts at Stockholm. So moved was the King when Ole Bull played before him at the palace, that he rose and stood until the "Polacca" was finished. He presented the artist with the Order of Vasa, set in precious stones.

Despite the honors heaped upon him by almost every European country, there was in Ole Bull a strong love and pride in his native land. Once he wrote tenderly to his wife, saying, "I work, not for myself, but for you, my family, my country, my Norway, of which I am proud." At the summit of his fame, he played as often for the peasants of Bergen and Oslo as he did for the rich who could pay fabulous sums for his performances. He was essentially a democratic artist who loved people for their own worth. Hans Andersen and Bertel Thorwaldsen were his devoted friends. He was humble in his admiration for the immortal Mozart; once he was heard to say that no mortal man could write Mozart's "Requiem" and live.

In November, 1843, the now celebrated Norwegian was invited to come to America. At first, some of the prominent musicians in New York were critical of him, saying that his style was meretricious and flamboyant. But when James Gordon Bennett offered him the columns of the *Herald* that he might reply to his critics, Ole Bull said simply: "I think, Mr. Bennett, it is best that they write against me and I play against them." Soon everyone succumbed to the brilliance of his playing, and one distinguished critic wrote of his first performance in New York, "His bow touched the strings as if in sport and brought forth light leaps of sound, with electric rapidity, yet clear in their distinctness. He played on four strings at once and produced the rich harmony of four instruments. His audience was beside itself with delight, and, as he finished his playing, the orchestra threw down its instruments in ecstatic wonder."

At once, all America took the brilliant artist to her heart. In all, he gave more than two hundred concerts throughout the country and received tremendous ovations everywhere he went. In spite of his grueling schedules, Ole Bull played with undiminished vigor and artistry, yet managed to find time to give extra performances at many hospitals and charitable institutions along the way.

On his return to Norway, Ole Bull attempted to fulfill one of his lifelong dreams. In the nineteenth century, it was all too frequently impossible for the average person to enjoy great art and great music. Only the rich and powerful could afford such pleasures. Ole Bull had long dreamed of founding a National Theatre in Bergen for the advancement of music and drama in Norway. Now, rich and renowned, he set aside a considerable share of his personal fortune for this purpose, and in 1850, the theater was opened. Unfortunately, however, the Norwegian Parliament refused to grant an appropriation for the continued support of the institution; Ole could not carry the burden alone, and, after a few seasons, the enterprise died out.

America and its sturdy democracy made a profound impression on Ole Bull, and he often spoke of himself as her adopted son. A few years after his

triumphal American tour, the great violinist conceived the idea of founding a Norwegian colony in
the United States, "consecrated to liberty, baptized
with independence, and protected by the Union's
mighty flag." For several years he devoted all the
proceeds of his concerts to the project; and at last
he was able to purchase one hundred and twenty-
five thousand acres of land along the Susquehanna
River in Pennsylvania. He laid out five villages in
which a church, a school, a store, and some three
hundred houses were built; and he took out patents
for a new smelting-furnace. A few families had already come from Norway, when a crushing blow
fell upon the little colony. It was discovered that
the title to the land which Ole Bull had purchased
was not clear, and that the kindly man had been de-
frauded of his entire fortune. Saddened by the failure of his plan, and worried by years of legal wran-
gling, Ole Bull now went back to Norway, only to
find that some of his countrymen thought him
guilty of improper speculation, a fact which almost
broke his heart.

During the Centennial year, he returned once
more to America and made his home with his second wife, an American woman, in Cambridge in
the house of James Russell Lowell. The world-
famous musician, now failing in health, loved the
quaint little city of Cambridge where he delighted

in the friendship of such men as Longfellow who wrote of him in his *Tales of a Wayside Inn:*

> "The angel with the violin,
> Painted by Raphael, he seemed."

Old and tired though he was, Ole Bull never lost his human touch. Near his home, he was approached by a young barber who had heard him play. "Mister," said the lad, "can't you come down to my shop tomorrow to get shaved, and show me those tricks?" Obediently, the master went to the barber shop the next day and showed the young novice the secrets of his skill.

In 1880, Ole Bull sailed, for the last time, to Europe to his lovely home at Lysö, an island in the sea, eighteen miles from Bergen. He was ill throughout the voyage, and longed only that he might see his native land once more before he died. His wish was granted, and he lingered on for a few weeks at Lysö in the beautiful house which he himself had planned and built. After his death, all Norway joined in honoring Ole Bull, who was not only a world-famed musician, but a great-hearted man.

Charles Dickens

T HROUGH the quiet English countryside near Chatham in the 1820's, a lively brown-haired boy liked to roam. Often his feet led him to a stately manorhouse that overlooked the main road between Rochester and Gravesend. Crowning the highest hilltop, it seemed to embody all his dreams of honor and achievement. The little boy of Chatham would grow up to become master of the house on Gad's Hill. And his imagination would enrich the lives of parlor-maids and princes. For Charles Dickens became one of the best-loved novelists of all times.

Charles John Huffam Dickens was born on February 7, 1812, at Portsea, a suburb of Portsmouth. The son of a clerk in the Navy Pay-Office, he spent his early childhood chiefly in seaport towns. When the boy was two, his father, John Dickens, was transferred to London, and shortly thereafter to the Kentish port of Chatham. In a plain little cottage with a front of whitewashed plaster and a tiny garden at each end, the Dickens family settled. Bur-

dened with the task of caring for a numerous family, his mother had little time to devote to her second child, Charles.

His father, however, was less preoccupied. A very agreeable man, John Dickens loved to tell amusing stories, and gaily brewed a lemon punch on the slightest provocation. Father and son became good companions, making long expeditions about the countryside together. Often they stopped for refreshment at a neighboring inn, where Charles, strongly gifted as a mimic and comedian, would be lifted to a table to perform.

The observant boy was soon aware of his charming parent's irresponsibility. John Dickens was a "gentleman," who found it hard to live within an income that at best amounted to three hundred pounds a year. A simple woman of unmethodical mind, Mrs. Dickens was not equal to the difficult task of making ends meet. And the frequency with which new little Dickenses were added to the household hastened their impoverishment. The result was a steadily rising tide of debts.

Next door to the little white cottage in Chatham stood a Baptist meeting house, whose minister, a Mr. Giles, undertook the education of Charles at the age of nine. A musty heap of books which the boy discovered in the attic of his home yielded up many treasures. The adventures of *Robinson Cru-soe, Gil Blas, Tom Jones, Don Quixote,* and *Rod-erick Random* were quickly digested, as well as the lore of *Arabian Nights* and the contents of miscel-laneous newspapers.

Soon the Dickens brood grew to eight, and the family fortunes declined in inverse ratio to the number of mouths to feed. Harassed by rapidly mounting debts, the family moved to London, where John Dickens had been recalled. Prosperity continued as far around the corner as ever. But as he plunged deeper and deeper into debt, John Dick-ens, with the boundless optimism of a Micawber, never despaired but that something would "turn up." Composing a "deed" which signed away his salary to creditors, he hinted darkly of sacrifices to come. Eventually the "deed" passed from the realm of fantasy to reality.

The family larder became increasingly bare, and the little Dickens grew daily shabbier. Clutching at a last straw of hope, Mrs. Dickens resolved to open a school for young ladies. She moved the family to Gower Street and hung out a plate em-blazoned in shiny brass with the words, "Mrs. Dickens' Establishment." Charles was sent out to distribute the prospectus from door to door. No stu-dents were forthcoming, however, and all hope soon vanished. The furniture was seized by bailiffs. On a flood of debts, John Dickens was swept into debtors' prison, the Marshalsea.

At the age of eleven, Charles found that his relatively carefree childhood was over. Numerous household tasks occupied his days. He must go to market, mind his brothers and sisters, visit his father in prison, and, most important of all, deal with the pawnbroker. Soon the few remaining possessions of the family had found their way into the latter's hands. The boy was stung with shame at his father's predicament, and troubled with anxiety about the future.

Then from a surprising source an unexpected offer came. A distant cousin of Mrs. Dickens owned a blacking factory on Old Hungerford Stairs, and he was willing to employ Charles. The boy's task was to wrap the jars of blacking in paper, tying them up and pasting on the labels. Soon he became so dexterous that a little circle of curious passers-by would gather around the window where he and a companion worked. But Charles dreamed of continuing his schooling, and of succeeding where his father had failed. In the dark, rat-infested old factory, surrounded by rough companions, the sensitive boy lavished on bottles of blacking the hours he longed to spend with his books. He earned his six shillings a week with a "secret agony of soul" that left per-

manent traces. So deep was the humiliation he suffered that for many years afterward he was unable
to talk of this experience. It was not until 1849 that
he eased the weight of these unhappy memories,
projecting them into an autobiographical novel,
David Copperfield.

The shadow of the Marshalsea loomed large in
Charles Dickens' mind. It was a grimly astonishing
place—the debtors' prison. An "oblong pile of bar-
racks buildings," shut off by high spiked walls from
the city of London, it was a little state within itself.
Humming with petty enterprises and centering
about a social hierarchy all its own, the daily life of
the Marshalsea was rich in human drama. A stream
of people crossed the prison threshold each day to
visit and sell necessities to the inmates. Upon pay-
ment of the required rental, the families of prisoners were permitted to lodge with them. And so, unable to sustain her large household single-handed,
Mrs. Dickens joined the improvident John Dickens
in one of the squalid houses of the Marshalsea. She
took the entire family with her, except for Charles.
Lodgings were found for him in Camden Town.
But he spent Sundays with his family at the prison.

After a scanty breakfast of bread and milk, the
boy would go trudging off to Old Hungerford
Stairs. Often the displays in the pastryshops along
the way tempted him to buy a stale cake. Then he

must do with only a slice of pudding for lunch, and bread and coffee at teatime. Moving closer to the Marshalsea, he was able to have breakfast with his family, waiting until the great gates swung open for the day. He would join them again after work until nine, when the last visitor had to be gone. The inner life of the Marshalsea was strangely absorbing. Many of the scenes he witnessed and the stories gleaned from his mother, the boy stored away in his memory. He was later to give a vivid picture of prison life in the novel, *Little Dorrit.*

At last the redoubtable optimism of John Dickens was justified by an unexpected windfall. A small legacy enabled him to leave the Marshalsea. But Charles was permitted to continue working at the blacking factory, until he despaired of ever continuing his education. A quarrel of John Dickens with his wife's cousin, however, brought about the boy's release. Charles then persuaded his father to send him to school. Accordingly, he found himself enrolled as a day student at the Wellington House Academy, whose tyrannical proprietor and headmaster, Mr. Jones, punctuated his lessons with resounding blows on the pupils' backs with a swordlike cane.

The medieval methods prevalent in such schools were to be described in later years by the author of *David Copperfield, Nicholas Nickleby,* and *Dom-*

bey and Son. Despite the school's drawbacks, however, the days passed pleasantly enough at Mr. Jones' Academy. Dickens' leadership asserted itself in the amateur theatricals he promoted, a newspaper published on bits of paper from his copybook, and various harmless pranks he instigated. But the legacy which had so opportunely released his father from prison was almost gone, and the boy's days at school were numbered. At the age of fifteen he was forced to return to work.

Since he had learned to read and spell correctly, and had acquired a smattering of Latin, he found a position as clerk for Mr. Blackmore, a solicitor at Gray's Inn. His weekly salary consisted of thirteen shillings and sixpence, later increased to fifteen. As he performed his daily tasks at the lawyer's office, he observed with fresh young eyes the fascinating ways of solicitors and clerks, and of the endless stream of clients in all walks of life who passed through the portals of Mr. Blackmore. Obliged to run errands which took him to all parts of London, he acquired an intimate knowledge of the city's life in all its varied aspects, which the novelist-to-be carefully amassed for future capital.

Spurred on by the exhaustion of the legacy, John Dickens had learned shorthand, and become a reporter at the House of Commons. Charles decided to follow his father's example. Investing his entire savings of one guinea in an old shorthand book, he plunged into the study with his characteristic intensity, stopping only when he had mastered it and become the best reporter in London. Employed first in the Lord Chancellor's Court, he later became a parliamentary reporter for several newspapers, beginning with the *True Sun* and the *Mirror of Parliament*.

In 1830, at the age of eighteen, shortly before he became a parliamentary reporter, Dickens met Maria Beadnell, the daughter of a moderately well-to-do banker, and promptly fell in love. "All was over in a moment," he was to write in *David Copperfield* of a character which he identified with Maria. "I loved Dora Spenlow to distraction. She was more than human to me. She was a Fairy, a Sylph." The family of the sylph, however, although friendly to Dickens, did not look upon the penniless young man as a likely suitor for their daughter's hand.

Maria was sent to the Continent to attend a finishing school. Upon her return, her reception of Dickens was pointedly cool. After a number of vain efforts to win back her affections, Dickens abandoned his suit. Maria married Henry Winter, a business man, and Dickens was not to see her again for many years. The profound effect of this loss may well be measured by his heartfelt declaration on re-establishing contact with Maria twenty years later. "I have never been so good a man since, as I was when you made me wretchedly unhappy," he wrote. "I shall never be half so good a fellow any more."

The *True Sun* and the *Mirror of Parliament* soon closed their doors. In 1834 Dickens joined the staff of the *Morning Chronicle* as special reporter. A rare opportunity now presented itself to hear the heartbeat of a great city. Holiday revels, brawls and riots, local elections—all stamped lively pictures on his impressionable mind. Snatches of Cockney wisdom overheard on the London streets lingered in his ears. He posted madly about the countryside, in his calling of reporter, observing provincial life, and racing his professional rivals to beat their stories to press.

His earnings had now reached the comfortable sum of five guineas a week. For the first time in his life, Dickens' mind was free of financial anxieties, and he could pursue his long-cherished ambition to write. At the age of twenty-two, he tremulously posted to the *Monthly Magazine* a short story he had written, signed with the pen name of "Boz." Much to his surprise and delight, the story was printed in the following issue. The young reporter then continued writing, in the same vein, little vignettes of life in London and the provinces. Soon he transferred the series to the *Morning Chronicle,* whose publishers offered him two guineas a week for the sketches. Added to his income as reporter, this made a grand total of seven guineas. The *Sketches by Boz,* later published in book form, were enthusiastically received by London readers. Dickens soon decided to give up the profession of reporter altogether, and devote his efforts to writing books.

The historian, Thomas Carlyle, who met "Boz" at a dinner party as he stood on the threshold of fame, described him as having "clear, blue intelligent eyes, eyebrows that he arches amazingly, large protrusive rather loose mouth, a face of most extreme mobility, which he shuttles about—eyebrows, eyes, mouth and all—in a very singular manner while speaking." Only twenty-four, Dickens already impressed everyone he met with his vitality and purposefulness. The youthful author was now asked by a firm of London publishers, Chapman and Hall, to write a group of humorous sketches built around a sporting club. These were to be published serially, featuring the illustrations of the well-known artist, Seymour. Dickens agreed, and *Pickwick Papers* came into being.

After the first number, which met with little success, the artist, Seymour, committed suicide. The fate of the venture hung in the balance. Then another artist was discovered whose work was peculiarly in accord with Dickens' literary qualities. Hablot Browne, or "Phiz," was to illustrate many of the author's novels with eminent success. As the subsequent numbers of *Pickwick Papers* appeared, the comic genius of Dickens won an increasingly greater number of readers. From the moment when Sam Weller was introduced, after the publication of five or six installments, the success of *Pickwick Papers* was assured. The latest Wellerism was heard on everyone's lips. A vogue for goods of "Pickwick" brand spread like a fever among the London shopkeepers. Although only 400 copies had been published for the first number of *Pickwick,* the fifteenth exceeded 40,000 in advance sales alone.

The historian, Carlyle, reported a story told him by a clergyman concerning a dying man whose final hours he had been attempting to comfort. "Well, thank God," whispered the patient weakly as the minister left the room, *"Pickwick* will be out in ten days anyway!" Thus in his early twenties Dickens had already won a generous measure of fame. He was destined to live the rest of his life in the public eye.

Early during the publication of *Pickwick Papers,* Dickens had married. His bride was Catherine Hogarth, eldest daughter of George Hogarth, one of the publishers of the *Morning Chronicle.* A pretty blue-eyed girl, Kate had proved a sympathetic audience to the rejected suitor of Maria Beadnell. Her general lack of purpose and competence, however, was irritating to so exacting a man as Dickens. The courtship was not smooth. On April 2, 1836, the ill-suited young couple were married. Kate's younger sister Mary, to whom Dickens was deeply devoted, became a member of the household. But in May, 1837, after a gay evening at the theater, Mary Hogarth died of a sudden illness. The shock and grief of Dickens were so intense that publication of *Pickwick Papers* had to be halted for a month. "I can solemnly say," he was to write many years later of this unfortunate event, "that waking or sleeping, I have never lost recollection of our hard trial and sorrow, and I feel that I never shall." And in the year of his own death, he wrote again with reference to Mary: "She is so much in my thoughts at all times . . . that the recollection of her is an essential part of my being, and is as inseparable from my existence as the beating of my heart." For in Mary Hogarth Dickens saw his ideal of perfect womanhood. Her face was to brighten the pages of his novels again and again —as Little Nell in *The Old Curiosity Shop,* as Amy in *Little Dorrit,* and as Agnes in *David Copperfield.*

Following the death of Mary, Kate's second sister,

Georgina, went to live with the young couple, and Dickens turned to his work once again. His debt to Georgina was to increase with the years, for she was to prove the mainstay of the household. As the bond between Charles and Kate crumbled, Georgina kept order in domestic affairs, and mothered her rapidly growing brood of nieces and nephews.

Dazzled by the success of *Pickwick*, London publishers now vied with each other for more of Dickens' stories. In *Oliver Twist*, published in 1838, he wrote of an orphan boy whose early years were spent in a public workhouse. Written in a grim vein that contrasted sharply with the light-hearted satire of *Pickwick*, the novel exposed the faults of the institution to the public eye. Dickens' literary reputation was now solidly established. And before the final numbers of *Oliver Twist* had rolled off the press, the installments of a third book, *Nicholas Nickleby*, began to appear. The major portion of Dickens' work was to be similarly issued in installments.

The ten years that followed were a time of astonishing productivity for Dickens. Out of this period came five great novels and miscellaneous stories. Mornings were usually devoted to writing, while the printer's messenger cooled his heels, waiting to receive his copy. In the afternoon and evening, Dickens loved to take long, rambling walks.

Particularly was he fond of prowling the streets of London, for without the stimulus of "that magic lantern" his imagination found it hard to glow. In a wry phrase, Dickens described himself during this period as "a gentleman with rather long hair and no neckcloth, who writes and grins, as if he thought he was very funny indeed." But the extravagant velvet waistcoat he wore about London, with a long gold chain and as many as two underwaistcoats, signaled the triumph he felt in the vigorous maturity of his powers.

Following the publication of *Nicholas Nickleby*, a serio-comic romance which was to set the pattern of much of his later work, he published a book based on the No Popery riots of 1780, entitled *Barnaby Rudge*. Suspending an unsuccessfully miscellany known as *Master Humphrey's Clock*, he continued one of the stories as an independent novel. The resultant book, *The Old Curiosity Shop*, won the immediate sympathy of the public for its heroine, Little Nell, an innocent young girl beset with many dangers. It was with much "agony of spirit" that Dickens concluded the story with the death of Little Nell, for she was a personification of Mary Hogarth. "Old wounds bleed afresh when I only think of the way of doing it," he wrote. "What the actual doing it will be, God knows.

Dear Mary died yesterday, when I think of this sad story."

Dickens' fame was enhanced in America, as well as England, by *The Old Curiosity Shop*. Many a sober housewife and businessman had waited at their pier for the ship bearing the final number of the novel to arrive, in anguished suspense to learn the fate of its delicate heroine. They wrote to the creator of Little Nell, urging him to visit America. In 1842, Dickens made his first trip to the United States. He was eager to observe at first hand the new, democratic state which had sprung up in a wilderness, unhampered by the heavy chains of tradition. The warmest of receptions was accorded him.

Unfortunately, he found the free American ways and manners offensive. Nor did the new democracy correspond in every way with the perfect ideal he had conceived in advance. Particularly was he shocked by the flourishing system of slavery. He denounced this abuse, as well as the pirating of English copyrights by American publishers. And staid New Englanders were startled to see the author of *Oliver Twist* appear at a ball in Boston, attired in a vivid green waistcoat, crimson tie, and lavender trousers, sporting "a regular flower-garden" in his lapel. The sympathy of the press and many of the public was alienated. "This is not the Republic I came to see," wrote the disappointed Dickens to friends back home. "This is not the Republic of my imagination. . . . England, even England, bad and faulty as the old land is, rises in the comparison." After completing his tour, which took him as far west as St. Louis, he returned to England, where he published his *American Notes,* describing the United States in somewhat acidulous terms. He was to return to America again, however, when old scores were forgotten in an atmosphere of mutual understanding and appreciation.

Dickens now set to work on another novel, *Martin Chuzzlewit,* published in 1844, attacked hypocrisy and self-absorption, traditional English failings. Whether because of the complex plot or the subject of the satire, the book failed to maintain the level of popularity set by the preceding novels. Dickens decided to take his family abroad for a while. Following the publication in 1843 of *A Christmas Carol,* probably the most famous and best-loved Christmas story in English literature, he set out with his household for a prolonged stay on the Continent.

Although Dickens had gone abroad, among other reasons, for the express purpose of extending his experience and sources of description, the books which he brought back with him from his residence in France and Italy were characteristically English in setting and background. And they were woven about the usual Dickensian themes. The clanging of the church bells at Genoa had inspired *The Chimes,* written in 1845; and the remainder of Dickens' stay in Italy was devoted to completing the series of Christmas stories introduced by *A Christmas Carol.* During his sojourn in Paris he had visited, in the approved English fashion, all the spots of interest, including the Morgue, the Louvre, Versailles and the site of the Bastille. But his serious concern was with a new novel, *Dombey and Son,* in which he attacked the excessive pride of a rich business man in his firm, and in his son as the next of his dynasty.

For the publication of this novel, Dickens returned to London. The success of the book restored him to the tidal crest of popularity again. A maidservant in the school attended by one of Dickens' sons was awestruck at meeting "the man who put together Dombey." Although she herself could not read, her landlord read out the serial issue of *Dombey and Son* at a regular monthly teaparty. "Good gracious!" she exclaimed, astonished to find the author an ordinary mortal. "I thought it would have needed at least three or four men to put together Dombey!"

London now drew Dickens into a whirl of ac-

tivities unrelated to his writing. Always strongly
attracted to the theater, he now organized with a
few friends a charity performance of Ben Jonson's
"Every Man in His Humour." Besides taking the
leading role, Dickens supervised the entire production, assuming a variety of duties ranging from
stagehand to wardrobe master. So great was the
success of the play that performances had to be
given elsewhere, even in the provinces. Under this
strenuous regime, Dickens' health suffered, and
he became subject to severe headaches and eye
troubles. Despite this, in 1850 he undertook the
editorship of a newspaper, the *Daily News,* which
with customary zeal he dedicated to "combatting
evil and advancing the welfare of the poor and
the happiness of society." After a few months of
this ambitious program, however, he concluded
that his abilities did not lie in this field. Resigning,
he founded a weekly, *Household Words,* which,
publishing only creative writing, was more in accord with his talents. This publication continued
with all success for eight years, until it was reorganized in 1859 under the name of *All the Year
Round.*

Using his early life as material, Dickens now
embarked on a novel of a new type. In *David Copperfield,* which marked the peak of his powers, he
told the story of his blighted childhood. Maria

Beadnell, the sweetheart of his youth, served as the model for Dora Spenlow, while John Dickens, his father, appeared as the always bankrupt but irrepressibly hopeful Micawber. *David* was followed by *Bleak House* (1853), a satire on certain aspects of the law; *Hard Times* (1854), an attack on the *laissez faire* theory of economics; and *Little Dorrit* (1857), a story of life in the Marshalsea.

Dickens' lifelong need for constant activity now began to intensify, as his imaginative faculty became more sluggish. Whether editing a newspaper, rearing his family, or promoting amateur theatricals, he was always the hub of the undertaking. Absorbing himself in work, he tried to blot out his growing personal disquiet. "Why is it that, as with poor David," he wrote, "a sense comes always crushing on me now, when I fall into low spirits, as of one happiness I have missed in life, and one friend and companion I have never made? . . . However strange it is to be never at rest, and never satisfied, and ever trying after something that is never reached . . ." At the root of his dissatisfaction lay his failure to achieve a happy domestic relationship. Early in his marriage, Dickens had realized the error of his choice. "Amiable and complying" though she was, the mother of his ten children lacked the ability to be an understanding companion to such a man as he, while her competence in household matters was question-able. The impatience of Dickens with his wife's shortcomings added to the disharmony between them.

During these troubled times, Dickens was surprised to receive a letter from Maria Beadnell Winter. After a lapse of some twenty-two years, she was anxious to renew their acquaintance. The warmth of his replies to her letters suggests the untarnished light in which he had preserved her image through the years. But that he was considerably disillusioned upon meeting her again might be surmised from the passage in *Little Dorrit* depicting the encounter of Arthur Clennam with the sweetheart of his younger days: "Flora, always tall, had grown to be very broad, too, and short of breath . . . Flora, who had seemed enchanting in all she said and thought, was diffused and silly . . . Flora, who had been spoiled and artless long ago, was determined to be spoiled and artless now: that was a fatal blow."

The shattering of the illusion which had enveloped the love of his youth, however, wrought no improvement in his home life. In 1858 Dickens and his wife agreed to a separation. The eldest son, Charles, went to live with his mother. The other children remained with their father, who shortly thereafter purchased the house on Gad's Hill, satis-

fying the ambition of his boyhood. Settling in the
big house with his children and their aunt Georgina, Dickens set about reorganizing the pattern
of his daily life. The same bustling spirit which
always hovered about him pervaded the air at
Gad's Hill. No petty detail was too small for his
interest. Numerous guests filled the house at holi-
days, and the indefatigable host would arrange
charades and theatricals with his familiar gusto.

But these domestic pursuits were soon inter-
rupted, as the conquest of a new field beckoned.
A reading from *Pickwick Papers* which Dickens
gave for a charitable cause met with such enthusiasm that he was asked to tour England and
Scotland professionally, giving readings from his
books. Succumbing at last to his long-repressed
love of the footlights, he took to the stage with the
ease of the born actor. But no applause fell more
pleasantly on his ear than the words of the old
man in Belfast who asked to shake his hand, muttering, "God bless you, Sir . . . for the light
you've been in me house," or of the woman in
York who approached him on the street exclaim-
ing, "Mr. Dickens, let me touch the hand that has
filled my home with many friends." In the inter-
vals between his public readings, he was writing
the last of his novels: *A Tale of Two Cities* (1859),
a romance of the French Revolution; *Great Ex-*

pectations (1861) and *Our Mutual Friend* (1865), in which snobbery was his target.

Hardly was the ink dry on *Our Mutual Friend,* when Dickens was off on another series of readings. His tour took him to the United States, for the second time, in 1867; and a new generation, oblivious of past misunderstandings, welcomed him enthusiastically. It was the dead of winter when he arrived. But so widespread was his renown that "people slept on mattresses before the booking-office windows, and neighboring restaurants sent meals to sustain them. No hall was big enough, and in Brooklyn the writer was given a church for his performance. From the pulpit he read the adventures of Oliver Twist and the death of Little Nell." His health had begun to fail while working on *Our Mutual Friend,* and these exertions rapidly undermined it still further. He took sedatives in order to sleep at night, then found it necessary to rouse himself with stimulants in order to endure the strain of reading. After visiting New York, Boston, Philadelphia, and Washington, the exhausted Dickens returned to England, where he made his final public appearances in 1870.

He now began work on a new novel, *The Mystery of Edwin Drood.* A departure from his previous pattern, it was to be a type of detective story, reminiscent of the work of his friend, Wilkie Collins. Dickens was destined never to complete it, however. On June 8, 1870, after writing all day in the chalet of his garden at Gad's Hill, he collapsed of a stroke at the dinner table. Lapsing into unconsciousness, he died the following morning, at the age of fifty-eight. His death was doubtless hastened by the permanent shock suffered from a bad railway accident in 1865, as well as the extravagant outpouring of energies that had characterized his adult life.

The bountiful teller of tales that stirred the heart and conscience of nations was buried in the Poet's Corner of Westminster Abbey. His books had advanced the cause of human brotherhood, crystallizing public opinion against abuses in debtors' laws, the school system, the public almshouses, employment of child labor in industry, and other current institutions. It was not in his achievement as a pleader for good will among men that his greatness primarily lay, however, but in his peculiar genius as a storyteller. Such was the exuberant power of Dickens' caricatures that Mr. Micawber, Pecksniff, Uriah Heep and Scrooge became popular symbols of the human frailties they displayed. And for the enduring charm and vitality of Sam Weller, Little Nell, and David Copperfield, successive generations, like the stranger in York, honor the hand that peopled with many friends the magic world of books.

John D. Rockefeller

THE stories of the nineteenth century novelist, Horatio Alger, had as their heroes humble young men who through sheer pluck and ability rose to a position of wealth and respect in their communities. Of all those whom the United States has afforded such an opportunity, perhaps the man whose rise most nearly exemplifies that of an Alger hero was the modest young clerk who lived to build one of the most powerful industrial empires in America—John D. Rockefeller.

Rockefeller was born in Richford, New York, July 8, 1839. When he was fourteen years of age, the family moved to Cleveland, where the boy attended public school. At sixteen, however, his school days were over, and in September, 1855, he took a job as clerk with a firm of commission merchants. So earnestly did he concentrate on the task of getting the job that not a word was said about

CJNAAR

the salary he was to receive for his services. Such an unbusinesslike procedure, however, casts a light on the motives of the man who was to retire as the wealthiest man in America, and perhaps of modern times. For, more than the mere satisfaction of accumulating wealth, John D. Rockefeller enjoyed the battle, the sense of achievement, and the exciting game of protecting his domain, once he had conquered it. For his first three months of work, his employers paid him a total of $50. Then his perseverance was rewarded with a regular salary of $25 a month. At last the firm's bookkeeper resigned, and the new clerk took his place with a compensation of $500 per year, one quarter of his predecessor's salary. For several years he plodded along conscientiously in his new position, scrupulously saving a part of each month's pay. At the end of the third year, the young bookkeeper mustered up the courage to ask for $800 a year. The firm countered with an offer of $700 and Rockefeller promptly resigned.

A young friend, M. B. Clark, now proposed that the two of them start a general commission business of their own. In addition to his savings, young Rockefeller needed $1,000 to enter the partnership. He therefore borrowed the funds from his father, at ten percent interest. And such was the enterprise of the new firm that before long Rockefeller had paid off his debt, established a bank credit, and was borrowing considerable sums for the expansion of his business. With this auspicious beginning, the partners continued their venture with the greatest success for a number of years.

In 1859 an important event occurred: the first oil well was drilled in the United States. Some 2,000 barrels were produced that year. The new product quickly became popular as an illuminant, replacing the tallow candles then universally used for lighting, and annual production began to leap. It looked as though there would be a great future for petroleum and its by-products.

The discovery of oil in Pennsylvania aroused the interest of John D. Rockefeller. He went down into the western part of the state to investigate. At Titusville, he was met by Mr. Breed, a miller with whom his commission firm had done considerable business. Breed had two saddle horses waiting, and together the two set out on a twenty-mile ride over snow-clogged roads that were hardly more than trails. Petroleum Center, where the wells were in operation at the time, was a veritable wilderness. Finding the last quarter-mile of their approach impassable, Rockefeller and Breed prepared to finish the journey on foot. The final lap of the journey proved to be a foot-log spanning a gully which was filled with refuse from the wells. Eyeing the improvised bridge dubiously, Rockefeller inquired, "Isn't there some way of going around this thing?"

"No, we will just have to make it!" responded his companion, leading the way forward. Once safely across, he turned to help Rockefeller, just in time to see the latter lose his balance and slip off into the greasy, ill-smelling sludge. "Well, Breed," said Rockefeller drily, as soon as he stood on firm ground, "I guess you've got me in the oil business, head and feet." And scraping off the tarry mixture with barrel staves, he insisted on seeing everything connected with the wells, since he had "dipped into the business."

Before he left Titusville, he had to buy an entirely new outfit of clothing. But the trip evidently convinced him entirely. "It was only a day or two afterward," commented Breed, "that I got an order from Mr. Rockefeller for a carload of oil, and I got more after that. He always maintained every time I met him that I was responsible for making him an oil refiner and an oil merchant."

At any rate, in 1862 Rockefeller and his partner invested $4,000 with Samuel Andrews, who had invented a more economical process for refining crude oil. The business of refining oil was then in its infancy, but it was to grow into a healthy giant. His firm expanded, and by January, 1870, Rockefeller, Andrews, and Flagler had taken over one-fifth of the oil refining business of Cleveland, then the principal oil-refining center of the United States. In that year, with his brother William and others, Rockefeller organized the Standard Oil Company, of which he became president. Within ten years he was to control the petroleum industry of America.

Chaotic conditions prevailed in the oil business of that era. Competition between the numerous small producers was bitter and unscrupulous. Risks of unproductive drilling, fires, and other hazards were great. No controls operated over the production and distribution of the "black gold." Rockefeller saw an opportunity to stabilize production and prices by gaining control of the numerous small producers.

Meanwhile improvements in production and transportation methods, as well as the development of new uses for petroleum, provided a great stimulus to the oil industry, which boomed as never before.

Evidence though it was of great business acumen and powers of organization, Rockefeller's success in gaining control of the oil business was nevertheless an obstacle to free competition. Following a congressional investigation and much public protest, he reorganized his interests in 1875. Unfortunately, the "trust" into which he welded them was even more powerful than his earlier organization, and in 1892, the Ohio Supreme Court declared the Standard Oil Company illegal. Although it was reorganized a second time, a later court decision was equally unfavorable. An interesting sidelight on the oil magnate's character is provided by an anecdote connected with these reverses. On the date that the federal circuit court reviewed the imposition of a $29,000,000 fine on the Standard Oil, with a decision expected in the afternoon, Rockefeller spent the day with a farmer cousin, William Humiston, at his farm a few miles southeast of Cleveland. "He talked of nothing but farming and gardening and early day conditions during the visit. Lunch was invitingly spread by the Humiston daughters under the trees in the farmhouse yard, and Mr. Rockefeller ate sparingly, drank copiously of spring water after the meal, and lectured Cousin William seriously upon the evils of over-eating. For Cousin William had a true farmer's appetite."

At one time Rockefeller nearly became a power in the iron trade. He had invested a considerable amount in various rich mines in the Lake Superior Ore district. During the panic of 1893, this district was hard hit. In order to save his own holdings, Rockefeller had to buy up a controlling interest. The stock was easy to acquire; it was literally "tossed at him in bundles." But considerable capital was required to purchase it. Rockefeller had always been an accomplished borrower. On one occasion "his ride from bank to bank was something on the Paul Revere order." At each one he stopped just long enough to find out how much he could get. After making the rounds, he got off on the train he had to make, and put his deal through. This borrowing ability now stood him in good stead. At panic prices he bought up ore lands now worth millions of dollars. Then, with his usual enterprise, he set out to make good his investment. The mines were put in operation, and he began building vessels to transport his product to market. In 1900, when this property was sold to the U.S. Steel Corporation, Rockefeller had in operation a fleet of fifty-six vessels, of the largest and most modern type known in the lake ore trade.

Essentially a "home man," John D. Rockefeller derived deep satisfaction from his family life. "People tell me I have done much in my life," he once said, "but the best thing I ever accomplished, the thing that has given me the greatest happiness, was to win Cettie Spelman." He had married his boyhood sweetheart, Laura Celestine Spelman, in 1864, about the time of his first plunge in oil. Four children, Elizabeth, Alta, Edith, and John D. Junior, were born to this union. All married, and

Rockefeller was many times a grandfather. Keen of wit, good humored, and with a rare faculty for "hitting the bull's-eye of observation nine times out of ten," he was much beloved by his children and grandchildren.

Aside from business and family, he had a passion for landscape gardening, and gained the greatest pleasure from personally supervising the planning and laying out of the beautiful grounds on his two estates, at Forest Hill, Cleveland, and Pocantico Hills, Tarrytown. A master hand at executing winding drives, and in arranging artistic effects of shrubbery, he was excellent at tree groupings too. He was glad at all times to have distinguished visitors and delegations shown over his grounds, but on such occasions remained carefully in the background. An ardent golfer, he liked nothing better than to trim an opponent on the links.

As early as 1890, Rockefeller had begun to establish a system of organized philanthropy. He was to distribute "the largest group of gifts ever made for the promotion of the well-being of mankind throughout the world." For, during his declining years, he lost interest in the accumulation of wealth. After the dissolution of the Standard Oil Company in 1899, Rockefeller had reorganized his holdings as the Standard Oil Company of New Jersey. In 1911, however, this organization was declared illegal under the Sherman anti-trust act. Rockefeller retired from the presidency and gave his interests over to the management of his son. The company was dissolved, and the control of the stock held in thirty-seven different companies went back to the shareholders. "The literal truth," commented one who knew the oil magnate in his years of retirement, "is that Mr. Rockefeller has for many years been largely concerned with golf, his health, and the giving away of money. What motives or what conditions made it possible for him to accumulate a vast fortune thirty or forty years ago are now only of historic interest."

In disposing of what was perhaps the largest fortune in modern history, estimated by some as high as one thousand million dollars, Rockefeller reinvested a large portion in industrial enterprises. A total of $530,853,632, however, was donated to numerous philanthropic and charitable causes. Of this amount, about four-fifths was earmarked for the four large corporations which he established for benevolent purposes: the Rockefeller Foundation, the General Education Board, the Laura Spelman Rockefeller Memorial (later merged with the Rockefeller Foundation, the new Spelman Fund of New York being created in 1928), and the Rockefeller Institute for Medical Research. These gifts were outright, and bore no restrictions. The principal, as well as the income, of these funds is at the absolute disposal of the trustees. At the same time, Rockefeller was responsible for numerous individual benefactions, among the more noteworthy of which were the gifts of $23,000,000 to the University of Chicago; $1,000,000 or more to Barnard College, Harvard and Yale Universities, and the Southern Educational Board, as well as various juvenile reformatories; and land for park purposes to the city of Cleveland in the value of $1,000,000.

Rockefeller died in May, 1937, having seen almost a century of the nation's history, and having been for many decades an important factor in its industrial life. But by the great mass of people all over the world, his memory is honored, less as an industrial giant, than as the philanthropist who gave so much of his wealth for the promotion of the welfare of mankind.

Thomas Alva Edison

At the age of six Thomas Edison made his first scientific experiment, spreading his skirt over a nest of goose eggs to keep them warm. In his

CJNaar

CJNaar

eagerness to learn how a goose became the proud mother of goslings, he had placed food for himself nearby, so that the experiment might be carried through to its conclusion. Although the plan was thwarted by his astonished parents, the thirst for discovery never left the little experimenter. He grew up to become one of the greatest inventors of modern times.

The quiet little town of Milan, Ohio, was the birthplace of Thomas Alva Edison. He was born February 11, 1847, to Samuel and Nancy Elliott Edison. His father was of Dutch ancestry, the family having come to America from Amsterdam in 1737. His mother was a Canadian of Scotch descent.

Early in his life the child evinced a great fondness for reading. This was encouraged by his mother, who had been a school teacher. Like other children of active mind, he was always inquiring how things were accomplished. When the boy was seven, the family moved to Port Huron, Michigan. Here he was placed in school, but remained only three months. Regarding his school days, Edison remarked years later: "I remember I used never to be able to get along at school. I don't know now what it was, but I was always at the foot of the class. I used to feel that the teachers never sympathized with me, and that my father thought I was stupid."

Fortunately for the boy, his mother was always sympathetic and understanding. He was reluctant, however, to confide in her about all his difficulties in school, for fear she too might lose confidence in him. One day he overheard the teacher tell the school inspector that he was "addled," and it was useless to keep him in school any longer. "I was so hurt by this last straw," commented Edison, "that I burst out crying and went home and told my mother about it. . . . She came out as my strong defender . . . and I felt that I had someone to live for, someone I must not disappoint. . . . I did not have my mother very long, but in that length of time, she cast over me an influence which has lasted all my life. The good effect of her early training I can never lose. If it had not been for her appreciation and her faith in me at a critical time in my experience, I should very likely never have become an inventor."

Thus the boy's school days came to an early end. His education was continued, however, by reading with his mother. Between the ages of nine and twelve, he read such books as Hume's *History of England, The Penny Encyclopedia,* Gibbon's *Decline and Fall of the Roman Empire,* Ure's *Dictionary of the Sciences,* and Newton's *Principia.*

This last work was difficult for him to digest. "It gave me a distaste for mathematics from which I have never recovered," he later said.

Systematic reading soon had to be discontinued, for it became necessary for Tom to contribute to the support of the family. For a while he sold papers on the street. Then his application for the position of train boy on the Grand Trunk Railroad was accepted, and he found himself making the daily run between Port Huron and Detroit. His pleasant manner won him friends on the train, as he sold his books, papers, toys, packages of prize candy and peanuts. Although in constant anxiety lest an accident should occur, his mother encouraged and cheered him in his work.

His personal appearance was of secondary importance to the enterprising young candy butcher. "His mother always kept him supplied with clean shirts," said a friend, "and he always washed his face and hands, but I think in those days he did not often comb his hair. He would buy a cheap suit of clothes and wear them until they were worn out, when he would buy another. He never by any chance blacked his boots."

The nation was now in the early days of the Civil War, and papers sold well to a news-hungry public. The ambitious Tom decided to establish a paper of his own. Buying some old type from the *Detroit*

Free Press, and a printing press formerly used to print bills of fare at a hotel, he printed his *Weekly Herald* on the train. The first copy appeared February 3, 1862, twelve inches by sixteen in size. So novel and unique was the paper that it soon had five hundred regular subscribers at eight cents a month, while two hundred copies were sold on the train at three cents each. From this venture the boy earned forty-five dollars a month. In four years his earnings totaled two thousand dollars, all of which he turned over to his parents.

Meanwhile, his urge to experiment could not be stifled. In the comparatively unused car of the train where he kept his printing press, the lad had also established a laboratory consisting of telegraph apparatus, bottles of chemicals and other articles needed for his investigations. Here he measured and stirred busily in his spare moments, oblivious of his strange surroundings. All went well until one day, as the car sped over a rough road, a bottle of phosphorus fell to the floor and set the woodwork on fire. The fire was soon extinguished. But the conductor, indignant at the danger to his passengers, boxed the lad's ears and at the first station, Mt. Clemens, threw him off onto the platform, printing press, type, laboratory and all. In boxing Edison's ears, the irate conductor produced permanent deafness in his right ear, which inconvenienced the inventor all his life. No surgery was of any avail to restore hearing.

This setback to his scientific career left Edison downcast, but not discouraged. His father offered him a room for his experiments near the roof of their house, and the work went on enthusiastically. Using an ordinary stovepipe wire insulated by necks of bottles, he strung telegraph lines from tree to tree between his home and those of other boys. One night a cow wandering through the orchard knocked down the telegraph poles and became entangled in the wires. Her frantic bellows alarmed the neighbors, resulting in liquidation of the home telegraph.

In the newspaper field, too, Edison suffered a reverse. At the request of a friend, the *Weekly Herald* had been discontinued in favor of another paper called *Paul Pry*. Unfortunately, a personal gossip note so annoyed one man that upon encountering Edison he threw him into the St. Clair River. This dampened the young columnist's journalistic ardor, and his editorial enterprise came to an abrupt end.

One day in 1862 the fifteen-year-old Edison happened to be at the Mt. Clemens railroad station, where he had once been thrown off the train by the angry conductor. A train was speeding rapidly up the track. Suddenly Edison noticed that the baby son of the station master, J. U. MacKenzie, had run out onto the track before the approaching train. Without a moment's delay he sprang for the child. Both were thrown upon the gravel ballast, the wheel of the car striking the heel of Edison's shoe. They emerged with some cuts and scratches, but the child was saved.

The grateful father, eager to help the boy who had risked his life, offered to teach him how to become a telegraph operator. He gave Edison lessons four days a week after working hours, and in three months, according to MacKenzie, the pupil excelled his teacher. On the latter's suggestion, Edison applied for a position as night operator at the Port Huron station. He obtained it, receiving a salary of twenty-five dollars a month. Once again, however, his devotion to his experiments resulted in the loss of his job. Working in his laboratory all day, he was not always able to keep awake at night, and so his career as telegraph operator came temporarily to an end.

From Port Huron Edison went to Sarnia. Here his preoccupation with experimenting got him into the usual difficulties. Absorbed in his researches, he allowed a train to pass by his station, while another train was just ahead. Realizing the danger, he rushed down the track. Fortunately the engine drivers had heard each other's whistles, and so prevented a rear-end collision.

In November, 1864, Edison, now a little over seventeen, began work as a telegraph operator in Indianapolis. Although he received about seventy-five dollars a month, he sent home all he could possibly spare, spending the remainder for second-hand books and materials to experiment with. As a result, he was always low in funds.

In Detroit, while working on the Grand Trunk, he had resolved to read the Public Library entirely through. After reading about "fifteen feet" of books, he reconsidered, concluding that the task was too great for the most indefatigable reader. In Cincinnati, however, where he worked at the age of eighteen, he bought for two dollars at an auction a great pile of *North American Review*'s. Loading them in his arms, he took them home at three o'clock in the morning. An alert policeman took him for a thief, and commanded him to halt. Because of his deafness, Edison failed to hear the command. A bullet soon whizzed by his ear, just missing him. Had the policeman been a better shot, Edison might have been killed.

From Cincinnati, Edison journeyed to Memphis, and from Memphis to Louisville. With almost no money in his pocket, due to his generosity with "tramp operators," he had to walk one hundred miles of the journey, obtaining free transportation the rest of the way. Edison was very shabbily dressed, and carried his scanty possessions tied in a handkerchief over his shoulder. His rapidity and skill in telegraphy soon obtained a position for him, and he was at one time the fastest operator in the employ of Western Union.

As usual his inquiring mind created difficulties for him. One night he went into the battery room to obtain some sulphuric acid he wished to use in his experiments. "The acid in the carboy tipped over, ate up the floor, and went through to the manager's room below, ate up his desk and all the carpet," Edison related. "The next morning I was summoned before the board and told that what they wanted was telegraph operators, not experimenters, so that I was at liberty to take pay and leave."

With his health somewhat impaired, Edison returned to his home in Port Huron for eighteen months. He was now twenty-one. The financial position of his parents had improved. The young man was now given a free pass to Boston by the Grand Trunk Railway Company. They had adopted a little invention of his, "an ingenious device by which a single submarine cable could be utilized for two circuits." When Edison arrived in

Boston, the operatives were amused at his shabby clothes and unkempt appearance. Their attitude underwent a change, however, when they saw his skillful work.

Edison soon fitted up a small workshop for his experiments in electricity. "One day," reported his friend, Milton Adams, "he bought the whole of Faraday's works on electricity, brought them home at three o'clock A. M. and read assiduously until I rose, when we made for Hanover street (a mile away) to secure breakfast. Tom's brain was on fire with what he had read, and he suddenly remarked to me: 'Adams, I've got so much to do, and life is so short, that I am going to hustle.' And with that, he started on a dead run for his breakfast."

At nights he worked in the office of the Western Union Telegraph Company. He spent his days, however, in the Public Library, in second-hand bookshops, and in his laboratory. His first patent, taken out in 1869, covered an electrical vote-recording machine. To his great disappointment, the Massachusetts Legislature failed to adopt it.

Invited to speak on telegraphy before an academy, Edison allowed the appointment to slip his mind. When summoned by his friend Adams, he was found on the roof of a house putting up telegraph wires. He and Adams hurried over to the academy in their working clothes, and were astonished to find an audience, not of boys, as they had expected, but of well-dressed young ladies.

Edison was now two or three hundred dollars in debt, his mind full of inventive plans that he could not carry out for lack of funds. Tired of working as an operator, he went to New York in 1869. For three weeks he had little food, and prospects were discouraging.

At last one morning he entered the office of Law's Gold Reporting Company on Wall Street. The stock quotation printer in the central office had suddenly collapsed, leaving five or six hundred brokerage offices in distress. "I think, Mr. Law," said Edison, "I can show you where the trouble lies." His diagnosis was successful, and soon he was offered a position as manager of the service at three hundred dollars a month.

Some time later he became associated with General Marshall Lefferts, then president of the Gold and Stock Telegraph Company. During this period he invented several stock printers and private printing telegraphic appliances. On being asked the price of these inventions, he said, unaware of their value, "Make me an offer."

"How would forty thousand dollars strike you?" the prospective purchaser replied.

Regarding this incident, Edison commented in later years, "I believe I could have been knocked down with the traditional feather, so astonished was I at the sum." With this forty thousand dollars, the former "addled" schoolboy from Port Huron was able to open a factory at Newark, New Jersey, with a force of three hundred men.

During these early years after his departure from Boston, Edison produced several important inventions in the field of telegraphy. After inventing a duplex system of telegraphing by which two messages could be sent in opposite directions over the same wire simultaneously, in 1874 he invented his quadruplex system by which four messages were sent over a single wire, two in each direction. Both were sold to Western Union. The thirty thousand dollars which he received for the quadruplex system, he used entirely in his efforts to invent a six-message system. These inventions resulted in his saving many millions of dollars for Western Union. Edison also perfected an automatic telegraph system which the papers of 1873 characterized as "incredible."

How tirelessly the inventor worked during that period is described by his friend and associate, Charles Bachelor. "I came in one night," he related, "and there sat Edison with a pile of chemistries and chemical books that were five feet high when they stood on the floor and lay one upon the other. He had ordered them from New York, Lon-

don, and Paris. He studied them night and day. He
ate at his desk, and slept in his chair. In six weeks
he had gone through the books, written a volume of
abstracts, made two thousand experiments on the
formulas, and had produced a solution (the only
one in the world) which would do the very thing
he wanted done—record over two hundred words a
minute on a wire 250 miles long. He ultimately succeeded in recording 3,100 words a minute."

Meanwhile an important event had occurred in
Edison's personal life. In 1873 the twenty-six-year-
old inventor married Mary E. Stillwell, one of his
working force at Newark. Until her death in 1881,
she proved an admirable wife and mother to their
three children, Mary Estelle, Thomas Alva Edison,
Jr., and William Leslie.

The year 1876 saw Edison established in Menlo
Park, an estate twenty-four miles from New York
on the New York and Philadelphia Railroad. Here
he built a workshop one hundred feet long by
thirty-five feet, an extensive laboratory, and a costly
scientific library. In these surroundings he hoped to
work and think in quiet. But so revolutionary were
the inventions that issued from his retreat that the
"wizard of Menlo Park" was never to achieve the
quiet life he sought.

For years scientists had been considering the possibility of using electricity to convey speech over

great distances. On the same day, February 15, 1876, two men who had worked independently, Alexander Graham Bell and Elisha Gray, applied for patents in Washington covering inventions for "transmitting vocal sounds telegraphically." The patent was awarded to Bell, who had applied a few hours earlier. At first the public had little faith in the telephone, which was considered a novel toy. Bell found it extremely difficult to gain supporters for his enterprise. An offer of a half-interest for $2,500 was declined by a friend. A tenth interest which Bell offered an official in the patent office for $100 was likewise rejected, although in fifteen years it was to become worth $1,500,000.

At this point Edison devised a carbon transmitter which according to the *Scientific American* of April, 1909, "is universally acknowledged to have been the needed device that gave to the telephone the element of practicability that made it a commercial possibility." The resultant rivalry is described by the inventor himself: "Bell's instrument was taken up by Boston capitalists, while mine was adopted by Western Union, and a fierce competition ensued. It was seen by the Bell people that their instrument was impracticable for commercial purposes without my transmitter, and pro contra by the Western Union that without Bell's receiver, which they did not own, my instrument was not available without extensive litigation, so a consolidation of interests took place."

Electric lighting, too, had long been a subject of study by great scientists. In 1878 Edison was shown the first arc lamp he had ever seen by Professor Barker at Philadelphia. "Then a little later I saw another," related Edison, "—I think it was one of Brush's make. . . . It was easy to see what the thing needed. It wanted to be subdivided. The light was too bright and too big. What we wished for was little lights, and a distribution of them to people's houses in a manner similar to gas."

Thirteen months of tireless experimenting now began for Edison. Over two thousand substances were tested in an effort to find a durable filament for the vacuum in his glass globes. Fine platinum wire melted; carbonized cotton thread broke. "We saw that the carbon was what we wanted," related Edison, "and the next question was, what kind of carbon." Among the substances which he now tested was a strip of bamboo from a Japanese fan. The result of this experiment showed that he was close to success. The proper fiber now had to be obtained. One of his men went twenty-three hundred miles up the Amazon River; another traveled thirty thousand miles through India and China. A third searched Japan, where the coveted bamboo was found. About one hundred thousand dollars were spent in this exhaustive search.

In January, 1880, Edison obtained a patent for his electric light. A bulb factory was begun at Menlo Park, and a central station was built in New York, which would supply consumers with electric power for their lighting. Sleeping at night on piles of pipes in the station, Edison supervised it all. A number of serious obstacles arose. Scientists declared the new light would not work. When this was disproved, litigation began. Edison was to fight for his electric light fourteen years, finally emerging victorious.

His first patent for the phonograph had been obtained by Edison two years before that for the electric light, in 1878. "I discovered the principle by the merest accident," he commented. "I was singing to the mouth-piece of a telephone, when the vibrations of the voice sent the fine steel point into my finger. That set me to thinking. If I could record the actions of the point, and send the point back over the same surface later, I saw no reason why the thing would not talk. I tried the experiment first on a strip of telegraph paper, and found that the point made an alphabet. I shouted the words 'hello! hello!' into the mouth-piece, ran the paper back over the steel point, and heard a faint 'hello! hello!' in return. I determined to make a machine that would work accurately, and gave my assistants instructions, telling them what I had discovered. They laughed at me."

But as soon as the first crude model was tested, the phonograph was an assured success. Numerous improvements in later models perfected the machine, which gave rise to various industries in which millions of dollars were invested.

Shortly after the invention of the phonograph, Edison wrote an article for the *North American Review* listing some of the uses he visualized for it. He saw it as the perfect complement to the telephone and the telegraph in the field of communications. It could be of value in the courtroom for recording the testimony of the witnesses and the judge's counsel, thus establishing a full and permanent record of all law cases. It could be of untold service in asylums and hospitals for the recreation of the sick and the blind. It could be a useful instrument for teaching elocution or languages. By means of it, speakers could reach unlimited audiences. Finally, it could be a valuable device in offices, eliminating the necessity for a stenographer.

The phonograph was to prove useful in many of the ways he predicted. It now occurred to Edison that it ought to be possible "to do for the eye what has been done for the ear." Bringing to the problem a highly trained mind and a resourceful laboratory, he produced another significant invention: the kinetoscope, forerunner of our modern motion pictures.

In approaching the task of indicating natural movements successfully, Edison realized that pictures would have to be taken with great speed, from forty to sixty a second. In this way alone could the eye be prevented from detecting the change. Furthermore, it would be necessary to devise some kind of machine which would project the pictures, once they were taken. Altogether the problem promised to be intensely interesting. But it involved a field of science to which Edison was a stranger: photography. He had never before taken a snapshot or developed a plate. In fact, he had rarely seen a camera. Immediately, with his characteristic ability to "hustle," he plunged into the study of photography. Soon he had mastered all that was known concerning the essential details.

"We shall never get anywhere with cumbersome glass, plates, and a multiple of cameras," he reasoned. "We must have films, capable of taking one impression after another with great rapidity." But when he searched about for film material, there was none to be had. Without delay, a photographic laboratory was added to his establishment, and a train of experiments set in motion to produce the needed film. Finally, a film was evolved which suited his purpose; and the machine for projecting the pictures, the kinetoscope, was also developed. Now Edison began to take miles and miles of films for demonstration. His laboratory assistants turned somersaults, stood on their heads, played leap-frog, and performed all sorts of stunts for the camera. Later, as the machine approached its modern form, a stage was set up in the Orange laboratory, and various celebrities came down from New York to appear before the camera. Such a project was costly indeed. A hundred thousand dollars is said to have been poured into this invention. The export of several of these machines gave impulse to the development of motion pictures in England and France. They formed an important chapter in the history of movies in the United States.

Not content with this, Edison turned his attention to the talking motion picture, a combination of phonograph and kinetoscope. Certain difficulties prevented Edison's machine from becoming a commercial success, although similar devices were perfected which made possible the talking pictures of today.

Countless other valuable inventions sprang from the mind of the man who said, "Genius is two per cent inspiration and ninety-eight per cent perspiration." Among them may be listed the tasimeter, by which the heat of the stars can be measured; the megaphone for conveying sound to distant points; the aerophone by which the voice is magnified two hundred times; and the mimeograph for reproducing documents. In addition, he made a magnetic ore separator which separated the iron from low-grade ores by an electromagnet. He also secured twenty patents on his storage battery. "I believe that the problem of vehicular traffic in cities has at last been solved," declared Edison in 1906. "The new electric storage cell weighs forty pounds per horse-power hour. . . . I believe that the solution of vehicular traffic . . . is to be found in the electric wagon. Leaving off the horse reduces the length of the vehicle one half. Electric power will double the speed. With the new electric wagon, the vehicular traffic of cities can be increased four times without producing any more congestion than at present." Thanks to Edison's electric storage battery, the revolution which he prophesied came about, in the form of modern trolleys and subways.

His experiments in the construction of cement houses aroused wide attention. A method was developed whereby cement was poured into a steel mold for the proposed structure. After the cement hardened, the mold was removed for use elsewhere; and the complete structure, except for trim and finish, was ready in a few days. Although the idea met with small success during Edison's lifetime, a similar method has been developed for the rapid production of concrete houses during the postwar period.

In 1886 Edison moved from Menlo Park to a large laboratory and factory built at the foot of the Orange mountains in Orange, New Jersey. Here, surrounded by models of his various inventions, he spent days and nights working in his chemical laboratory, often foregoing food and sleep. On one occasion he worked for sixty hours without stopping, sleeping nearly thirty to recuperate.

The same year saw his marriage to Miss Mina Miller, daughter of an Akron, Ohio, manufacturer. Soon afterward, Edison purchased "Glenmont" at Llewellyn Park, near his laboratory, a graceful house of brick and wood in Queen Anne style, set in thirteen acres of park and garden. Here were born three more children, Madelyn, Charles, and Theodore. At "Glenmont" were to be found gifts from all over the world: statues of serpentine marble from the Russian emperor; Japanese vases from the Society of Engineers in Japan; a Krupp inkstand composed of miniature guns and shells from the German munitions makers. Included in the collection were a Prince Albert gold medal from the London Society of Arts, awarded in 1892; the three degrees of the Legion of Honor; the bronze medal of the Photographic Society of France; the Order of Commander of the Crown of Italy; medals from the American Institutes of Boston and New York; and from the Expositions in Australia, Austria, England, France and America.

For the numerous applicants for positions as his assistants, Edison had prepared an examination which usually produced disastrous results. Always thorough and painstaking himself, he had little patience with workers who were forgetful or who had only a smattering of knowledge. When his questionnaire was finally published in 1921, it aroused much controversy. Educators and journalists denounced it as an unfair test, although the questions seemed innocent enough, ranging from the location of a certain town or river to facts about a famous man. Edison, however, came to the defense of his test, declaring that it was calculated to surround him with men of accurate and acute memories. Lapses of memory on the part of his assistants had proved costly. "Of course I don't care directly," he argued, "whether a man knows the capital of Nevada, or the source of mahogany, or the location of Timbuctoo. Of course I don't care whether he knows who Desmoulins and Pascal and Kit Carson were. But if he ever knew any of these things and doesn't know them now, I do very much care about that in connection with giving him a job. For the assumption is that, if he has forgotten these things, he will forget something else that has direct bearing on his job."

Despite the astonishing number and scope of the inventions already to his credit, the aging Edison never abandoned the quest for discovery that had begun in his earliest years. At all hours of the day and night, he was to be found working in his laboratory, with such devotion to the problem at hand that even on his birthday he stopped to eat lunch only with reluctance. His tireless labors were ended at last by his death on October 18, 1931, at the age of eighty-four. The world paid homage to the man who had illuminated cities and brought in such abundance to the everyday lives of men the benefits of applied science.

Pope Pius XI

NEXT door to the octagonal-domed church in the village of Desio, Italy, stood a small factory. Here, on May 31, 1875, a fourth son was born to the manager, Francesco Ratti and his wife Teresa, pious, hard-working folk engaged in the

silk-weaving industry. This child was named Am-
brogio Damiano Achille Ratti. He lived with his
three brothers and sister beneath the rustic beams
of the factory, in three rooms with whitewashed
walls and red brick floor. All day long they could
hear the clatter of the looms in the adjoining room
where Francesco labored twelve hours a day.

About the church, the villa, and the factory clus-
tered the roofs of Desio; beyond stretched the fertile plains of Lombardy to the Alps. Achille gazed
upon these blue, snow-capped peaks with wonder
and delight, and felt a great longing to climb them.
Thus was born the intrepid Alpinist. He began
very early to scale the hills of Desio; by the time he
was eight years old he had a reputation among the
young climbers. One time he was seen to linger far
behind while his comrades went forward until they
reached a height from which it seemed they could
go no farther. Soon he caught up with them, and,
as they turned to descend, continued the ascent by
a careful plan until he reached the highest peak.
What a perfect parallel to the whole course of his
life: He hung back in comparative obscurity and
humble service while his friends were achieving
great honors, and then, when he was an old man,
passed them all and rose to the highest fame.

Every summer Achille would visit his uncle, Don
Damiano Ratti, the Provost at Asso, a village which

CJNAAB

is situated on the heights that separate the two arms of beautiful Lake Como. Here, in the foothills of the Alps, Achille made many happy climbs, hardening his muscles and learning the holds which would one day help him to conquer Mont Rosa, Matterhorn and Mont Blanc. He became observant and self-reliant. He developed the independence of judgment that characterized him in later years and his sturdy good health. It was probably here, too, as he watched his uncle go about the duties of a parish priest, that he first formed the intention of entering the priesthood.

About this time a copy of Milton's *Paradise Lost* in Italian came into his hands, and he studied it carefully. No doubt his imagination was enchanted by the grandeur of the figures and the excitement of the conflict. Shortly afterward, during his first trip to the Alps, he met an English clergyman, and heard the English language spoken for the first time. He resolved to learn English in order to read *Paradise Lost* in Milton's own language. He applied himself so diligently to the study that he neglected his meals and his play in the effort, but he was soon able to read some of the simpler passages. In later years, when he became Pope, the ease and fluency of his English always astonished his American visitors, as did the many questions he asked about America itself.

For Achille was adventurous. Just as his feet explored his native hills, his mind explored books, and his eager curiosity embraced the whole world. His fellow students called him "Africanus" because of his keen interest in Africa. He never became so preoccupied with his studies as to forget the affairs of the outside world, but he was grave and studious. So much so that the Archbishop of Milan, who was visiting his uncle at Asso, struck by such ability, knowledge and force of character in one so young, called him his "young sage." Thereafter Monsignor Calabrini took great interest in the young boy, who was now sent, after a year of schooling from the village priest and two years at the Seminary of Saint Peter the Martyr, to the Seminary at Monza. In all his work he made perfect marks; he was chosen as a brilliant candidate for theological honors and sent to Rome to study at the Lombard College.

City of Martyrs, Cradle of Christianity, how Rome must have thrilled the mind of this young man. His daily walks led him through the Colosseum, where thousands had died for their faith, or through the Catacombs, where the early Christians practiced the precious rite of their religion. Now Achille knew what he wanted to do. Refusing an appointment as Professor of Mathematics at the University of Turin, he became a priest. He was ordained in the Chapel of Saint John Lateran in 1879, his father and brother receiving his first blessing. Fifty years later, when he celebrated the Mass of his golden jubilee as a priest, it was a triumphal event, the first time in sixty years that a Pope had been carried in procession through the streets of Rome.

He continued his studies and at the end of a year he received the degree of Doctor in three subjects: Canon Law at Gregorian University, Theology at Sapienza and Philosophy at the new Academy of St. Thomas Aquinas founded by Pope Leo XIII. As a first and exceedingly brilliant graduate of the Academy, Dr. Ratti was received in private audience by the Pope. Leo XIII took particular interest in the young priest and conversed with him for some time. This was a great honor.

During these years there had been a wave of Anticlericalism in Italy. Ever since Achille was thirteen years old, and the Italian army had entered Rome to make it the capital of Italy, thus taking it from the Pope, the clergy had been in danger of their lives when they appeared in cassocks on the streets. Perhaps it was this early experience that made young Achille forever afterward the champion of all persecuted peoples, of whatever race or faith. Yet danger of persecution meant little to a mountaineer who loved to defy steep glaciers and sheer cliffs. He was not deterred from his desire to be a priest and serve the people.

But a humble priest must serve where he is needed. Dr. Ratti was now made a professor, first of Hebrew and later of Philosophy, at his old seminary at Milan. After five years he was appointed to the vacant position in the Ambrosian Library of Milan. The Ambrosian Library, founded in 1609 by Cardinal Frederigo Borromeo, is one of the great libraries of the world, ranking with the British Museum, the Bibliothèque Nationale at Paris and the Vatican Library. With the exception of the Bodleian at Oxford, it was the first genuinely public library in Europe, where any who came was supplied with the volumes he wished, and pen, ink and paper as well. Through the centuries the library grew in fame and wealth of books. To the book-loving young man it must have seemed a paradise on earth. For twenty years Dr. Ratti delved in these riches and published many learned treatises on the early history of Milan and other subjects.

One of his first discoveries was the finding of four maps of Milan. These he published with a scholarly explanation and a touching tribute to his mother. "It is to you, Mother of a rare and ancient pattern, I dedicate these maps (the oldest known) of our great and loved Metropolis of Lombardy, our Mother-city—and I like to think that some learned man, perhaps even some generations hence, will there read your name and find in it a testimony of the love and veneration in which your children held you." His mother and his youngest brother had come to Milan, his father having died. In spite of his arduous duties of librarian and priest, he visited her every day.

During the next thirty years or so, he was a busy librarian carrying out profound researches, being friendly and helpful to students in the library, answering queries from all the world, re-arranging the vast library according to modern methods and writing an excellent guide to it—for which services he was made a Knight of the Cross of St. Maurice by the Italian government in 1907. Dr. Ratti was also chaplain of the Cenacle of St. Charles Borromeo, putting into practice the ideal of priesthood learned from his uncle. He conducted classes for women and children of the working classes, building up what would correspond to a social center today.

One day a ragged little urchin straggled into confirmation class, black with soot. As it was obvious that the boy was more in need of bodily than of spiritual aid, Father Ratti went to him after class, and fed him and talked to him. He was a chimney-sweep, one of the poor, migrant boys who leave their parents' farms in winter to gain a miserable

pittance in the cities. Father Ratti now tried to help
these boys, finding them better jobs and teaching
them. They idolized him and his fame spread
among them so that as older boys outgrew the trade
there were always younger ones coming to take
their places. When he was Pope, Pius XI once saw
at an audience a man who had assisted him in this
work. "Remember the chimney sweeps," the Pope
said to him, his eyes lighting up. "That was real
charity."

During these years Dr. Ratti was becoming
known to Alpinists for his daring ascents. With
three companions he set out to conquer Mont Rosa
from the Italian side. This was a feat considered too
dangerous to try, since many good Alpinists had
lost their lives in the attempt, and none had succeeded. Careful planning such as had won him the
peak in that childhood climb now made possible
this more daring success. After twelve hours of
steady climbing they reached the first peak, but it
was evening, and they were forced to descend a
little and spend the night on a narrow ledge. They
could only sit dangling their legs, or stand and
stamp carefully to ward off the cold, which had
frozen their wine and coffee. Sleep was impossible.
"But who could have slept?" Father Ratti wrote of
the adventure. "In that pure and clear atmosphere,
beneath that sky of deepest sapphire, illuminated

by a crescent moon, and, as far as the eye could reach, dotted with twinkling stars, in that silence . . . we felt in the presence of a novel and most imposing revelation of the omnipotence and majesty of God."

A few moments later, the perfect silence was broken by the thunderous crash of an avalanche below them. At dawn the party retraced its steps and went across a saddle to the next peak. The descent was even more perilous than the ascent had been, and they were forced to spend another night on the mountain. But they had conquered the highest peak in the Italian Alps on its most dangerous face, and they had made Alpine history. The very next week Dr. Ratti and his friend assayed Mont Blanc. On the way down, they discovered a new descent. This trail was put on military maps; the Italian Alpine Club named it Ratti Trail.

Now it seemed that Dr. Ratti was reaching the highest point of his career. He became Prefect of the Ambrosian Library. Then he was called to the even greater Vatican Library, of which he became Prefect in 1914. At fifty-seven years of age what more could he expect but to live out his life in the highest post of his profession, enjoying his fame as a librarian, and Alpinist? But now he was called to serve as a diplomat in an atmosphere utterly different to any he had known. He was made Apostolic

Visitator to Poland. His command of languages (and he quickly added Polish to a list that included French, German, English and Hebrew), his unfailing courtesy and tact, and his imperturbable good humor in trying situations made him a very successful diplomat. When the new Republic of Poland was formally recognized in 1919, the government at once suggested to Pope Benedict XV that Visitator Ratti be made permanent Nuncio to Poland. Amidst much pomp and splendor in the Cathedral at Warsaw, in the presence of Pilsudski, the government representatives and the diplomatic corps, Achille Ratti was consecrated Archbishop of the Titular See of Lepanto, and made Nuncio to Poland.

In comparison with his thirty long years of comparative obscurity, how rapid now was his rise to fame. After three years of brilliant diplomacy, Achille Ratti was called home to receive the red hat of a cardinal, and to become Archbishop of his native Milan. He entered Milan amid rich and colorful pageantry and was received with great enthusiasm by the people. But fate had other things in store for him. Within a few months, Pope Benedict XV died, and Cardinal Ratti hastened to Rome for the Papal conclave from which he was never to return, for in that election the choice fell upon him. The little cloud of white smoke rising from the Vatican, which tells the waiting populace that they have a new Pope, ushered in a new and great epoch in the history of the church, the reign of a vigorous Pope of Peace.

"Pius is a name of peace," said Achille Ratti to the Cardinals, his eyes bright with tears. "Since I desire to consecrate my labors to the peace of the world, I choose the name of Pius XI." Then, after a moment of thought, he added, "I desire that my first blessing shall go, as a pledge of that peace to which the whole human race aspires, not merely to Rome and Italy, but to the whole Church, to the entire world. I shall give it from the outside balcony of St. Peter's." Since 1870, when the Italian army entered Rome and the Popes became voluntary prisoners, no Pope had been seen outside the Vatican and St. Peter's. When Pius XI appeared on the balcony in his shining, white, papal robes, there was wild cheering, then reverent silence. The people knelt to receive his Benediction; the Italian Troops presented arms. It was the first Italian homage to a Pope for over fifty years. Thus, in his first act as Pope, Pius XI showed his power as a leader for peace.

That influence for peace was sorely needed, for after the Armistice, which was the prelude to no lasting peace such as the world desired, but a mere cessation of hostilities, the nations continued their bitter, uncompromising struggles with each other in the so-called peace conferences. How many unhappy developments in recent years might have been avoided had the nations paid heed to the message which Pius XI now sent to the Genoa Conference. "We pray and confidently expect that the envoys of the Powers will consider the tragic situation . . . with a willingness to make some sacrifice on the altar of common good, because international hatreds, the sad legacy of the war, work to the detriment even of the victors, and prepare a future fraught with fear for all."

Peace, like charity, often begins at home. Pius XI set an example of peace to the world by settling the ancient dispute between Italy and Rome. He relinquished all claim to the large territory that had belonged to the Holy See for over a thousand years, asking only one hundred and twenty acres of churches and buildings in Rome—Vatican City—and independence as a neutral, sovereign state. We, in America, who knew that we must set aside a separate territory under the jurisdiction of no state, the District of Columbia, for our national government, understand very well what the Pope meant when he insisted that the head of a great international church must have "real, visible independence" from all governments. Much preliminary negotiation and revision of a welter of laws was necessary.

After seven years, the Lateran Pact, guaranteeing the Vatican inviolability as a neutral state, was signed by Cardinal Gasparri and Premier Mussolini. There was great rejoicing.

Peace was now needed along another front, for as the owners continued to amass wealth at the expense of the workers, the struggle between the classes became increasingly bitter. In 1924 striking textile workers in France appealed to the Pope to define their rights in order to settle the dispute. Five years later, for a Pope whose word carries much weight throughout the world must consider those words deeply, they received their reply. The principles of social justice set forth in that letter were elaborated in his formal encyclical, *Quadragesimo Anno*—"In the Fortieth year"—commemorating the fortieth anniversary of Leo XIII's great encyclical on the rights of the working man. Pope Pius reaffirmed the rights of workers to organize. He condemned atheistic communism, but he did not condone the evils of capitalism, for he said, "Far more severely must be condemned the foolhardiness of those who neglect to remove or modify such conditions as exasperate the minds of the people and so prepare the way for the overthrow and ruin of the social order." The wisdom of this great encyclical which shows a path between the extremes of unrestrained capitalism and of socialism will make Pius renowned for many years to come.

In other encyclicals—*Non Abbiamo Bisogno,* written when Mussolini tried to suppress the youth organizations known as Catholic Action; *Mit Brennender Sorge,* "With Burning Sorrow," delivered by secret messengers in the dead of night to the pastors of Germany; *Revini Redemptoris,* attacking atheistic communism—he denounced "nationalist-religion" and "the ideology which clearly resolves itself into a true, a real pagan worship of the State." At the time of his death it was recognized that Pope Pius had been the first and clearest voice raised against the totalitarian philosophy which makes the individual the helpless slave of the State. Wherever anti-semitism appeared, the Pope denounced it, saying that anti-semitism was incompatible with Christianity. He established the Feast of Christ the King to remind us that the kingdom of God includes all men, and we should live in peace.

Achille Ratti was now an old man, and though he insisted that "the Pope must not be sick; the Pope must be Pope," he was growing infirm, and was confined often to his bed. His mind remained young. He who had broken precedent in his first blessing, in bringing his old nurse to the Vatican, in driving in a modern automobile, in cataloguing the Vatican Library according to the most modern method, in installing telephone, elevators, and a broadcasting station in the Vatican, would never grow old and unadventurous. As he lay dying, as it was thought, in 1936, he broadcast a Christmas Eve plea over an international hook-up for peace. The world that had felt his keen interest through his care for foreign missions, in his questions and words to the million and a quarter pilgrims from every part of the earth who visited him during the Holy Year of 1925, and in his letters to nations in trouble, still felt his eager participation in the concerns of all mankind. As the world faced the "future fraught with fear for all" which he had predicted, he continued to struggle for peace and justice. In February, 1939, after many relapses and valiant recoveries, murmuring, "I have still so many things to do," a tired old man closed his eyes.

All the world mourned a great man, who, though he might have made his mark in any field, chose to serve God and Peace, devoting the Papal income to the poor and his whole strength to the cause of Peace. Perhaps, of the many saints he canonized during his reign, he himself will one day be considered the greatest.

The Mayo Brothers

THE story of the Mayos is an unfinished one which stretches far into the future of medical science.

It began on a day in 1845, when William Worrall Mayo walked down the gangplank of the ship that had brought him to America. He was no unschooled immigrant. He was a young doctor who had received his medical training in the best hospitals of Manchester, Glasgow and London, and who had studied and worked for a number of years with the great English chemist, John Dalton. The young man's reasons for coming to the new world were not immediately apparent. It may have been that he was tired of the crowded, caste-ridden cities of England. Or it may have been the immemorial urge of youth to seek out the land beyond the horizon.

Three years later, Doctor Mayo was established at Lafayette, Indiana, not—to be sure—as a physician, but as the successful proprietor of a tailor shop. And this fact throws a remarkably revealing light

upon the medical practices of the day. Only a few
eastern states maintained any regulations over the
medical profession. Elsewhere, the trained physician found himself in competition with a whole
horde of faddists, cultists and quacks who set themselves up as healers of the sick. Since the charlatans
felt no compunction about advertising and promised their luckless patients the most dazzling cures,
they often acquired tidy fortunes, while the legitimate doctor was left to starve. More cautious people
became increasingly skeptical of all medical assistance. They dosed themselves and clung to home-
made remedies.

It may well have been a natural revulsion against
these traffickers in human suffering that made Dr.
Mayo decide to return to medicine. At any rate, he
went down to the University of Missouri in 1853
and took a second medical degree. Then, with his
wife, he set out for the territory of Minnesota—the
last outpost of the American frontier. In Minnesota,
he spent the first few months, not in setting up his
household, but in exploring the wild regions which
surrounded the isolated villages, and in studying
the habits and customs of the Indian tribes. The information he gathered seemed rather wasted at the
time. But a few years later, during the great Sioux
Outbreak, it was to prove invaluable to him, when
he was one of a band of men who rescued the be-

DOCTORS WILL (LEFT) AND CHARLIE MAYO

sieged villagers of New Ulm from the enraged Sioux Indians.

During the Civil War, Dr. Mayo was appointed as an examining surgeon for the Union Army, and this required him to take up residence in Rochester. When the war was over, Dr. Mayo found that he liked the little town which showed promise of becoming a thriving grain center, and he hung out his shingle on a little house on Third Street. Before long, people all along the frontier began to talk of the "little doctor," as they called him. They liked his brisk, competent manner, his shrewd, unerring diagnoses, and, what was more, they liked the remarkable number of recoveries he had to his credit.

Their confidence in the "little doctor" was well placed. For, although he loved the free, democratic life of the frontier, Dr. Mayo had no backwoods mentality. Every year he took a trip back East to keep himself abreast of the new ideas in medical science. But no idea passed his critical mind unchallenged. In the small laboratory in the back of his home, he spent hour after hour studying and analyzing the surgical techniques he had learned, sifting out the impractical ones, and adopting only those of proved worth.

Nor did the "little doctor's" reputation rest upon his skill as a surgeon alone. Always a progressive thinker, he was aware, as few men born in the

United States could be, of the tremendous responsibilities of citizenship in a democracy. In spite of the demands of his growing practice, Dr. Mayo was a tireless worker in community activities. He took a vigorous part in state politics which he did not relinquish until he retired as state senator at the age of seventy-four. He was a member of the school board, and he planned a new and improved system of sanitation for the city. He founded a book fund as the nucleus of a public library, and he arranged to have visiting lecturers include Rochester on their circuit.

Two sons were born to the Mayos, William James in 1861, and Charles Horace in 1865. From the beginning, their choice of a profession was inevitable. As Will Mayo said in reminiscing over his boyhood: "It never occurred to us that we could be anything else but doctors." Certainly by the time they were in their teens, the two boys had a background of medical experience which many a doctor might envy. They became accustomed to going with their father on long trips into the country where, in some lonely farmhouse, they acted as their father's assistants. Will soon learned the names of all his father's instruments, kept them sterile, and handed them to his father in the proper order during the most intricate operations. The story is told of how Charlie was pressed into service as an anesthetist when he was only nine. The young man who was giving the anesthetic suddenly fainted in the middle of an operation. With scarcely a flick of his wrist, Dr. Mayo motioned to young Charlie to climb up on a box and take over. Startled, but confident, the youngster climbed up and went to work. In the next few minutes, the patient was quietly asleep, and another Mayo had been launched upon his medical career.

With his European background and his broad education, Dr. Mayo could give his sons a thorough grounding in the sciences allied to medicine as well as practical experience. He taught them chemistry, interspersing his lectures with stories of his old friend, John Dalton, and he introduced them to the recent discoveries of Huxley, Darwin and Spencer which were then making scientific history. And the boys learned their anatomy, bone by bone, from an old Indian skeleton which their father had articulated and hung in his office.

Very early in their lives, the two Mayo boys realized that their father's profession was one of service with only meager material rewards. They remembered how excited their father had been when he returned home after one of his trips to the East. Bursting with enthusiasm, the "little doctor" told his assembled family of a new microscope he had seen and of how much such an instrument would help him in his clinical and pathological exam-

inations. Mrs. Mayo, always an understanding
woman, asked him why he had not ordered one
immediately. The doctor hesitated only a moment,
took a deep breath, and blurted out: "Well, it costs
about six hundred dollars, and would mean mort-
gaging our home." As the boys recalled the story,
Dr. Mayo got his microscope and it was more than
ten years later that the mortgage on the Mayo house
was paid off. But the microscope became an important fixture in the household, and who knows how
many times over it may have repaid its cost in the
training in scientific analysis that it afforded the
young Mayos?

Dr. Mayo guided his sons' choice of their medical schools as carefully as he had guided their early
education. After looking over the possibilities, he
decided that the University of Michigan which was
one of the few schools to offer clinical courses in
surgery was the right school for Will. And, in order
that the Mayos should not become ingrown in their
professional training, he sent young Charlie off to
the Chicago Medical College where he would acquire a different viewpoint.

The year 1883 is an important one in the Mayo
annals. It marked Will's graduation from medical
college, and it was the year of the Rochester tor-
nado, an ill-wind which resulted in the founding of
St. Mary's Hospital. The storm struck late on the

afternoon of August 21, and, within a few minutes, had leveled a good part of the town. As soon as they could get through the shambles, Dr. Mayo and his two sons set up an emergency hospital in a local dance hall, and cared for the injured as they were brought in. The doctors could patch up their patients' broken limbs and battered bodies, but the nursing problem they presented was a different story. The "little doctor" had an idea. Early the next morning, he went up the hill to the Convent of St. Francis and suggested to the Mother Superior that some of the sisters be sent to the hospital to serve as nurses. Mother Alfred agreed at once and, from then on, the nursing at the emergency hospital was taken over by the sisters of St. Francis.

Once the emergency had passed, Mother Alfred gave a great deal of thought to the possibility of establishing a permanent hospital in Rochester. She spoke to Dr. Mayo about it. At first, he did not approve. He pointed out that Rochester was a small town, that hospitals were costly to maintain, and that the public in general had a great aversion to hospitals, preferring to be cared for in their own homes. Still Mother Alfred was persistent. She said that her Order would guarantee to build and equip a modern hospital, if Dr. Mayo and his sons would agree to take charge of it. Six years went into the planning and building of St. Mary's Hospital, dur-

ing which Dr. Mayo and his son, Will, made many
trips to the East to study the best methods of hospital administration and design. But in October,
1889, St. Mary's opened its doors, dedicated to the
care of the sick regardless of their color, sex, financial status, or religion. And, in the service of that
common ideal, the Protestant Mayos and the Catholic sisters of St. Francis worked side by side in
perfect collaboration for many years, unmindful of
any differences in creed.

When Doctor Will and Doctor Charlie came
back to Rochester from medical college, they were
faced with a problem as old as medicine. They were
too young! Patients felt no confidence in these
young men who looked like mere schoolboys. Old
Doctor Mayo resorted to stratagem. When a call
came for Doctor Mayo, he had one of the boys answer it, and, if the patient did not actually throw
him out, the young doctor proceeded to take charge
of the case. Thus the young doctors overcame the
handicap of their youth and the Doctors Mayo became a trio. All three now worked upon an equal
basis of partnership, but Old Doctor Mayo still insisted upon two things: that his sons spend a part
of each day in study and research and that they keep
up with the new developments in medicine and
surgery.

The young Mayos were too much their father's

sons to have to be urged to take time off for study and travel to the big medical centers of the East. Whenever they could be spared from their duties in Rochester, they took alternate turns at haunting the clinics where they could observe famous surgeons at work. Dr. Price of Philadelphia hardly counted a clinic complete unless one of the young doctors from the West was in attendance. Dr. Halsted of Johns Hopkins became their life-long friend. In the clinics of New York and Boston, they were accorded special opportunities to study new surgical procedures. But, like their father, the young men were chary of accepting new ideas only because of their novelty. They brought back and utilized only those techniques that had proved their worth.

The surgical patient of the 1890's enjoyed no such privacy as he does today. Reports of operations were considered legitimate news, and the newspapers were full of such stories, complete down to the last gory detail. In Minnesota and the surrounding states, the name of Mayo began to figure prominently in these accounts for the reputation of the young doctors as skilled and cautious surgeons was growing fast. Medical doctors from all over the state referred their difficult cases to the Mayos of Rochester, confident in the knowledge that the Mayos would not operate unless it was absolutely necessary. As these sick people made their way to

Rochester, stories of Doctor Will and Doctor Charlie took on almost legendary proportions. Railroad men told of seeing a hopeless invalid borne into St. Mary's Hospital on a stretcher only to have him emerge a few weeks later, sound and whole. On one train, they said, they had come upon a little blind boy, quite alone, wearing a tag around his neck with the words: "Take me to Rochester to Doctor Mayo" written on it. Such tales as these, some true, some apocryphal, brought an avalanche of patients to Rochester and forced the Mayos to an important decision.

With the retirement of William Worrall Mayo, Doctor Will and Doctor Charlie were left to carry on at St. Mary's by themselves, and they now had to decide whether to restrict their practice so that they could handle it alone, or whether to add new members to their staff. Both the Mayos had been brought up on the axiom that no man is big enough to be independent of others, and they knew that if they added to their staff they must accept the new members as equal partners, not as mere interns or medical assistants.

Largely because of this enlightened policy the Mayo Clinic evolved from the small group of offices on the second floor of the Masonic Temple building into the world's most famous diagnostic center, equipped with every facility known to science and housed in a modern structure which covered a full city block. Typical of the men who came to the Mayos was Henry Plummer. Dr. Plummer was a brilliant scientist and a highly original thinker for whom there was no greater delight than to isolate a disease and to seek out a method of cure. Turn of the century laboratories were for the most part crude affairs where only the most routine analyses were attempted. Under Dr. Plummer's guidance, the Mayo laboratories became scientific workshops which gave invaluable diagnostic aid to the examining doctors. In time, there were more than five hundred members on the Clinic staff, but these men, given independence of action and an opportunity for creative work, threw themselves enthusiastically into the co-operative effort that was to make the Clinic a beacon of hope for the sick and ailing all over the world.

One day, Doctor Will posted a manuscript describing his work in gall-bladder operations to an eastern medical journal. When the manuscript came to his desk, the editor snorted. Here was a country doctor in a town with a population of only a little over a thousand who claimed to have done a hundred and five gall-bladder operations. Incredible, the editor thought. The man must be an outrageous liar, for this was an operation attempted, in those days, only by surgeons of the highest skill.

The editor wrote "not suitable for our publication" across the face of the manuscript in a flourishing hand, and sent it back in the next mail. But, not many months later as the name *Mayo* kept cropping up in the reports that crossed his desk, the editor decided to go and see for himself what was happening in this "clinic in the cornfields." Skeptically, he set out on the long hot journey to the Minnesota prairies. Some of his skepticism disappeared as he stepped from the train. In Rochester, he saw a pleasant, modern city that had grown up around the Mayo Clinic. Here was St. Mary's Hospital with its new additions. There were several smaller hospitals to house the overflow; convalescent homes, and hotels to take care of the ambulatory patients. Even the trains made special stops to accommodate those traveling to Rochester. The next morning, the editor visited St. Mary's and the Mayo Clinic and was taken through the great laboratories, the record rooms, the library and the museum. Finally, he entered the surgical amphitheater, and watched as Doctor Will performed one of the gall-bladder operations at which he had scoffed. Months later, a considerable part of the space in the editor's journal was devoted to a discussion of all that he had seen at the Mayos'.

The editor was only one of thousands—many of them eminent surgeons—who poured into Rochester to observe the surgical wizardry of the Mayo brothers. One distinguished doctor, asked which of the brothers he thought was the better surgeon, thought a little and then said:

"Well, Doctor Will is a wonderful surgeon, and Doctor Charlie is a surgical wonder."

Some of the visitors to Rochester could never forget that memorable day when Doctor Will began to perform an operation for the removal of a tumor that had displaced all of the patient's organs. Suddenly, a large vein ruptured and the blood spurted forth in a dangerous stream. Doctor Will looked up at the surgical gallery.

"Gentlemen, I have torn the *vena cava* and it will be necessary to make another incision to repair the vein." With a quick movement, he set the damage right, and went on. As the large mass came loose, a section of the small intestine was torn away. Again Doctor Will looked up at the tense men in the gallery:

"This, gentleman, is a much more serious accident than the injury to the vein. I have torn a long rent in the duodenum and, if it is not made intact, the contents will leak out and the patient die." Then, with infinite skill, he stitched the rent and finished the operation. Three hours later, while the surgeons in the gallery wiped the beads of perspiration from their brows, Doctor Will walked calmly from the room, assured of his patient's recovery.

Seldom do two brothers differ as radically in appearance as the Mayos. Doctor Will was tall and blond with an innate kindness hidden beneath a rather austere manner. Doctor Charlie, on the other hand, was short and dark with many of the bluff characteristics of the country doctor. He couldn't be made to dress up, however august the occasion. Sometimes he would illustrate a delicate operation with a homespun turn of speech that made his remarks stick in the observer's memory for all his life. Doctor Charlie had a gift for dealing with his patients that was often half the cure. And he was not above using some plain horse sense in place of a more elaborate technique. A neurotic woman who had plagued the Clinic doctors with her tale of imaginary ailments, came at last to Doctor Charlie's office. He pondered over her case history, looked grave, and, after considerable thought, gave her a prescription. "One half bag of plain popcorn to be taken every afternoon," it read. In a week, the woman was back jubilantly announcing that Doctor Charlie had saved her life.

In their private lives, Doctor Will and Doctor Charlie were a team just as they were in their work. So close was their relationship that for many years they pooled their incomes and raised their families out of a common fund. Toward their patients, their policy was simple: Each paid according to his ability to pay. No one was ever turned away from the Mayo Clinic for lack of funds; and there was only one instance of preference. A patient who could not afford the expense of a long stay in Rochester was placed at the top of the list of appointments. Sometimes a farmer who had mortgaged his farm to come to the Clinic went to the office and paid his bill; and then found, when he reached his home, that his check had been returned uncashed and another added to "tide him over" his convalescence. Perhaps the Mayo boys remembered that six hundred dollar microscope that their father had spent ten years paying for.

In a speech before a medical society, Dr. Will once formulated an ideal.

"What a man may do with his own hands is small compared with what he may do to impart ideas and a scientific spirit in many men who in endless chains will carry on the same endeavor."

As the Clinic grew, the Mayos realized that its enormous facilities for research and study ought to be put to work. For it was a rare disease indeed that did not appear in some form in the Mayos' minute and painstaking records. Once again, they pooled their resources and, in 1917, with a fund of a million and a half dollars, set up the Mayo Foundation to endow a graduate school of medicine which would have all the facilities of the Mayo Clinic at its disposal. The school was to be affiliated with the University of Minnesota and the University was to supply the faculty, while the clinical work in research and diagnosis was to be done in Rochester at the Clinic. After a hesitant trial period, the Mayo Foundation and the University of Minnesota Medical School became the finest center of graduate medical study in America.

Doctor Will and Doctor Charlie both died suddenly in the summer of 1939, and only Doctor Charlie's son was left to carry on the tradition of the name in Rochester. But in the Clinic and in the Foundation, the Mayos were assured that the work which their father had begun before them would go on in the "endless chain."

The Mayo Clinic grew out of the American frontier, through the efforts of men who looked to the future. Today, the young doctors in Rochester carry on the work of eradicating illness and disease. Their eyes, too, are turned to the future and to the new frontiers of medicine.

George Washington Carver

The life of George Washington Carver is a simple demonstration of the fact that high ability and great spiritual gifts know no bounds of race, creed, or color.

Ironically enough, this gentle Negro scientist whose talents were to enrich all mankind was born in the midst of the American Civil War. His birthplace was Diamond Grove, Missouri, but the exact date of his birth is obscure and he had scarcely even a name. Because his mother, Mary, had been the slave of Moses Carver, the little fellow was known simply as Carver's George. Not until his school days did he attain the dignity of George Washington Carver.

Nevertheless, George had a happy childhood. Moses Carver was a good man, a hard-working farmer, who did not approve of slavery. He had been driven to purchasing a few slaves because he could not get help in any other way. He and his wife had a particular fondness for the small, wiry George whom they had rescued from kidnapers

CJNAAR

in his infancy by dint of trading him for a horse. They treated him much as they would one of their children. He had a few light chores to do around the house, feeding the chickens and weeding the garden patch, but after that he was free. This meant that George would go scooting off into the woods for there—even in childhood—he found his own special world of magic. He had a way with all growing, green things; and he rambled happily about among the trees, now stopping to pick up a bright stone or gathering a herb he had not seen before. His pockets became a miniature laboratory in which he stuffed all his treasures, to be taken out and examined minutely at his leisure. The neighbors smiled at the comical little lad and dubbed him The Plant Doctor.

The whole world became a question mark for young George. Mrs. Carver gave him an old speller that had been around the house for years, and the boy was launched irrevocably upon his insatiable quest for learning. Reading was fun and taught him the names of things, but it was not enough. George wanted to know the why of things. For many miles around there were no schools for Negro children, and it was not clear how the youthful naturalist expected to get the education he craved. George solved his own problem. He went to the Carvers and told them he would like to go away in search of schooling. The Carvers looked at the child, saw the eagerness in his face and the terrible yearning in his eyes. They could not say no.

George had no doubts about his future. Like a small, brave gargoyle, he went out in search of his destiny. His first stop was the town of Neosho, Missouri and his first bed away from home was a log pile that kept slipping out from under him. But Neosho had a school, and the next morning George walked into its one crowded room in a state of trembling excitement. In less than a year he had learned all that the little school could teach him and he had discovered a lot of wonderful things that were not in the books. He tasted the joy to be found in humble tasks well done. To earn his living he worked as a cook, a houseworker, and a laundryman. He found that he had strong, deft fingers with which he could create beautiful things. He became expert at sewing, embroidery and knitting; he copied intricate patterns in crochet. It did not occur to him that these were unusual occupations for a boy; they were all a part of his restless urge to learn.

The pattern of George's wanderings was becoming clear. He would come to a town, set up a small laundry business, and make for the nearest school. When the school could teach him no more he was off again. There were some dark moments along the way when he encountered cruelty and prejudice toward his race; but mostly he found that people were kind and eager to help him. Over his laundry tub and a bar of soap George made many of his life-long friends.

The young journeyman was never sure just what the requirements were for college. But one day he thought himself ready and he wrote out an application for Highland University. In a few days he heard that he had been accepted. When he presented himself for registration, George noted that the man behind the desk seemed strangely embarrassed. He twisted in his chair and slithered over his words. But his meaning was clear enough. He was sorry that George had not been told, the school did not take Negroes. George felt no bitterness, only a kind of pity for the white man's discomfiture.

George Carver simply marked this down as one of life's experiences. He did not even bother to explain that this rejection would mean a serious setback in his plans. He had spent all his money on train fare to the college; now he must wait another year.

Fifty years later, it was a proud boast of Simpson College at Indianola, Iowa, that George Washington Carver had been one of its early students. In 1890, even this liberal college did not know what to do about George when he came trudging in one day to apply for admission. They liked his spirit, but they could not ignore the fact that his scholastic background was erratic. And he insisted on taking the wrong courses. Instead of choosing subjects that would help him to earn his living, he wanted to enroll in the art classes. Finally, they settled on a compromise. He could register, but he must take the practical courses.

George was a gentle man but he was also a stubborn one. He did not intend to be cheated out of this opportunity to create the beautiful things of which he had always dreamed. Little by little, he worked himself into the good graces of Miss Etta Budd, head of the art department. Reluctantly, she agreed that George might attend her classes for a trial period. If he showed only a slight talent he was to go back to his practical work. George stayed in Miss Budd's classes for as long as he remained at Simpson, and in 1893 one of his paintings received honorable mention at the exhibition of the Chicago World's Fair.

To his friends back home, the young student wrote glowingly of his college days. The first weeks had been hard and he had nearly starved until word had been spread about of his laundry business. Soon he was a familiar and popular figure on the campus. In the discussion groups, in the college glee club, on the baseball field, his classmates simply forgot about his color and accepted him for the merry, warm-hearted lad he was. Under such treatment, George flourished.

It was Miss Budd who asked George point blank what he intended to do with his education. And he had been rather surprised at his own answer. Up to this time, he had thought vaguely that he might become a teacher or an artist. Now, with his new maturity, an ideal took hold of him, the desire to serve the people of his race. Clearly, it was in agriculture that he could serve his people best.

It was quite a wrench for George to break off at Simpson, but in 1891 he entered the Iowa State College of Agriculture and Mechanic Arts. Under the direction of James G. Wilson, director of the Agricultural Station, and Henry Cantwell Wallace, professor of agriculture, young Carver was soon absorbed in his new studies. These two men, among the ablest in their field in the United States, were to play no small part in shaping his future. They were not only his teachers, but his friends. Thirty years later, the three men were still exchanging ideas and threshing out the problems that beset them in their work.

George Carver was graduated from Iowa State College in 1894 and was immediately appointed a member of the faculty in charge of systematic botany. He thought sometimes that he would like to remain among these congenial people with whom he felt so strong a sense of kinship, but in 1896 came the call for which he had been waiting. Booker T. Washington wrote to ask if young Professor Carver could be persuaded to come to Tuskegee Institute. He needed small persuasion.

The founders of Tuskegee Institute thought of it as a nucleus of progressive education for the Negro race. Its graduates were to go out to teach other students, and they, in their turn, were to pass on their knowledge, until the influence of the school had permeated into the lives of a whole generation. When the Institute appointed George Carver to head its newly formed department of agriculture, it could scarcely have realized how momentous a step it had taken. For in the years that followed, the department of agriculture at Tuskegee became an important influence in the economy of the South, an influence shared by Negro and white alike.

But, for the moment, Dr. Carver's department existed largely on paper. No cupboard had ever been barer than the laboratory which confronted him; there were no tools, no course of study; and the thirteen eager-eyed pupils who presented themselves for instruction were an oddly assorted lot. A really sensible man would have gone scurrying back to the efficiency and the well-equipped laboratories of Iowa State.

Sensible or not, George Carver plunged, with hardly a backward glance, into the work that was to occupy him for nearly half a century. Within a year, he had formulated a well-rounded course of study that was flexible enough to meet the needs of all his students, and he had built a fine laboratory out of the odds and ends he found around the campus—bits of wire and string, old broken bottles, cast-off jars, scraps of tin, and bottle tops. He loved his students and felt a high sense of responsibility for these young people who had come to the college over so hard a road. Into his classes crept much of his zest for everyday living, and the sly bantering quality of his humor. Nor did the young professor mind when his pupils turned the tables on him and he became the victim of a hoary joke. When a big, smiling boy walked up to his desk, and laid before him a strange looking insect that seemed part fly, part beetle and part spider, he regarded it seriously.

"Professor Carver, will you tell me what this bug is?" asked the lad.

"That, my young friend, is a humbug," quipped the teacher.

Teaching was the work he loved. Yet in a very short time the young scientist found that his classroom work was not enough.

George Washington Carver loved the South as

one loves the home of his youth, but its poverty haunted him. The farmers looked at their sterile soil, their scorched fields, and they saw nothing but despair for the future. With his peculiar gift of second sight, George Carver saw the South as a land of abundance if only men could learn to use its rich resources wisely. At Tuskegee he set up an agricultural experiment station and he began a campaign of education for every farmer who would listen.

Up and down the South he went in every moment he could spare from the college, attending farmers' meetings, visiting at county fairs, or sometimes just dropping in to see some isolated farmer who was having trouble with his crops. And everywhere he demonstrated the foolishness of planting only cotton. Rotate your crops, he told the the farmers, give the soil a chance to breathe, substitute sweet potatoes or peanuts for the cotton which was draining the land of its richness. He talked to men who had come miles to hear him, to men who had to memorize all that he said because they could not read or write, even to men who jibed at him because of his color. But gradually the farmers came to do as he told them, because they saw that there was common sense and hope in it.

One problem brought another, and the next one was really a poser. The farmers had taken Dr. Carver's advice, they had put vast numbers of acres into peanuts. Now there was no market for their abundant crop. Quietly and prayerfully, Dr. Carver took a basketful of peanuts into his laboratory and studied them. The story of that study did not end until one day in 1921, when Professor Carver of Tuskegee Institute was asked to go to Washington and testify before the House Ways and Means Committee in support of a tariff on peanuts. The Congressmen displayed little interest as the tall, aging Negro laden down with heavy bags, entered the committee room. Probably some crank or faddist, they thought, and allotted him ten minutes in which to speak. The Professor met this rebuff with his usual patience. He opened one of his bags and pulled out a small glass jar. One hour and three quarters later, he was still talking, his voice a hoarse whisper by this time, and every Congressman seemed glued to his seat. Before his awed audience, the Negro scientist had displayed more than one hundred and forty-five useful products made from peanuts, and some one hundred more made from sweet potatoes for good measure. The variety was staggering: flour, coffee, milk, cheese, face cream, pickles, shampoo, bleaches, ink, polishes, on and on endlessly. The problem was no longer to find a market, but to supply enough peanuts.

Everything that Dr. Carver touched turned into a kind of riches. Nothing that went into his laboratory came out without having found its proper use. Paving blocks came from cotton, rubber from sludge, potent medicines from barks and herbs. In the clays of Alabama, he found dyes and a blue pigment whose secret had long been lost in history. His paints and color washes became a matter of deep interest to one of the country's leading paint manufacturers. He could have a fortune for the asking, he was told. All such offers met a firm "no"; never once in his career could Dr. Carver be persuaded to take out a patent or to commercialize any of his products. Neither could any high paying job entice him away from his beloved Tuskegee. He was interested in the problems of industry only as they affected human beings.

With all this came fame, which was to George Carver only an annoying invasion of his privacy. He clung to his simple ways and might be found, fresh from some college commencement at which he had received an honorary degree, down on his knees in the earth peering intently at some odd fern he had found. At one of these commencements, a reporter caught up with him and asked him for his philosophy of life. Dr. Carver thought a while and then he said with the simplicity of a man who is not ashamed of a deep and honest faith:

"I go into the woods and there I gather specimens and study the great lessons that Nature is eager to teach us. Alone in the woods each morning I best hear and understand God's plan for me."

In the world of science, there is only one criterion —ability, and George Carver's fellow scientists were quick to recognize his genius. In 1916, he was made a fellow of the Royal Society of England. In 1923, he was awarded the Spingarn Medal for distinguished service in agricultural chemistry. In 1935, the government honored him and he was appointed collaborator in the Bureau of Plant Industry, U.S. Department of Agriculture. Franklin Delano Roosevelt and George Carver were men who understood one another, for each man, in his own way, was working to make it possible for people everywhere to be better fed, better housed and better clothed.

In 1940, when he was ill and near the end of his life, George Washington Carver did a characteristic thing. He directed that his life's savings, some thirty thousand dollars, be applied in setting up the Carver Foundation for agricultural research. With the money and endowments which have poured in from all sides, this center now offers unexcelled facilities for graduate studies for young Negro scientists from all over the country.

George Washington Carver died in 1943. Much of his life is epitomized in a small brick building,

the Carver Museum, on the campus at Tuskegee.
Here on exhibit are the hundreds of useful products that George Carver created from waste materials; here are examples of the delicate handicrafts
he loved; here are the paintings which were his life-
long hobby; and here is his dream of America as a
land of opportunity and growth for all men.

Edward Bok

LIKE many another pioneer, Edward
William Bok proved that his friends were wrong.
For they thought that he had surely taken leave of
his senses, when in 1889 he announced that he was
leaving the publishing house of Charles Scribner's
Sons in New York to go to Philadelphia to accept
the editorship of a magazine for women. Why,
they asked astounded, did he want to throw away a
promising career in New York—the center of the
publishing world—to undertake what must prove
a hopeless enterprise in Philadelphia? But never
once in his more than thirty years as editor and pub-
licist did Edward Bok regret his decision. He be-

came one of the trail blazers for modern American journalism; and he introduced into the American scene a distinctly new type of civic awareness.

Edward Bok's boyhood accustomed him to abrupt changes in his environment. He was born in Helder, Holland, on October 9, 1863. His family had been distinguished in the Netherlands for many generations, but a series of unfortunate investments had swept away their entire fortune. When Edward and his parents arrived in America in 1870 they had little more than the meager possessions they carried with them. Mr. Bok was not a man to waste time sighing over a vanished past. Since his sons were to be Americans, he decided that the process had better begin at once. Accordingly, six days after their ship had docked in New York harbor, he took his two sons around to the neighborhood public school in Brooklyn. Although they spoke not one word of English, the two small boys were graded by age and marched off unceremoniously to face the hostile stares of separate classrooms.

Seven-year-old Edward made the best of a bad situation. He sat stoically through his classes, and endured the taunts of his schoolmates in a necessary silence. But he was a pleasant, friendly lad; and before long the other boys discovered that the little Hollander knew some very interesting and novel

CJ NAAR

tricks that he had picked up along the dykes in his native land. Promptly they accepted him as their friend.

Nor did the Bok boys find the struggle with classroom work as difficult as it might have been. Their father had learned English as a boy in Holland, and they demanded lessons of him. Every evening for many months afterward, the Bok living room was turned into a schoolroom with a gay babble of Dutch and English flying back and forth. Edward in particular had an inherent linguistic sense, and he was soon leading his class in the public school. But, although the boy was an excellent student, he could not be forced to do anything that went against the grain of his good Dutch common sense. One evening during his English class, his father noticed that the boy's hands were bruised and swollen. He asked why. Young Edward's explanation was matter of fact and to the point. In writing class, he had been required to write in the Spencerian style which was then popular; he had refused to do so; and had been summarily punished for his obstinacy.

"Why did you refuse?" asked Mr. Bok.

"Because that way of writing is silly," the boy maintained stoutly. "Who is going to use such funny scrolls and curlicues in everyday business?"

Edward then showed his father a style of "plain"

writing that he had determined to adopt for his own use. Mr. Bok said nothing, but the next day he went to school with the boys, and spent some time in the principal's office. A few weeks later, new copy books appeared for the whole school. The style of writing used in the books was the one that Edward had recommended so heartily. Years later in the days before the typewriter had come into general use, Edward Bok found his clear, legible handwriting an important asset in his quest for work.

Although Edward and his brother took rapidly to American life, affairs in the Bok household were not going too well. Mr. Bok, a man of a fine liberal education, lacked the specialized training necessary for a job; and he brooded over his apparent inability to support his family. His wife, worn out by the difficult task of transplanting her family to the new world, became seriously ill.

The two boys felt sure that their mother would feel better if her house were clean. With a true Dutch zeal for cleanliness, they fell to, and scrubbed and polished and burnished until every corner of the house glistened and shone. Then they began to think about the problem of earning some money.

Edward's first job came by chance. He was walking along the street one morning, when he paused before a baker shop to admire the fine array of pies and cakes that the baker was setting out. "Look pretty good, don't they?" asked the man, joining the boy outside. "They would," answered the candid Dutch lad, "if your window were cleaner." "True enough," agreed the baker, "Perhaps you will clean it?" The boy attacked the job then and there. When he saw his sparkling window, the delighted baker lost no time in arranging to have Edward work for him every Tuesday and Friday after school for the sum of fifty cents a week.

Edward might soon have been spending all his spare time working for the baker. But he had other ideas. The Boks lived near the horse-car line from Brooklyn to Coney Island, and always through the summer heat the horses were watered at a certain watering-trough. While the horses drank, the men in the horse cars usually jumped off and went into a nearby cigar store for a drink of ice water. For the women and children this was not possible. They were forced to take the long ride in thirst and discomfort. So Edward bought a new tin pail and some glasses, and soon worked up a fine trade selling ice water to the thirsty passengers. When competitors appeared, he thriftily added sugar and lemons to his drink, raised the price, and went right on making money.

Young Bok was now doing very well for a school

boy, but further opportunities kept cropping up all about him. He was invited to a party and his latent journalistic sense prompted him to write it up for publication, including the names of all those present. He took the article to the Brooklyn *Eagle*, with the remark that every name mentioned in the paragraph meant another buyer for the paper. No other paper had such a department and the editor was quick to see its possibilities. He promptly offered Edward three dollars a column for all the society reports he could secure. The boy began to turn in from two to three columns each week, and the sales of the paper increased to such an extent that his pay was raised to four dollars a column.

Now with his chores at home, his work at the bakery, his sale of cold drinks, and his journalistic efforts, Edward found that he had no time left for school work. He asked to be allowed to leave school altogether, but his mother objected. Edward said little more about it, but inwardly his mind was made up. Meanwhile, Mr. Bok had become a translator for the Western Union Telegraph Company, a position for which his easy command of languages admirably fitted him. One evening at home, he casually mentioned that the office boy in his department had left. Immediately, Edward was all attention; nothing would do but he must have that job.

So at the age of thirteen, Edward Bok found himself working for Western Union at a salary of six dollars and a quarter a week.

Although the boy had now left school for good, he did not feel, by any means, that his education was at an end. He had an alert and eager mind; and, somehow, he told himself, he would acquire the equivalent of college training. In the evenings, he began to study the careers of famous men to see how they had made their way. At the time, the only available biographies were the short sketches in *Appleton's Encyclopedia* in the public library. Edward was not free during library hours so he decided to buy a complete set of the encyclopedia for himself. For this purpose he set aside a part of his lunch money, and he walked the five miles to work and back that he might save carfare. At last he had enough money for the set and proudly made his purchase.

One day it occurred to him to test the accuracy of one of the biographies. James A. Garfield was then being mentioned for the presidency. Edward wondered whether it was true that the man who might become President of the United States had once been a poor country boy on the tow-path. He sat down and wrote to General Garfield, telling him what he had read and asking if the story were true. The General was vastly pleased with the boy's

innocent letter. His reply was prompt, and so full
and complete that the lad hurried to show it to his
father.

"Why, my boy," cried Mr. Bok, "this is very
valuable. You must put it away very carefully, and
take good care of it."

"So?" said Edward to himself. "Well, why not
begin a collection of autograph letters?" Everybody
collected something. And actual letters from famous people would surely contain a great deal of
information.

The results were most interesting. General Grant
sent the lad a sketch of the exact spot where General
Lee surrendered to him. Longfellow told him how
he came to write his poem "Excelsior." Tennyson
sent him a stanza or two from "The Brook" together with some good advice against the use of
slang. Then, one day, came a letter from the Confederate General Jubal A. Early telling the boy
why he burned Chambersburg; and a friend suggested that this interesting bit of history would be
enjoyed by the readers of the *Tribune*. This letter,
which the paper ran together with a feature story
about young Edward Bok and his unique collection, became a subject of national discussion. Soon
references began to creep into letters from famous
persons to whom he wrote, saying that they had
read about his collection and were glad to be in-

cluded in it. Not a few expressed a desire to know the boy personally. So Edward began to watch the papers for the arrival of distinguished people in New York. Then he would go and call upon them. In this way he made friends with General and Mrs. Grant, General Sherman, Mrs. Abraham Lincoln, Jefferson Davis, and many others.

Edward's autograph collection was an absorbing hobby and was proving to be an education in itself. Still, like most hobbies, it was expensive; and Edward, on his slender pay, found this disturbing. He was thinking about this at lunch time one day when a man near him tossed away a picture from a package of cigarettes. Almost mechanically, the boy picked it up and found that it was the picture of a well-known actor. A line beneath the picture advised the purchaser that if he would keep the pictures included in each package of cigarettes, he would soon have a valuable album of the leading actors and actresses of the day. Turning the picture over, Edward found the other side a blank. Why, he thought to himself, they don't even say who this actor is. Suddenly, he came up with a start. Here was a way to finance his hobby. Fired by his idea, he hurried off to the Knapp Lithographic Company which produced the pictures and explained his plan. Mr. Knapp's answer was instantaneous. "I'll give you ten dollars apiece if you will write me a hundred-word biography of one hundred famous Americans. Send me a list and break them down into groups as statesmen, authors, soldiers, actors and so on."

Thus did Edward Bok get his first real literary commission. It was almost too successful for the young editor's taste. The work began to pile up so, that he found it necessary to hire two assistants to gather material for the biographies, while he contented himself with the editorial part of the venture.

Edward's hobby was now responsible for one of the greatest occasions of his young life. Some months before he had taken a course in stenography to enable him to make rapid notes when he was interviewing people. On the strength of his shorthand, he received a momentous assignment. He was to attend a state dinner in New York and report on a speech by President Hayes. The young reporter set off in high spirits, and whipped out his notebook as soon as the President rose to speak. All went well for a minute or two; then Edward realized that the President was speaking far too rapidly for his pencil. It seemed to the agitated boy that hours passed before the dinner was over and the guests had left the table. At last it came to an end, and Edward, still undaunted, quickly sought out the President and introduced himself. He told him of his assignment, and of how much it meant to him. Was there, he asked, some way in which he might get a copy of the speech? Something in the boy's earnest, forthright manner appealed to the President; he called one of his aides and told him to see that the lad got a copy of the speech at once. The next day, Edward's paper was the only one to carry a verbatim report of the President's address.

Nor was this the end of the incident. The next evening when he came home from work, the boy found a note from the President and Mrs. Hayes, asking him if he would not come to see them that evening at eight-thirty. Edward quickly put on his very best clothes and set out on a great adventure— a call upon the President of the United States. It was the beginning of a precious friendship. From that time on, the President took an unflagging interest in the lad's career, and gave him much sound advice. His last letter came in 1892 not long before his death, and was signed "thankfully your friend, Rutherford B. Hayes." A brief postscript was added, "Thanks, thanks for your steady friendship."

It was natural that Edward Bok's passion for autograph collecting should lead him to read the works of the authors with whom he corresponded. He became particularly attached to the New England group: Longfellow, Holmes, and Emerson.

The extraordinary force and power of Emerson's philosophy had a peculiar appeal for the boy; and he was seldom without a volume of the great philosopher's essays in his pocket to read on the long rides back and forth to his office. Since New England authors rarely came to New York, young Bok got a week's vacation and went up to Boston to see them. He had breakfast with Dr. Holmes, and spent most of the day with Longfellow who took him to the theater that night. He met Wendell Phillips and Phillips Brooks, Louisa Alcott and the Emersons, William Lloyd Garrison, Lucretia Mott and many other famous people. On his way home, the lad sat up all night in the day coach, not so much to save pullman fare, as for the chance to set his notes in order and to relive mentally the most wonderful vacation he had ever known.

A little while later, Edward became the editor of a local church paper, the *Brooklyn Magazine*. Overnight, the magazine leaped to national prominence, for its table of contents was sheer magic. The first issues carried articles by President Hayes, Wendell Phillips, William Dean Howells, General Grant and Marion Harland—a truly arresting array of celebrities. "How do they manage it?" people asked one another. "Surely the church can't afford to buy such material." Bok grinned to himself. Every one of the articles had come to him as a gift from friends who wanted him to make a success of his new vocation.

The young editor's experiences on the *Brooklyn Magazine* convinced him that the right career for him lay in publishing and editing. He gave up his work with Western Union, and went to the publishing house of Henry Holt and Company. From there he moved on to Charles Scribner's Sons. At Scribner's he became secretary to the two chief editors. In the course of a year or two he learned every detail of the publishing business and he met the cream of the literary world. He seemed assured of a bright future with an old, established firm. Then one of his numerous little side ventures came along to change all that.

About a year before, he had conceived the idea— unheard of at the time—of selling the same articles to a number of widely scattered newspapers for publication on the same day. The plan worked well, and soon the Bok Syndicate Press was organized with a New York office and with Edward's brother in charge. One of their leading features was a woman's page, the first of its kind, for it was an intrepid man who would undertake to write such a page. To cynics who pointed out that the women of America were not, in general, newspaper readers, the youthful editor retorted: "Of course not, there's nothing in the papers to interest them."

Whereupon he proceeded to write a page of such interest to women that letters of praise poured in from all over the country. In Philadelphia Cyrus Curtis noted the page and paid a hurried visit to New York. He posed his question briefly: Would young Bok come to Philadelphia as editor of the *Ladies' Home Journal?*

Edward Bok was confronted with the greatest decision of his career. There was an element of challenge in the new venture, but if he failed he would not only sacrifice his future, but expose himself to all sorts of ridicule. In his practical mind, he weighed the situation carefully. The next morning he took a train to Philadelphia to begin a career that lasted thirty years.

Under Bok's aegis, the *Ladies' Home Journal* developed into one of the most progressive magazines in the country. Its aims were democratic; it was designed for the average intelligent reader rather than for the select few. And for the average reader Bok decided that nothing was too good. He sought out the best in literary talent. He presented informative, yet entertaining articles on important questions of the day. And always he campaigned through his editorial page for a better America. There was hardly a phase of American life upon which his restless mind did not touch. His bitter attack on the cruel and misleading advertisements of the patent medicine dealers aroused public sentiment for the passage of the Pure Food and Drug Act. The ugliness of the typical American home distressed him; soon there appeared in the pages of the *Ladies' Home Journal* complete architectural plans for a series of small attractive houses for people of moderate income. A few years later, he started the conservative by inaugurating a department where young mothers could obtain sound, scientific advice on the care of their babies. He was instrumental in introducing art to the American public; for many months the *Ladies' Home Journal* carried a series of handsome reproductions of great masterpieces, many of them never before seen in America.

One of the strongest traits of Edward Bok's character was his deep sense of responsibility to his readers. He knew all too well that the editor of a magazine that reached into hundreds of thousands of homes could exert a tremendous power for good or evil. Through all his editorship he used all the force and energy he possessed to make his magazine an influence for betterment and progress.

Although Bok's professional duties were rigorous and exacting, he found time for a full, rich personal life. In 1896 he married Mary Louise Curtis and his two sons, Curtis and Cary, became a source of great happiness to him. His estate at Marion, a suburb of Philadelphia, was never a show place, but a gracious American home abounding in warm hospitality. One of his best friends was Theodore Roosevelt; and the two men spent many evenings together threshing over the affairs of the world "as one Dutchman to another," for both were proud of their Dutch ancestry.

It had never seemed to Edward Bok that a man ought to go on working at top speed to the very end of his life. He saw around him too many worn out old men who had tried that. For himself, he felt that twenty-five years of editing were enough. But World War I intervened and it was not until 1919 that he vacated the editorial chair. When he did, the circulation of the *Ladies' Home Journal* had risen to over two million and it was one of the most valuable magazine properties in the world.

Retirement did not mean idleness to Edward Bok. It meant merely another chance for service to others. His interests were boundless; and with his wealth and influence, he now strove to enrich the lives of everyday people. He gave a large endowment to the Philadelphia Orchestral Association on condition, however, that it open its doors to popular subscription. He campaigned vigorously for better parks and playgrounds in every community. In his hatred of war, he offered a huge prize for the best plan for permanent peace.

Edward Bok died on January 9, 1930 and was buried at the foot of his Florida Singing Tower, a wonderful sanctuary for birds, patterned after the "Island of Nightingales," his ancestral home in Holland. His story is not one of cheap and quick success. It is the story of a stalwart immigrant boy who brought to America almost as much as he took from her. In his famous book, *The Americanization of Edward Bok,* he wrote his credo: "I ask no greater privilege than to see the America that I like to think of as the America of Abraham Lincoln and of Theodore Roosevelt become not faultless but less faulty. It is a part in trying to shape that America that I ask in return for what I owe her. A greater privilege no man could ask."

Henry Ford

WITH the possible exception of Edison, Henry Ford's name is known to more human beings in the world today than that of any other American. A few years ago, a fellow countryman, traveling abroad, pasted Ford's picture on an en-

CJ Naar

velope and mailed it without a name or address. It
went straight to Detroit and to Henry Ford.

Much of what Henry Ford stood for he owed to
the sturdy Dutch traits inherited from his mother,
Mary Litogot. She was the daughter of a well-to-do
farmer who lived near Dearborn, Michigan. As a
child of six, dangling over a fence, she first noticed
a neighbor's son, William Ford, who was working
for her father. William grew fond of the little girl
who tagged after him while he went about his farm
chores. He saved his money, bought a forty-acre
tract from Mr. Litogot, and, when little Mary grew
up, he asked her to marry him.

Their marriage took place just at the outbreak of
the Civil War, and on July 30, 1863, the first of their
six children was born and was christened Henry.
His mother died when Henry was thirteen, but her
memory had a lasting influence on his whole life.
"I try to live as I know my mother would wish me
to," Henry Ford once told a friend. One of the
things that Mary Litogot Ford had impressed
upon her son was that, if you are dishonest, or do
an unkind act, you, yourself, will suffer most
from it.

William Ford was a quiet, hard-working farmer
who provided well for his family. There were no
luxuries in the modest home, but there was an
abundance of simple comfort.

Henry was five when he began his schooling at the village schoolhouse. Each day he trudged two and a half miles to school, and back again at night, carrying his lunch in a little tin pail with a cup on top. In three years, he was transferred to another school, but it was just as far away in the opposite direction.

Even as a very small boy, Henry showed a keen interest in machinery of all kinds, to the distress of his father who wanted him to be a farmer. His curiosity got him into some serious scrapes.

Henry watched with deep fascination the workings of the steam in the kitchen teakettle, just as another boy named Watt had once done in England. The small boy named this power "Mr. Steam," and he determined to find out how it would behave under certain handicaps. He got a thick earthenware teapot, filled it with water, stuffed up the spout, tied down the lid, and smuggled it into the dining room, where a brisk fire burned in the huge old fireplace. Then he sat down to wait. Presently the sound of an explosion and young Henry's cry of pain brought Mrs. Ford hurrying from the kitchen. All about the room lay the fragments of the teapot. One piece had knocked a chunk out of the mirror, another had broken a window, while a third gashed the young investigator's face. He was badly scalded, too, and to the end of his days a faint scar reminded him of "Mr. Steam."

One day an irate farmer appeared in young Henry's classroom at school. He brought a tale of woe. The boys had dammed up the water in a creek near his property, until it had overflowed into his cellar and made a mess of things generally. "What about this, Henry?" demanded the schoolteacher, turning instinctively to the Ford youngster for he knew he was the ringleader.

"Why-ee," said Henry, "I never thought about the water backing up and doing any damage. We built the dam to get water enough to run a water-wheel. We used an old rake handle for the shaft and a coffee-grinder for the other end. You ought to see how beautifully it works."

Interested in spite of himself, the schoolmaster still had to maintain discipline. He gave the boys a stern lecture on respecting the property rights of others, ordered them to tear out the dam, and told young Ford that he might remain after school each day until he grew tired of his company.

All his life Henry Ford loved to be reminded of these boyish escapades. Among his most treasured possessions was a picture of the old creek, showing the dam, the water wheel, and the childhood chums who had helped arouse the farmer's ire. In later years, he took a great deal of pleasure in restoring the old Ford home and furnishing it so that it looked exactly as it did in his mother's day. The carpets, the dishes, the lamps, the pictures on the walls and an old sampler with its homely motto worked in red thread are the same; while down by the barn, in the old carpenter shop, are the counterparts of the tools his father used.

After his adventures at the creek, water power grew tame for Henry Ford. He turned to watches. In school one day, he and his desk mate, John Haggerty, were happily "dissecting" a watch when the teacher swooped down upon them. "Well, Henry," said Mr. Brush in martyr-like calm, "are you two boys never going to learn why you are sent to school? Bring the watch to me. Now you may both stay after school tonight until you've put it together again." Little did the good man know how light was his punishment; Henry had the watch together again in ten minutes flat.

Before long the lad was repairing all the watches in the neighborhood with tools consisting of a screw-driver made out of a knitting needle, and a pair of tweezers fashioned from an old watch spring. William Ford had no intention of having a tinker for a son and protested mightily. Henry was obstinate. He was only doing the repair work for fun, he said. "But the laborer is worthy of his hire," said Mr. Ford, "and it's a different story, when you ride my horses nine miles into Detroit, after the day's work is done, just to get parts to mend other people's watches with. It's bad business and it's got to stop. Hereafter you stay at home nights."

William Ford wanted his son to be a farmer, and he hated the mechanical bent which he felt would in the end draw the boy away from the farm. Father and son had many bitter misunderstandings, which came to a climax when the boy was sixteen. Without saying a word to anybody, young Henry walked into Detroit, and got himself a job in a steam-engine factory. But the job brought only $2.50 a week; room and board cost $3.50. Without ado, the boy got another job, this one at $2.00 a week for evening work in a jewelry store. With a whole dollar's margin, the young man felt independent and unworried.

For nine months, Henry worked in the steam-engine factory by day and repaired watches at night. The lad was unusually proficient and was slated for a substantial promotion, when his father sent a message asking him to come home. Mr. Ford's health was failing and he needed his eldest son at home. Henry dropped everything and went back to the farm.

A season of plowing, planting, and harvesting went slowly by, but it was not the drudgery it would once have been, for young Henry had an idea. He was going to make a farm "locomotive" that would plow tremendously and eat nothing except when it was at work. Even at that age, Henry had little use for farm animals. It took so much time to care for them in winter-time which he could have used on his inventions—and all they did was to "stand around and eat their heads off." However, he managed to find an opportunity to keep his engine skill from getting rusty. He got a job as district road expert from the Detroit agent of the Westinghouse portable steam engine. Thereafter, when the farmers in the vicinity had trouble with their engines, Henry went out as the company's representative and took out the kinks. He was so skillful that many people said the engines limbered up of their own accord when Henry drove into the yard.

Making the best of his enforced stay on the farm, the young man turned his attention to the problems of the average farmer. He concluded that there was no need for farmers to spend more than twenty-four days a year in the actual work of raising food for the nation. Before the hard-bitten farmers of the neighborhood, he argued his case convincingly: "When it comes time to plow, cultivate, or harvest, farmers should go at the job with several tractors, plenty of machinery and do the thing in a hurry, hiring as much outside help as possible. Farm machinery can and will be made at a price low enough to make such methods entirely safe and sane. The more quickly the job is done, the sooner the farmer can be released from his farm to earn money elsewhere."

Henry Ford's first "farm locomotive"—the terms tractor and Fordson were then unknown—was built when he was twenty years old. The big cast-iron wheels came from a discarded lawn mower; he, himself, made the pattern and cast the cylinder for the steam engine which was to furnish the power. It all sounds very simple, but to those who know something about pattern-making and cylinder-casting, the wonder is how he could have produced a workable machine in his little country shop. On its first trial, the locomotive ran forty feet and stopped. "I thought my machine would plow up the whole farm in no time," said Mr. Ford, "but I found I did not have enough steam. Moreover, I felt that there was nothing I could do to make the engine generate steam rapidly enough to keep it going any length of time." But the young inventor knew that a machine that had run forty feet could, in time, be made to run any number of feet. What was needed was an internal combustion engine. One would be forthcoming some day and then he would build a machine that would revolutionize farming. His first farm locomotive was run back into the shed to await its day.

Just about this time, one of Henry's other interests was a girl over in Greenfield Township. But Clara Bryant, small and winsome with chestnut hair and bewitching eyes, cared not a hoot for him or his citified ways. "Hmmm," mused Henry, and he purchased a shining red cutter and a new set of silvery sleigh bells. Then he scrubbed his father's best pair of horses, until their coats shone like satin, and set out with a gay group of young people for a skating party at the Greenfield club. As a further blandishment, he carried in his vest pocket a beautiful watch of his own making, one with two sets of hands, to indicate standard and sun time.

"Mother," said Miss Bryant, the next morning, "that Henry Ford from Dearborn, is different from our boys around here. I shouldn't be surprised if some day he makes a mark in the world."

Henry was not slow in seizing his advantage. A few weeks later he approached his father resolutely. "Father," he said, "if I decide to marry, what will you do for me?"

Mr. Ford had long had this problem satisfactorily settled in his own mind, and his answer was prompt: "You can have that eighty acres facing Recknor Road, and all the timber you want to cut for buildings."

"Good," said Henry and started to saw lumber that very day. Soon there was enough for a frame house thirty-one feet square and a story and a half high.

Henry and Clara were married in April, 1888, and the new house, trim and modern, with its broad porches overlooking the rolling farm land, was waiting for them. In the back were the red dairy, the barns, and the workshop, where the young man hoped someday to perfect his scheme for revolutionizing industry. For three years, little was heard of these plans. He was busy with his farm, his "expert" work, and he had three sawmills in operation that he had to supervise. However, it was evident that he had done a good deal of thinking and planning. One evening he spoke out suddenly to his wife: "Clara, I believe we are going to have to move to Detroit. I want to get at my horseless carriage, and there are too many distractions here. I have hardly a moment to myself."

"Wh—at!" exclaimed Mrs. Ford, aghast. "Your *horseless carriage?* Whoever heard of such a thing!" and she looked at her husband quite as though he had taken leave of his senses.

He smiled quietly, "I've had it in mind for some time. Bring me a pencil and paper and I'll give you an idea of it."

Mrs. Ford took the first paper at hand, a sheet of music from the piano and passed it over mechanically. She had not yet recovered from the start her

husband's speech had given her; and she sat looking about her pleasant parlor with but one thought
uppermost in her mind—could she bring herself to
leave this cozy home where she had been so happy?
In the city, they would have to rent, and probably
nothing would be as she wanted it.

"You're not listening, Clara," reproached Mr.
Ford. "Come over here, and I'll explain the mechanism as the drawing takes shape."

Obediently, Mrs. Ford came to lean over his
shoulder, and watched, fascinated in spite of herself, as her husband drew quick sure strokes, his
eyes sparkling happily, and his voice filled with enthusiasm. He talked of steam cars, steamboats, and
fire engines; he mentioned a low-speed gasoline
engine he had seen running in a bottling works.
Steam had failed him as a motive power for his
farm locomotive; he felt assured that it would not
serve in the horseless carriage. But gasoline— Ah!
He talked a great deal about resilience and various
technical terms which Mrs. Ford did not understand in the least, but she caught his spirit, and at
midnight, when the drawing was finished, she said
slowly: "Well, if you want to go to Detroit, we'll
manage it somehow."

They moved to the city, and Ford got a night job
with the Edison Lighting Company and worked
on his horseless carriage in the daytime. It was two

years before he could make it run. He spent so much time in the little brick barn at the rear of his lot that the neighbors thought him a little crazy, and referred to his work as that fool project that would never come to anything. "A horseless carriage!" they jeered. "Who will want one of the things, if he does get it to go!"

But Henry Ford had vision and confidence. He had not only to invent his strange vehicle, but to build with his own hands everything that went into it, except the rubber-tired bicycle wheels and the buggy seat that he used. At length, the invention was taking all his time. He quit his job and settled down to work on it uninterruptedly. "What a silly thing to do," people said; and they took careful note that the Fords had no turkey that Thanksgiving. All that winter the wolf was never very far from the Ford door.

At last, at two o'clock one rainy April morning in 1893, the horseless carriage was ready for a trial. In spite of the darkness and the downpour, Mr. Ford climbed in and got behind the wheel. With a great deal of sputtering, smoke and noise the engine got under way, and he clanked out of the barn into the street. For a moment, fear clutched Mrs. Ford's heart; then she caught up an umbrella and followed. Before she had gone a few steps, she became aware that the horseless carriage was returning. Flushed with pride and excitement, her husband drew up along side of her and got out. It is probable that the engine balked, for we are told by a witness that "the inventor pushed the strange little machine into the barn, locked the doors and went into the house." We now know that it was impossible to turn the car around. Mr. Ford had to get out and swing the back around. But the machine had *run,* and there was no doubt that it would run again. The happy inventor drank a glass of hot milk, spread his dripping clothes before the fire, and went to bed to enjoy the best rest he had known since the Fords had left their farm.

The next time the "gasoline buggy" went out, Mrs. Ford was a passenger. Such a sensation they created! Heralded by its unearthly clank and rattle, the horseless carriage attracted people all along its path. Horses dashed into fences or climbed the curb as it went by. When the engine stalled, as it often did, little knots of people gathered around and criticized. Several times the inventor came within an ace of getting into serious trouble. "But Maybury told me he would protect me," said Mr. Ford naively. And this first automobile license, though issued verbally, was quite effective. People knew and had confidence in Mayor Maybury. If he thought Henry Ford's horseless carriage was not the nuisance it seemed, then it had to be put up with, that was all. But what good was a horseless carriage that would not back up, nor make steep grades, even if it could run twenty-five or thirty miles an hour on the level? The thing had no commercial value, that was plain. Henry Ford would have done better to have stuck to his job.

But the inventor did not think so. "She runs," he said, "and she can be improved. Name any invention you please, and then turn backward and study its beginning: Edison's first incandescent lamp gave no more light than a glow-worm; the phonograph was a particularly awkward and useless-looking cylinder of tin foil; the first telephone looked like an old fashioned clothes wringer. Just wait!"

"I never thought of money in connection with my invention," he said repeatedly. "All I thought of was making an automobile." But it was a long grade up to the top of the hill. Altogether twelve years passed from the time the first plans were drawn on that piece of sheet music until the perfected machine appeared. It was an invention which in both its economic and financial returns has proved to be—in John D. Rockefeller's words —"the industrial marvel of the age."

Everyone knows of the amazing growth of the Ford factories from that first car. Fortunes were made for all those connected with the enterprise.

The Dodge brothers were mechanics and they had agreed to make ten thousand dollars' worth of engines for Ford and to take their pay in stock. A few years later they sold out to Ford for thirty-four million dollars, and founded their own motor works.

A few years ago it was announced that the *forty-two millionth* Ford car had been produced, and the Ford factories now turn them out at the rate of thousands every day. Meanwhile, the price of the Ford cars has been lowered whenever and wherever possible. Ford's idea of mass production and low costs has been carried out with his tractor as well as with his automobile. "If I hadn't cut my prices as often as possible," he once said emphatically, "a relatively small factory would still be large enough for us."

The achievements of the Highland Park plant, where Mr. Ford brought standardized production to an unparalleled peak of efficiency, are known wherever manufacturing is known. Ford automobiles come out of this factory at the rate of eight thousand a day. There are five hundred departments in the factory which spreads over one hundred and ninety-nine acres. Here industrial experts come from all parts of the world to study Ford methods. Many of these men work in the factory for a time in order to get a first-hand knowledge of the practical organization of the system.

The River Rouge tractor plant, on the outskirts of Detroit, covers six hundred and sixty-five acres and is lined with a network of twenty-one railroads. It cost forty million dollars to build, and is so equipped that, working at capacity, one million tractors a year can be turned out. Each part of the tractor is made in a separate department, and taken by a conveyor system to an initial assembly and then on to where various "assemblies" meet in a final assembly. Mr. Ford himself once said: "Just as I have no idea how cheaply the Ford automobile can eventually be made, so I have no idea of how cheaply a tractor can eventually be made. It is important that they be cheap. Within a few years a farm depending solely on horse and hand power will be as much of a curiosity as a factory run by a treadmill. The farmer must either take up power or go out of business. The cost figures make this inevitable."

Before the United States entered the first World War, Henry Ford was the victim of an international hoax. He had set out with a number of other prominent Americans in the now famous "Peace Ship." The idealists who started out on this voyage planned to carry a direct appeal for peace to the warring nations of Europe. Before he was half-way across the Atlantic, Mr. Ford awoke to the fact that the whole plan had been a monstrous joke, engineered by those who wished to delay American aid to the Allies. In Christiania, he paused only long enough to verify his new understanding of the real situation. Thoroughly angry at the manner in which his desire for peace had been abused, and convinced that the United States would inevitably be drawn into the War, Henry Ford returned home and began to make immediate plans for putting all the resources of the Ford Motor Company to work for his government. When the War came, and a committee of Congressmen asked him how soon he could begin shipping cars and munitions, he drew out his watch and made a brief calculation: "Within five minutes, after my telegram is received, gentlemen," he said, "the factory will start filling war orders. Our first shipment should be ready by three o'clock tomorrow afternoon."

It was in 1914 that the world first began to hear of Henry Ford, and then in ways they found difficult to believe. He proposed to cut the working day from nine to eight hours, to pay his workers a minimum of five dollars a day, and to distribute ten million dollars a year in bonuses among his men. Workmen stormed the Ford factory to get jobs, until a fire hose had to be used to disperse the crowd. Newspapermen rushed to the scene, and clamored for interviews with Ford. Economists and bankers deplored the effect of such action on the labor market, and were loud in their denunciations. Ford, unmindful of praise or criticism, carried out his plan, remarking only that it was better to make fifteen thousand families happy than to make a few people millionaires.

After 1914, people everywhere became accustomed to hearing of Henry Ford as a pioneer in industrial relations. One of his favorite welfare projects was a hospital for his employees, a "garage" where the human frame could be cheaply and quickly repaired. He reasoned that, if he maintained a service station for his cars, why not a hospital for human beings where the best of care and attention could be had at nominal cost. Another favorite idea was employee education, and the Ford vocational schools have become so famous that educators come from all over the country to study the methods used in the Ford system.

"Not show, but service," said Ford, and everything he planned was substantial and worth while. "If I can make men of my people," he believed, "my business will take care of itself. Everything I do for them, benefits me as well."

In the light of his achievements, Henry Ford may be pardoned for what has been called his "pigheaded" autocracy. Even as a boy his playmates knew that he was inclined to get "set" every now and then, and when this happened, "all heaven and earth couldn't make him let go." It has been said of him that, in all the years when he was in active control of the Ford enterprises, he never gave a command. Nevertheless, every employee—whether an executive or a laborer—knew what would happen if his "requests" were not carried out to the letter. He was never in any sense a team man. Intense individualist that he was, he rarely sought advice and was intolerant of interference.

Henry Ford was a man of many sides and of warm, deep friendships. Their mutual love of birds and wild life formed a strong bond between him and John Burroughs, the great naturalist. On the Ford estate in Florida there were, at one time, more than five hundred bird houses. At a point on the grounds, called the "Hotel Ponchartrain," was a martin house with seventy-six apartments where innumerable birds could find food and shelter all through the year. John Burroughs said he found more birds on the Ford farm than he had ever seen in any one locality.

Another of Ford's best friends was Thomas Edison. Ford, Edison, Burroughs and Harvey S. Firestone used to form a happy quartet that delighted in making vagabond trips in motor caravans, sleeping outdoors and cooking their own meals.

Henry Ford died on April 7, 1947, at Dearborn, Michigan, at the age of eighty-three.

In spite of the enormous number of newspaper stories and books that have been written about him, Henry Ford remains an enigma to the public at large. In his heyday, he was, to many people, an impractical idealist. To others, he was a dangerous demagogue. At one time he had senatorial aspirations, and his name was mentioned for the presidency. But even his best friends shook their heads at this suggestion.

"I should never vote for him for president," said Edison, "but as a great industrialist I should vote for him—twice."

Henry Ford saw the United States emerge victorious from two World Wars, largely because of the miracles of production accomplished by American industry. He believed in the tremendous power of private industry, but he also believed in the simple democratic way of life. In Dearborn Village, he assembled, somewhat nostalgically, a replica of a colonial American town, for the qualities he valued most highly were those of a simpler, less complex America: honesty, hard work, and individual initiative.

"What is the secret of Henry Ford?" asked a writer in the *New Republic*. And he proceeded to answer by saying that Mr. Ford was the sum of a great number of contradictory things. "A portrait of that side of himself which Ford, the manufacturer, presents would be puzzling enough, for it would have to contrive to show him as at once brilliant, hardheaded, flexible, obstinate, fearless, ruthless, domineering. Such a view would be only a profile. Another side of him, which is quite apart from his business life, reveals unplumbable depths of idealism, good-will, simple-mindedness, foresight and credulity, imagination and utter lack of it. . . . We must take him as he is, one and indivisible, a hard-boiled idealist."

The Wright Brothers

IN THE fall of 1903 an eminent scientist published an article proving conclusively that human flight was impossible. For centuries men had dreamed of imitating the flight of birds, and many keen minds had tried to solve the problem. But although ascents had occurred in lighter-than-air craft, and strides had been made in the field of gliding, at the opening of the twentieth century no man yet had succeeded in making a controlled flight in a heavier-than-air plane which rose and progressed under its own power. Scientists and laymen alike, with few exceptions, shared the conviction that flying was forever denied to mankind. Three months after the learned scientist's statement, however, the impossible was achieved. The miracle of flight was accomplished by two unassuming bicycle-makers —the Wright brothers.

Ohio was the birthplace of Wilbur and Orville Wright. The sons of Reverend Milton Wright and Susan Koerner Wright, Wilbur was born April 16, 1867, on a small farm near Millville; and his brother Orville on August 19, 1871, in Dayton. On both sides of the family, their ancestors were among the early pioneers who settled Ohio and neighboring regions. The Reverend Milton Wright, a minister of the United Brethren Church, had at one time taught in his college at Hartsville. In 1869, he assumed editorship of a religious paper published by the United Brethren, at Dayton. His work, however, soon took the Wright family to Cedar Rapids and Richmond, where Wilbur and Orville spent their early childhood, in the companionship of their elder brothers, Reuchlin and Lorin, and their younger sister, Katharine.

While their father's interests provided a stimulus to intellectual curiosity, it was Susan Koerner Wright who seemed to have the mechanical mind of the family. She displayed much ingenuity in converting household utensils to fresh uses, and in con-

WILBUR (LEFT) AND ORVILLE WRIGHT

structing things. Always the elder Wrights lent a sympathetic ear to matters important in the lives of their children—their diligent enterprises for earning pocket money, the neighborhood circuses they were forever promoting, and the amusing events of school life. Out of the countless everyday happenings that made up the childhood of the Wright brothers, one was to stand out later with special significance. Returning from a trip, their father, now Bishop Wright, brought back as a gift a small toy helicopter. A Frenchman, Alphonse Penaud, devised it of bamboo, cork and paper; it rose into the air by means of tightly wound rubber bands. The secret of this toy was the object of much speculation on the part of Wilbur, Orville and Katharine. It planted the seed of inquiry which was to blossom years later in epoch-making discoveries.

In June, 1884, Bishop Wright moved his family back to Dayton, where once again they took possession of their home, a simple frame dwelling of seven rooms. Here Wilbur, having finished his schooling in Richmond, continued his studies on his own, while Orville completed his high school course. On July 4, 1889, the family circle was broken by the death of their mother, Susan Wright. Soon Lorin and Reuchlin married, establishing homes of their own, and the bond between the remaining Wrights became stronger than ever. On the first floor of their home was a library into which Wilbur and Orville often delved, for it contained, among other books, Plutarch's *Lives,* miscellaneous fairy tales and romances, Gibbon's *Decline and Fall of the Roman Empire,* and histories of England and France. Particularly was their interest drawn to Marey's *Animal Mechanism,* and the scientific topics in the *Encyclopaedia Britannica* and *Chamber's Encyclopaedia,* which the library also included. Over and over again since early childhood, the two boys·had thumbed the pages of these books.

Early in his teens Orville Wright had become intensely interested in printing. Owning a succession of tiny presses, he undertook various small printing jobs and publishing enterprises, in which his brother Wilbur often assisted him. In the spring of 1888 the aspiring editor built the largest press he had ever had, and renting an office, he published a small weekly, *The West Side News.* The paper flourished for a year, until expanded into a daily, *The Evening Item.* After the suspension of the *Item,* however, the printing ventures of the younger Wrights continued in one form or another until 1894.

By this time, other interests had entirely supplanted printing. In 1892, when the fad for bicycles was at its peak, both Wilbur and Orville had invested in one of the new machines. Shortly afterwards, the brothers decided to enter the bicycle business, with a sales and repair shop for the better-known brands. Accordingly, the Wright Cycle Company opened for business in December, 1892, with offices on Dayton's West Third Street; and as their business expanded, they moved several times to larger locations. By 1895 they were conducting operations in a remodeled house at 1127 West Third, where in the slack winter season they now manufactured their own makes of bicycles. This venture resulted in several hundred bicycles made under their own trademark, one of which, the "Wright Special" sold at the bargain price of $18.00. But even so commonplace an object as a bicycle interested their inquiring minds, and as they manufactured their machines, they experimented with balloon tires, tandems and other variations. Orville, moreover, was drawn into experiments unrelated to bicycles, devising an improved kind of calculating machine, and attempting to develop a more practical form of typewriter.

But in 1895 an event occurred which doomed the Wright Cycle Company to a glorious death one day. For it was in this year that the Wrights' interest first turned to the momentous problem to which they would devote their lives—aeronautics. It began with an article in a magazine which told of the German Otto Lilienthal's experiments in gliding.

The thrills of bicycling paled beside such an exciting sport. Lilienthal's fatal crash aroused their interest still further. The brothers determined to find out what progress had been made toward flying.

Writing to the Smithsonian Institution in Washington, whose director, Professor Langley, was conducting experiments in this field, they requested sources of information. Back came a reply in June, 1899, recommending Langley's *Experiments in Aerodynamics;* Chanute's *Progress in Flying Machines;* recent volumes of Means' *Aeronautical Annuals,* covering experiments ranging back several hundred years. With the reply came numerous pamphlets published by the Smithsonian, including extracts of Mouillard's *Empire of the Air,* Langley's *Story of Experiments in Mechanical Flight,* and Lilienthal's *The Problem of Flying and Practical Experiments in Soaring.* Soon the Wrights were absorbed in the pursuit of the truths that had eluded man for centuries—the principles of human flight.

Their thoughts first centered around the vital problem of balance. Various unsuccessful systems had been devised in the past, most of which depended partly on shifting the pilot's weight about. The Wrights felt that the factors producing equilibrium should be inherent in the structure alone. A cardboard box which Orville happened to twist one day gave the brothers a clue to a new system. Evolving ideas for warping wings to adjust to the varying air pressures which might be encountered, the Wrights constructed a five-foot box kite which Wilbur flew on a public tract outside of Dayton. Balance was maintained by a series of cords which warped the wings, and by a rear "elevator" which the Wrights had added.

In the spring of 1900 a correspondence began between Wilbur Wright and the famous engineer, Octave Chanute, who was living in Chicago. Chanute had conducted experiments in gliding himself, and it was his history of aeronautics which the brothers had read earlier. Discussing a plan for building a passenger kite which would afford practice in manipulating an airship, Wilbur drew from Chanute suggestions for suitable localities. With the approach of the slack season in the bicycle trade, once again the brothers plunged into the problem of equilibrium, studying the possibility of various new devices. Drawing up plans for the new glider, the Wrights now began to search for the proper spot for their experiments. A study of wind velocities in various parts of the country led them to select Kitty Hawk, a remote point on the coast of North Carolina, as the place where conditions seemed most favorable. In September, 1900, therefore, the Wrights set out for Kitty Hawk.

Kitty Hawk proved to be on a dreary spit of beach, bounded on one side by the Atlantic Ocean, and by Albemarle, Pamlico and Roanoke Sounds on the other. The only signs of civilization were a life-saving station, the office of the U.S. Weather Bureau, and a few small fishermen's shacks. Building a crude camp, the brothers set about assembling the glider. Built of spruce ribs covered with white French sateen, the glider had a wing spread of 17½ feet. It featured the wing warping which had characterized the box-kite, and a front rudder. Instead of wheels, it had skids or runners for sliding over the sand. The Wrights were now ready for their experiments. But to their dismay, they found that the winds at Kitty Hawk were not strong enough to support the glider with a passenger. They were forced to fly it as a kite, instead, weighting it with fifty pounds of chain. In addition, they tried gliding from a hundred-foot sand dune known as Kill Devil Hill. These experiments indicated that their devices for maintaining equilibrium were a great improvement over the old systems.

The summer of 1901 saw them back at Kitty Hawk, with a new glider similar in design to the one of the year before, but a good deal larger. With a wing spread of 22 feet, and a greater "lifting area," it weighed 98 lbs. This year they were visited in camp by Octave Chanute, who gave them counsel and encouragement. They succeeded in surpassing all earlier achievements in gliding. The experiments of 1901 suggested that their devices for balance should be supplemented by a vertical tail. Probably the most significant result of all, however, was the error the tests indicated in previously published data on the center of gravity of curved surfaces. The Wrights returned home, filled with doubts concerning the accuracy of the figures compiled by authorities on which they had based their designs.

Determined to get at the truth, they now constructed, in the upper rooms of the Wright Cycle Company, a "wind-tunnel" consisting of a wooden box approximately a foot and a half square, with a wind created at one end by an engine-driven fan. Against this current they tested over two hundred types of wing surfaces, at various angles, to determine the ratios between curvature, angle and air pressure or "lift." From these experiments, conducted during November and December of 1901, with crudely improvised instruments, the Wrights arrived at figures concerning the center of air pressures on curved surfaces which proved the error of the previous tables, and whose accuracy has been scarcely improved upon by the elaborate testing apparatus available today. This information made it possible to predict the performance of a plane in the air, and without it no flight could ever have been accomplished.

The exciting new knowledge of the Wrights underwent trial in gliding experiments during the summer and fall of 1902. Except for an increase of ten feet in the wing span and the acquisition of a vertical rear fin, the new model resembled the previous glider. Some one thousand glides, many of them against a heavy wind, indicated the progress made through compilation of the new data on air pressures. In order to counteract possible "tailspins," the tail was converted into a movable rudder. Basing their application upon the construction of this glider, the Wrights applied for patents on March 23, 1903.

The secret of equilibrium was now theirs. The next problem was to build a plane which could lift itself and soar under its own power. A Dayton foundry made castings for an engine from specifications supplied by the Wright brothers. In the machining of the engine, which they did in their bicycle shop, they were aided by their assistant, Charlie Taylor. The finished machine, which developed about twelve horsepower, weighed less than 200 lbs. The next step was to design the propeller. Here again the brothers found little exact data to help them, for manufacture of propellers depended on trial and error. It was only after long study and experimentation that they learned enough about the action of airscrews to design one adapted to their purpose.

At last, in September of 1903, the new plane was ready for trial. With a 40-foot wing span and flexible wingtips, the machine weighed with pilot 750 lbs. Once again the Wright brothers journeyed to Kitty Hawk. Bad weather delayed the testing until December. On December 14th, however, taking off from Kill Devil Hill, Wilbur Wright, who had won the coveted privilege by the toss of a coin, attempted the first flight, in the presence of several witnesses from the nearby life-saving station. The launching was aided by the use of some steel track. Wilbur's flight lasted only three and a half seconds, and an accident in landing delayed the next flight until December 17th. On that day, the plane was taken up by Orville Wright, against a 27-mile wind. This time the pilot succeeded in making a flight of twelve seconds, described by him as "the first in the history of the world in which a machine carrying a man had raised itself by its own power into the air in full flight, had sailed forward without reduction of speed, and had finally landed at a point as high as that from which it started." Several other flights were made that day, the longest lasting fifty-nine seconds. Then the machine was damaged by the wind as it rested on the beach, and flying was over for the year. But in those historic days on the sands of Kitty Hawk, the first power flights known to man had taken place.

Despite the tremendous import of this news, only a few newspapers in the entire country made any report of the event, and of these only one accorded it any significance. Most of the accounts were highly garbled. The majority of diehards insisted that flight was impossible. That it had occurred did not alter matters. The Wrights were to encounter five long years of stubborn resistance to faith in the possibility of flight, of refusal to believe that it had been achieved. But in those early years immediately following their triumph, they had no time to lose in convincing the public. For while they had proved flight possible, they had yet to make it practical. And once more they returned to Dayton, where they set to work to develop the plane into a useful machine.

The construction of a new plane was undertaken in 1904, featuring various improvements over the Kitty Hawk plane. The brothers prepared to test it in a cow pasture at Simms' Station, eight miles from Dayton. Although they made no effort at secrecy, there was very little interest on the part of press or public, and the brothers were free to work unhampered. Again and again they made improvements in the plane, and hit upon the use of a launching derrick to assist the takeoff. The 1904 experiments were climaxed by two five-minute flights in which the maneuverability of the plane was demonstrated by circling the field repeatedly. By 1905 changes had been made in the propeller, the rudder, the wingtips, the engine, and other parts of the plane. So effective were these improvements that in the fall of the year the Wrights achieved a flight of 24½ miles in a little more than half an hour.

Reports now began to drift to the ears of the press concerning the Wrights' flying. However, they were either not believed, or no importance was attached to the facts reported. One evening an enterprising Dayton editor inquired of Orville Wright whether the brothers had accomplished anything of interest lately. Very little, replied the inventor, except to circle the field for almost five minutes. Accepting the latter's own modest appraisal of this event, the disappointed newsman politely replied that he would keep in touch with the Wrights, in case something unusual should develop.

But while the press in the United States remained steadfastly oblivious of the "scoop" that lay beneath their nose, European scientific journals, on the other hand, had begun to print accounts of the feats of the Wright brothers. Various clubs of aerial enthusiasts were aroused to controversy as the groups who believed the reports battled those who did not. It was not until 1906, however, that a scientific publication in the United States took cognizance of the great event that had occurred three years before.

The Wrights were now receiving frequent inquiries concerning their progress, to most of which they replied patiently, listing details and witnesses. And they were approached by unofficial missions on behalf of the governments of England and France, with a view to buying the brothers' invention for military purposes. Their invention had now reached the stage where experimentation was costly, and the Wrights were in need of funds to continue its development. They preferred, however, to sell their patents and secrets, not to foreign countries, but to the United States government alone. Accordingly, in January, and again in October, of 1905, Wilbur and Orville Wright conveyed their offer to the U.S. War Department to furnish scouting planes on contract, to be accepted only after due trial. As an alternative offer, the brothers were willing to furnish the government with the store of scientific data they had amassed concerning flying, together with permission to use their patents. The replies of the War Department, however, indicated that the claims of the Wrights were regarded as incredible, and the possibility of putting those claims to proof was not considered.

But as negotiations with foreign governments brought the prospect of foreign sale nearer every day, the Wrights continued their correspondence and representations to the War Department until as late as October of 1907. Although by this time the Ordnance Board was disposed to give serious consideration to the inventors' offer, various obstacles were permitted to delay decisive action in the matter.

In 1906, the Wrights were approached by a firm of New York bankers who offered their services as foreign agents. Upon their recommendation, Wilbur Wright sailed for France in June, 1907, to arrange the sale of the brothers' invention abroad. Instead of negotiating with the French government, it was thought advisable to sell the rights to private bankers or to a company formed for the purpose. Soon Orville arrived to join his brother, bringing with him a recently completed model of the plane, which was stored in Customs at LeHavre. It later became necessary to deal with the government, however, through one M. LeTellier. But matters dragged on without coming to a successful conclusion, and the plane remained in its packings at Customs. At last the brothers left Paris for Berlin, where their offers were received with interest. They were given a verbal assurance that upon a successful demonstration flight, Germany would purchase planes at the price named by the Wrights. But before the moment came to demonstrate their invention in Berlin, the long-awaited opportunity arrived to sell their planes to their own country, the United States.

During their sojourn in Paris, the Wrights had visited an acquaintance, Frank S. Lahm, a business man who was interested in the future of aviation. Here they met his son, Lieutenant Frank P. Lahm, of the U.S. Army. Shortly afterward, in September, 1907, Lt. Lahm was transferred to Washington. Returning from France, Wilbur Wright passed through Washington. This time he found that, possibly owing to Lt. Lahm's intervention, the Wright plane was regarded with serious interest. Talks were resumed with officials of the Ordnance Department and the Signal Corps, and Wilbur once again named the price of the first plane, $25,000. In addition to data regarding aviation, the purchase price was to include instruction of pilots. As a result of these talks, the government solicited bids for a military plane, with the belief that only the plane of the Wrights could meet the specifications. Even at this late date, the action of the Signal Corps was greeted with derision by the press, who dubbed the possibility of flight as a "delusion" and "hot air." Acceptance of the Wrights' bid was announced, however, in February, 1908, and plans were laid for the tests which were to culminate in triumph for the brothers.

Before trials got under way in the United States, Wilbur Wright had gone to France to conduct demonstrations of the plane. Arriving in May, 1908, he selected a race track at LeMans, 125 miles from Paris, for the scene of the test. On August 8, before a large group of skeptical spectators, the plane was launched by the derrick, circling the air for one minute and forty-five seconds. The excitement of the crowd knew no bounds, and when the modest pilot landed, he was overwhelmed with enthusiastic congratulations. Wilbur Wright remained at LeMans for some time, making flights of increasingly longer duration. After a while he shifted the exhibitions to the French Army artillery range at Auvours, where he continued his flying exploits. Soon the fame of the unassuming inventor had spread all over France, and thousands made the trip to Auvours to witness his flights. He was besieged by many distinguished visitors who wished to take their first plane ride, including Margherita, the dowager queen of Italy; Paul Doumer and Louis Barthou, French government officials; and numerous others.

Meanwhile, however, Orville Wright had arrived at Fort Myer, Virginia, for the scheduled U.S. Army test. As the crowd watched the plane circle the field for one minute eleven seconds, a hubbub broke loose. Formerly skeptical reporters were moved to tears at the tremendous significance of the spectacle they were witnessing. Orville continued making flights at Fort Myer, bettering his endurance record repeatedly. On one occasion he remained aloft one hour and fifteen minutes. The era of flying had indeed arrived.

Continuing his daring demonstrations abroad in France, Wilbur Wright won two prizes offered by aerial clubs. After recovering from an accident at Fort Myer, his brother Orville joined him; and the two resumed their exhibitions at the city of Pau, which offered a field and a hangar. At Pau they were visited by many notables, including King Alfonso of Spain, Lord Northcliffe of England, King Edward VII of England, and Lord Arthur Balfour. Many of these famous personages counted it a privilege to be a passenger of the Wrights, whose modest bearing, unaffected by renown, won the liking of all who met them.

After visiting Rome and London, where they were showered with honors, the Wrights returned to the United States in the summer of 1908. A grand reception awaited them in their native city of Dayton, climaxed by the presentation of the Congressional Medal of Honor. The final trials for the Army were now conducted, and the Wright

plane passed the tests with a speed of 43 miles per
hour, three miles faster than the minimum spec-
ified for acceptance.

The Wrights' invention now gave rise to a new
industry. In France and Germany companies had
been formed for the manufacture of planes. And in
October, 1909, the Wright Company was organized in the United States, with headquarters in
New York and plant in Dayton. In the early days,
before a great demand had been built up for air-
planes, part of the efforts of the Wright Company
were devoted to popularizing aviation through exhibitions all over the country. Although their new
duties kept them busy—Orville as chief engineer
of the factory, and Wilbur in charge of lawsuits
against patent violators—the brothers found time
to continue some of their experiments. Their invention was bringing them unexpected wealth and
honor.

But Wilbur Wright was not destined to enjoy
the rewards of his pioneering work. On May 30,
1912, he died of typhoid fever, at the age of forty-
five, leaving Orville Wright as the sole representative of a remarkable family team. He rejected the
role now offered him as head of a great industrial
empire, for the work that was closest to his heart,
experimenting and developing his invention. Or-

ville Wright sold out his interest in the Wright Company as early as October, 1915. The remainder of his life was to be devoted to the science he had served so well—aeronautics.

Symbol of the great advance made by the Wrights, the Kitty Hawk plane was still intact, and Orville Wright wished to present it to the Smithsonian Institution in Washington. But this institution, over-zealous in its efforts to glorify the role of its own Professor Langley in the field of aeronautics, was reluctant to accept the proffered gift. In 1928, therefore, its owner sent the plane to the Science Museum in South Kensington, London. Under the leadership of a new director, Dr. Charles G. Abbot, however, the Smithsonian Institution finally published in 1942 a statement recognizing the Wrights as the inventors of the modern airplane. In the summer of 1946, therefore, plans were under way to return the famous craft to its appropriate place in the native country of its inventors.

Today a tall granite shaft rising on Kill Devil Hill commemorates the achievement of Wilbur and Orville Wright. Not only in the development of aileron control and the principles of flight which enabled them to fly the first controlled and power-driven plane did their accomplishment consist. Their subsequent efforts in the development of a practical airplane also helped to earn a place in history for the men who as "Inventors, Builders, and Flyers . . . brought Aviation to the World."

Calvin Coolidge

IN THE early morning of August 3, 1923, Calvin Coolidge, Vice-President of the United States, lay sleeping in his boyhood home at Plymouth Notch, Vermont. Suddenly he heard an excited voice calling, "Calvin!" He jumped out of bed and flung open the door. His father thrust a telegram at him.

"Son, President Harding's died! You're President!" Coolidge, looking at his seventy-year-old father, thought only of the American people who now awaited his leadership.

The small farmhouse, nestling in the rugged Vermont hills, was soon jammed with reporters and photographers all clamoring for stories about the first son of New England to become President in two-thirds of a century.

By the dim wavering light of a little kerosene lamp, the President's father administered the oath

CJNAAR.

of office on the Coolidge family Bible. "Raise your right hand!" he ordered.

"So help me God!" concluded the new President. So with this simple ceremony, Calvin Coolidge was the first man ever to be sworn into the Presidential office by his own father.

Soon in the early morning light, little lantern-led groups of people could be seen walking swiftly toward the Coolidge farm. These were Calvin's life-long friends gathering to wish him luck. He shook hands and spoke to each one as simply as he had always done. Then he went to his mother's grave and knelt there for a few moments in prayer.

As the new President went with Mrs. Coolidge to the automobile which was to carry them toward Washington, he noticed a porch step displaced. "Better have that fixed, Father!" he called. Coolidge had just become the thirtieth President of the United States, but he was still a typical son of New England.

Calvin Coolidge was altogether American in background, spirit and life. "Vermont is my birthright. People there are happy . . . contented. They belong to themselves, live within their incomes . . . fear no man," he wrote. He was the ultimate example of this heritage. He had typical New England reserve, caution, modesty, and thrift. And from his sturdy New England ancestors came his industry, his dry humor, his loyalty to ideals, and his love of justice.

Born on July 4, 1872, in Plymouth Notch, a hamlet of some five houses in the Green Mountains, he came of a long line of hardy English Puritan farmers and fighters who cleared the wilderness and in later years fought valiantly in the American Revolution. They had fought and farmed their way north into Vermont and for four generations before his birth they had wrested a hard livelihood from the stony earth. They never went West, for they loved this free land that they had made their own with so much toil.

John Coolidge, Calvin's father, had plenty of Yankee ingenuity. He ran the local country store and worked his farm. He made his own buggies, and in addition was a skilled carpenter and stone mason. Like all New Englanders he took a deep interest in politics, and, when Calvin was two months old, John Coolidge was elected to the state legislature. Many years later when Calvin's own son was two months old, *his* father was elected to the same office.

Calvin's childhood was like that of any other country lad, except that his mother to whom he was devoted died when he was only twelve years old. Although she was an invalid for some years before her death, she influenced the boy deeply with her love of beauty and her goodness. "Red," as the other children called him, worked barefoot in the fields in a gray woolen smock and woolen hat. His people had worn similar home-woven work clothes for the past one hundred and fifty years. The maple sugar season saw the Coolidges making one thousand to two thousand pounds of sugar. "Cal could always get more sap out of a maple tree than any other boy," his father said. Young Coolidge also learned to use his hands skillfully. On the morning of his inauguration, a desk which he himself had built stood in the room in which he took his oath of office.

Although the boy learned early in life that work was important, he had a great deal of fun too. With his friends, he skated and swam. He had a pocket knife of his own before he could read. He cut pine and ash arrows, hickory bows, and hunted and trapped. He had a horse of his own—a calico, so like a circus horse that he rode it standing. He went to husking bees, the county fair, and to Sunday school picnics, but he did not dance for he had promised his grandmother that he would not do so and he kept his word.

As a child, Calvin was extremely shy. Even in his own home, he found it difficult to go through the kitchen door and to greet visitors sitting with his parents. He could do it, if he forced himself, but all his life he dreaded meeting new people.

By the time he was thirteen, the lad had learned all there was to learn in the village school of twenty-five pupils and one young woman teacher. Dressed in his Sunday suit, he was driven twelve miles through the heavy snow to Ludlow's Black River Academy. All his worldly possessions, in two small bags, shared the farm wagon with a calf headed marketward. In Ludlow, his father said laconically, "Goodbye, son. If you work hard you may some day get to Boston, but this calf's going to beat you there."

To the country boy, life in the Academy was a strange new world. Here, among many wonderful new things, he was wholly dependent upon himself, and he soon learned self-reliance and resourcefulness. Latin and Greek he found very difficult, but he took a great liking to Civil Government which soon became his favorite subject. On Saturdays he worked in a cab shop and this proved a valuable new experience. Besides the money he earned, he got first hand knowledge of factory workers' problems, and he met people very different from the Vermont farmers he had known all his life. Sometimes during the school term he trudged the twelve miles to his home for a brief visit. His long summer vacations were spent farming. Calvin graduated with honors.

After a spring term at the St. Johnsbury Academy, he entered Amherst. "Here," he said, "I went in more for educating my mind than my legs." He didn't need physical exercise. His body was fit from farm labor.

Young Coolidge got off to a poor start at Amherst. Although he studied hard, his marks were only fair and he became discouraged. However, his father encouraged him to continue, and, when he graduated, it was with honors. Then he came under the influence of Charles E. Garman, Professor of Philosophy, and this became the most important factor in his college life. Coolidge thought Garman walked with God. He taught that truth must be followed wherever it may lead, a lesson Calvin never forgot.

Socially, Calvin did not fare much better at first. He lived in a cheap boarding house far from the campus and took long walks by himself. He wanted to be a fraternity man, but the shy, lonely student did not seem a likely candidate. However, he faithfully attended all class functions. In his Junior year, he entered the traditional plug-hat race and fortunately came in last. For this he was penalized by having to make a speech; and it was so funny that it proved the turning point in his college career. He became a campus power and was soon invited to join Phi Gamma Delta.

By popular vote, in his Senior year, "Red Cal" was elected to deliver the Grove Oration, the humorous number on the Class Day program. The directness and wit he displayed that day were recalled many years later when Amherst graduates living in Spain invited the President to send a long message—cable charges free—to their reunion in Madrid. They received, "Greetings—Calvin Coolidge."

All his life he was noted for this dry Yankee humor. One morning, hash was served. "Where's the dog?" asked Calvin.

"In the kitchen."

"Bring him in." The beast appeared. "Pass the hash!" instructed Coolidge.

When he was handed his first Presidential paycheck, he smiled, "Call again!" His humor was as American as homespun.

When Commencement was over, Calvin went back to the farm, but not to stay. He had decided to become a lawyer. A classmate took him to the Northampton, Massachusetts office of Hammond and Field. The friend talked of Calvin's qualifications for twenty minutes. Coolidge briefly said, "Good morning"—his only contribution to the interview—and got the job.

This was great luck. Both employers were politically and legally important. Calvin absorbed every bit of knowledge he could, bought textbooks, and taught himself three years' work, everything necessary to pass the bar exams, in twenty months. "I had never seen just such a man—especially a young man. I couldn't understand how a man could be so quiet, and seem to care for nothing outside of his work," Judge Hammond said.

Shortly after Coolidge entered the office, Judge Field read in the *Springfield Republican:* "Sons of American Revolution award Calvin Coolidge $150 gold medal in nationwide collegiate essay contest on 'The Principles Fought for in the American Revolution.'"

"Are you this Coolidge?"

"Yes, sir."

"You never told us!"

"Didn't know you'd be interested."

Silence and reticence were Calvin's outstanding characteristics. Politicians, calling him "Silent Cal," soon realized that his was not the silence of stupidity. He knew every man has his destiny in him, and he wanted to be let alone to work his out. "I have never been hurt by what I have not said!" he wrote.

During his governorship a Massachusetts manufacturer had an important matter to discuss with him. Together they rode a hundred miles during which Coolidge said "Yes," seven times and "Good-day." In Washington a woman gushed, "Mr. President, you're so silent! I've wagered I'd get more than two words from you!" "You lose!" he replied.

He would ask Frank Stearns, his best friend, to sit with him. After an hour's silence, the President would say, "Thank you. Just wanted you here." Calvin Coolidge always knew that actions speak louder than words.

On February 1, 1898, he opened his own two-room office on Main Street, Northampton. It had taken only eleven years for the farm-boy to become a barrister. He knew the law; people depended on him. A proof of it was that he was soon self-supporting. He lived on thirty dollars a month and for relaxation translated Cicero at night.

His great interest was public affairs. It was in his blood. December, 1898; saw him elected to his Ward's Common Council, first rung on the political ladder. Nine years after he was graduated from Amherst, he became Chairman of the Republican City Committee, leader of the Republican party in a town of 30,000. Now he began to feel the need for his own home. He met Grace Goodhue of Burlington, Vermont. Soon he announced to the Goodhues, "I'm going to marry your daughter!" and on

October 4, 1905, he did. Their wedding trip to Montreal was the longest journey Coolidge had ever made.

Coolidge was elected to Massachusetts' House of Representatives by a margin of some 260 votes and was re-elected. He went to Boston with only two rusty suits, but an observant higher-up wrote, "Like a singed cat, he is better than he looks."

Professional politicians couldn't understand how this silent poker-faced ex-farmer swayed elections. He made none of the usual political noise. For fourteen years he commuted in the day coach. He was completely unostentatious, but he knew people, and he kept his faith in them to the end. "I have generally been able," said the young Representative, "to make enough noise to get what I wanted." The year 1910 saw him Mayor of Northampton. "Success lies in conscientious work," he wrote.

"Conscientious work" gave him two terms in the Massachusetts Senate and twice the Presidency of that Senate, an office of statewide importance. His short inauguration speech told the whole story of how he had gained the confidence of his fellowmen and why he held their trust. "Do the day's work. If it be to protect the rights of the weak, whoever objects, do it. If it be to help a powerful corporation better to serve the people, whatever the opposition, do that. Expect to be called a standpatter, but don't be a standpatter. Expect to be called a demagogue, but don't be a demagogue. Don't hesitate to be as revolutionary as science. Don't hesitate to be as reactionary as the multiplication table. Don't expect to build up the weak by pulling down the strong. Don't hurry to legislate. Give the Administration a chance to catch up with Legislation." This was Calvin Coolidge's entire message to the Senate. It was the briefest ever delivered in those halls and expressed fully the only political creed and platform he ever knew.

In 1915 Coolidge issued a statement, "I am a candidate for Lieutenant Governor." His campaign speeches were unique in political history. He announced, "I want your vote. I need it. I shall appreciate it," and swept into office for his usual two terms. These same tactics made him Governor of Massachusetts.

He stepped into this high office with as great a simplicity as he had lived his whole life. He moved from one room in the Adams House in Boston at one dollar a day to two rooms at double the rate. This was to him splendor enough. He didn't lose his perspective. He received many requests to address gatherings. A typical response read, "Don't care to make speeches. Nobody cares to hear them."

Once, however, he had to attend a reception. Grand preparations were made to welcome him.

Meanwhile an unobtrusive man stood silently in the reception hall's lobby. Finally someone recognized Calvin Coolidge, the guest of honor. "Governor! Does anyone know you're here?"

"No, but they'll probably find me."

"When did you arrive? No one saw your car or staff!"

"Don't have a car, and no staff's with me. Wanted a night off, so I got on a trolley."

In September, 1919, the Boston Police went on strike, and one of America's great cities was completely terrorized. Governor Coolidge broke the strike with a single statement, "There is no right to strike against the public safety by anybody, anywhere, any time." Friends predicted this would finish him politically. "Very likely," he replied and was triumphantly re-elected by 125,101 votes!

The silent man knew when to speak and what to say when he did. This time he spoke himself into the Vice-Presidency of the United States!

During the Republican National Convention of 1920, Coolidge was nominated for Vice-President and got about three-quarters of all the votes cast. He toured a dozen states and delivered his usual brief speeches. A woman at Madison Square Garden, New York, told him, "I enjoyed your speech so much that I stood up all the time!" "So did I," answered Coolidge. Many people who had never before voted Republican enjoyed those speeches too, for the Republican ticket rushed victoriously into power, and the ex-farmer boy of Vermont was Vice-President of the United States. "Another duty to perform," he observed.

Calvin Coolidge always did more than his duty. He presided over the Senate and was the first Vice-President to be a member of the President's cabinet. "I made progress," he said, "because I studied subjects sufficiently to know a bit more about them than anyone else on the floor." He lectured throughout the country and familiarized himself with fellow citizens in the farthest corners of the nation.

In August, 1923, President Harding suddenly died, and Calvin Coolidge was immediately ready to take his place. His whole life had been a long preparation for this moment. His countrymen had voted him into nineteen offices before the ultimate honor. He had climbed the political ladder rung by rung, and now he was at the top. He had the nation's respect and he held it.

President Coolidge, living in the White House during six most prosperous years, knew that the high office he held was the gift of the people, and that he was their servant. "Government," he said, "is not, must not be, a cold impersonal machine, but a human and more than human agency, appealing to the reason, satisfying the heart, full of mercy, assisting the good, resisting the wrong, delivering the weak from the impositions of the strong."

Once a Senator and the President walked past the White House. "Who lives there, I wonder?" joked the Senator.

"Nobody," responded the President. "They just come and go."

Though his time was occupied to exhaustion that first week of his Presidency, he wrote to James Lucey, Northampton cobbler, "I want you to know that if it were not for you I shouldn't be here."

Unassumingly he moved into the Chief Executive's chair, causing no political upsets. He didn't give his friends offices they didn't deserve. "When I appoint a man to office, I don't want him to thank me. I want him to go and make good," he said. "The business of America is business," he announced and settled down to routine.

He spent each summer in a different part of the country getting to know the people. He was deeply interested in agricultural problems and called the ground behind the White House "the south lot," like any farmer. At the laying of a cornerstone he turned his spadeful of earth and looked at the dirt a long time. Finally he said with great interest, "That's a fine fishworm!" He was essentially a

Yankee farm boy no matter what high offices he held.

On his first trip on the Presidential yacht, *Mayflower,* he looked at the fancy menu and said, "I've studied Latin and Greek, but I can't make head or tail out of this. What I want is roast beef and baked potatoes, and please put them down so I'll know what I'm eating."

Coolidge did not campaign for re-election in 1924. Instead, he went about his job of conducting the country's affairs, which occupied all his attention. He needed no campaign; his countrymen, recognizing in him the best qualities of New England, elected him for another term.

As 1928 approached, it was obvious that Coolidge could easily win a third term. But in 1927, with characteristic terseness, he announced, "I do not choose to run."

"We draw our Presidents from the people," he said. "It is a wholesome thing for them to return to the people. I came from them. I wish to be one of them."

When Calvin Coolidge left the White House and returned to the modest Northampton two family house he had occupied, he left politics behind. He wanted to be an ordinary man again, but sightseers didn't permit him obscurity. A newspaperman visiting him said, "It must make you proud to see so many people coming through here just to look at you sitting on your porch. Look at those cars!"

"Not as many as yesterday. Sixty-three then," said Coolidge.

From then on, he concentrated on writing his autobiography, and a daily newspaper column, full of shrewd comment and dry Yankee humor. When his autobiography appeared, he willingly autographed every copy sent to him by a Northampton bookseller. For each book so signed brought an extra dollar which was contributed to a local missionary society.

Suddenly without warning, Calvin Coolidge dropped dead on January 5, 1933, in his sixty-first year. With the simplicity that marked his life, he was buried beside his long-dead mother in the New England hills.

Will Rogers

"How much lies in Laughter," wrote Thomas Carlyle, "—the cipher-key wherewith we decipher the whole man." In the humor of Will

CJ NAAR

Rogers, homespun sage of twentieth century America, lay a key to the nation's day-to-day philosophy, for it was rooted deep in the common sense of the average citizen. "Be yourself," was his guiding principle, and by adhering firmly to it at all times, the rancher from Oklahoma achieved world fame and honor.

Will Rogers was born November 4, 1879 on a ranch which stood "half-way between Claremore and Oolagah, before there was a town in either place." For convenience, he claimed Claremore as his birthplace, because strangers found Oolagah difficult to pronounce. This region was Indian territory, and Will was exceedingly proud of being "nine thirty-seconds Cherokee Indian." His father was a well-known ranchman of the northeast Indian territory. His mother, a quiet home-body and a devout Methodist, cherished the hope that her son would grow up to be a minister. When Will was in his early teens, however, he showed far more promise of being hanged as a horse thief, in the opinion of a relative. Indeed, on the big ranch at Oolagah, the boy was fast growing into a cowboy desperado. His eyes rudely opened by the pessimistic relative, Will's father declared forthrightly that there must be a change. It was decided that the lad should go to the Kemper Military School at Boonville, Mis-

souri. Here his father hoped that the strict routine
might discipline his unruly son.

To the range-riding boy the idea was distasteful.
There was no gainsaying his father, however, and
he resolved to keep a stiff upper lip and see the
thing through. On the appointed day, therefore,
the students and faculty of Kemper were astonished to see an authentic cowboy arriving to enroll
at the school. With his ten-gallon hat decorated
with a cord of braided horse-hair, flannel shirt, high
colored vest, knotted red bandanna, high-heeled
boots with shining spurs, and trouser legs tucked in
his boot tops in approved western fashion, Will was
a resplendent spectacle indeed. Coiled conspic-
uously on top of his luggage was his lariat. At one
glance the Commandant knew that the school
faced a problem of no small proportions. And he
was right.

"Stoop over, run down the hall, and beller like a
calf!" Will would shout to some gangling youth,
who dared not ignore the order. Then the young
cowpuncher would skillfully lasso his victim's foot,
an arm or two, or pin him up solidly, as the case
might be. Always an unwitting classmate was subject to his swinging lariat, and in the absence of a
human target, Will roped door knobs or any object
in sight. Confiscate his lasso as often as they might,

the boy turned up at the first opportunity with a converted trunk rope or a new lariat. Unhappy chance had placed him on the alien ground of a military school, but he was determined not to lose his skill with the ropes. Above all else, he was going to be himself, and that meant a cowman of no small degree. In later years a visitor to Will's ranch home out west was to find the famous humorist in a calf pen trying out a "twist of the wrist" he had recently seen a rope artist use. "I'd give a thousand dollars to get the trick," he confessed ruefully, "but I kain't do it just right to save my gizzard."

Maternal hopes that Will might develop a calling to the ministry were soon blasted. The boy was not cut out for bookish pursuits. "At Kemper," he often told his audiences years after, "I spent half the time in the fourth grade, the rest in the Guard House." The statement was not literally true, of course. There were no fourth-grade pupils at Kemper, and Will's engaging grin usually staved off actual confinement. The lad liked memory studies best. He had little use for arithmetic, developing a particular aversion to the partial payments problems in *Ray's Higher Arithmetic*. "Why in heck don't people pay cash instead of using partial payments!" he once complained wrathfully to a fellow scholar. The superintendent of the study hall was in the habit of calling on a boy to rise when he wished to administer a reprimand. "Mr. Rogers, stand up," was a frequent command. Instantly all the students were on the alert. For merely the manner in which Will would rise, hitch his belt, and say, "Yes, sir," was so amusing that even the Colonel often had to turn his head to keep from laughing out loud.

Will was a born wit, an actor who even in the taciturn surroundings of Kemper Military Academy never failed to get a laugh. Nobody then foresaw world fame for the guilefully awkward cadet from Oklahoma, however. "Just listen to that!" exclaimed one of his Kemper instructors, listening to the radio in later years. "There's Will Rogers drawing big money for saying the same things I used to give him demerits for in the mess hall!"

Once a week declamations were given at school. These opportunities Will hailed with delight. On such occasions the acknowledged gems of oratorical literature were brought out: "Spartacus to the Gladiators," Patrick Henry's "Give me Liberty or give me Death," and the like. These the boys recited with the grimness of a cavalry charge. Cadet Rogers, however, clowned through them, to the delight of his entire audience, and received the highest marks. His history textbook, often quoted in later days by the whole page in comic fashion, was much beloved by him, but for reasons unre-

lated to scholarship. Sixteen inches square un-
opened, when spread out on edge it made a highly
effective screen behind which Will could shoot
paper wads, whittle the desk, and carry on a great
range of forbidden activities.

Will had a special aversion for his cadet uniform,
which he seldom wore properly. At last the day
came when the soldierly garb and the irksome discipline it stood for could be endured no longer.
Will cast about for a means of escape. He sat down
and composed a heart-rending note to each of his
married sisters, setting forth his immediate need of
ten dollars. The use to which the money was to be
put was, needless to say, not made clear. His sisters
felt a warm affection for their only brother, and
each responded with the cash by return mail. Their
surprise and consternation were considerable when
they learned that both had been appealed to, and
that the boy had used the funds so acquired to leave
school and find work in the Texas oil fields.

This sort of life, however, proved to be not quite
so attractive as it had seemed from the comfortable
distance of Kemper. The prodigal son was heartily
glad when his father sent him the money to return
home. The elder Rogers decided to give Will some
responsibility. This, he thought, would put the required stiffness into the lad's backbone. Will was

accordingly made steward of the ranch, with power to check on the Rogers' bank account. Having settled things so satisfactorily, his father then left on an extended business trip. Very soon a dance pavilion was erected in the ranch yards, and all sorts of contests and roping shows held sway. Considerable skill was used in the arrangement of the sweepstakes, and Will took his full share of the prizes. Notwithstanding, the family bank deposit was lighter by some $1,000 by the time his father returned. It was an error not to be condoned. Will's stewardship ended in hot words and disgrace, and he rode off on his cow pony to work at a nearby ranch. This incident, however, had been worth the cost, for it had shown the young man that he did not really want to be a rancher. He wanted to be a showman, with excited crowds cheering as he swung his lariat.

It was not difficult to get into the Western rodeos, and from there into a circus that traveled around the world. Will appeared in Zack Mulhall's Wild West Show at the St. Louis World's Fair in 1904. The following year the show played at Madison Square Garden, New York. One night a wild steer suddenly went on a rampage into the crowd. Instantly the cowboy from Oklahoma sprang into pursuit, his lariat whirled, and the enraged animal was roped fast before the frightened crowd could gasp for a second breath. Next day Will Rogers' name was on the front page of the newspapers.

From the rodeo to the stage in "Westerns" was a natural step, and gradually Will's name became known to theater goers and critics. He appeared in his own role in "Ziegfeld's Follies." The audiences were delighted, but Ziegfeld himself could never understand why people laughed.

His success on the stage was assured, when he was persuaded to try his hand at the movies in 1918. But the silent films could not catch the familiar drawl and laugh-producing witticisms that were the real Will Rogers. After appearing in several silent pictures, among them "One Glorious Day," "The Texas Steer," and "Two Wagons—Both Covered," Will decided that the movies were out of his field, and returned to the Broadway "Follies" for six years. With the perfection of sound projection, however, and the firm establishment of the "talkies," he was persuaded to go to Hollywood and have another try at pictures.

Notwithstanding his protest that he would probably "mess things all up," his first movie, "They Had to See Paris," proved a tremendous success. He was immediately slated for another picture. Before work could be begun on it, however, a message came that his old friend, Fred Stone, a musical comedy star, had crashed in an airplane accident, breaking both legs. Stone's play, "Three Cheers," which had just opened on Broadway, would have to be closed. Instantly Will Rogers' chivalry to a friend in need sprang to the fore. Forgetting his own opening career in a new field, he chartered a plane, flew to New York, and after one day's rehearsing, stepped into Stone's role. He "pinch hit for Fred," as he expressed it, until the end of the season.

Despite the numerous offers which this success brought, Will returned to Hollywood and began work on his own belated production. "So This Is London," followed by "Happy Days," earned him widespread popularity among movie goers. In all, he appeared in eighteen movies after his first successes, each of which broke records at the box office. All his pictures were clean and wholesome. The kindly, rather bashful man in suspenders and stocking feet, who drawled his humorous philosophy in an over-the-back-fence manner, became a household institution.

It was in the newest medium of entertainment, radio, that Will Rogers earned the title of "court jester of the United States." His happy knack of aiming at shining targets kept his listeners continually alert. No one knew just where the Rogers shaft might strike next. Nobody took umbrage at his remarks, however, for behind the barb was a sound wisdom that was recognized even by those who were his targets. In fact, many felt it a distinct honor to be drawn into the limelight by Will Rogers. On one occasion when he had lampooned Senator Borah, another Senator who might have been included but wasn't, complained vigorously: "If only you'd have done as much for me as you did for Bill Borah, I'd be famous now too!"

On another occasion, early in his broadcasting career, he played a joke which might have had serious repercussions had it not been for the good sense of the principal. As master of ceremonies at a radio jubilee, Will introduced many notables, who made brief responses. Then came the climax. "Now, friends," drawled Will, "we have a pleasant surprise. The President of the United States will speak on national affairs from the White House." After a moment's pause, a voice rang out clearly with the New England accent of Calvin Coolidge: "It gives me great pleasure to report that the nation is prosperous on the whole, but how much prosperity is there in a hole?" A gasp of shocked surprise swept the nation, followed by hearty laughter.

Next day, however, protests poured in at the White House from those who thought the speaker was Coolidge himself. Will Rogers was much chagrined at the result of his prank. In fact, his normal composure did not return until Mrs. Coolidge herself assured him that she was not deceived for an instant. "Why," she teased, "I could give a much better imitation of Mr. Coolidge than that!" "Of course," retorted Will, "but look what you have had to go through to learn it!" The incident had its lesson, however. Never again did he use his power of personal mimicry before the microphone. His special forte was a genial raillery in which he deflated stuffed shirts and told Americans the earthy realities about themselves, their politics, their civic standards and their social habits. And his audiences learned to laugh at themselves, and approved the wisdom which pointed out their foibles.

By 1930 Will Rogers enjoyed wealth and fame in abundance. He was known and admired in every part of the world, which called him variously, "the ambassador of good will," "the prince of wit and wisdom," "a homespun philosopher," "the most widely read columnist," "the most popular radio entertainer," and so on. To all of these eulogies Will grinned infectiously and confided in his inimitable drawl, "Folks, what you say about me ain't so, but I'm happy to hear you say it." No amount of adulation or wealth could keep him from being himself, and liking people for their good qualities. "I just kain't seem to dislike anybody I ever met," he frequently observed. "If I want to hate a person, I've got to stay away from him." In overalls, high-heeled cowboy boots and a battered old sweater, he roamed the movie lots, getting more pleasure from hobnobbing with the extras than with the highest-salaried personages in Hollywood. If he had any impatience with human frailties, snobbishness would head the list. "Please understand," he frequently took care to state, "that while I joke about royalty and the moneyed class, society people, presidents and statesmen, I don't look down upon 'em. They'd be just as good as anybody else if they had an equal chance!"

An ambassador without portfolio, Will was welcomed in every country he visited. His journeys usually took on the nature of triumphal tours, with royalty and populace at large receiving him with equal warmth. When the Prince of Wales visited America, Will was the person he most urgently wanted to see. In his usual worn, double-breasted blue serge, Will arrived at the Long Island Country Club to chat with the Prince, and was not at all perturbed to find everyone else in the most correct formal attire. "Hello, old timer," he greeted the Prince, "how are you falling these days?" And the Prince—now Duke of Windsor—laughed delightedly. "All over the place," he responded. "I've had a broken shoulder since I saw you last." Both referred to the days when they had first met, when the Prince had begun to go in wholeheartedly for polo and the steeplechase, taking a legendary number of spills. Later on, when Will rose to speak, the Prince continually pulled at his coat-tail, prompting him, "Tell them that one you told me about—!" And no one at the table seemed more to enjoy the informal, rambling talk. "Best prompter I ever had," Will chuckled later. "Plugged my act both ways; furnished more material than I could use!"

Most of the people who knew Will Rogers—and the number was legion—knew him primarily as the showman. He liked to be the center of every gathering, the laugh producer, the stimulus. But there was another side to his personality that was not so well known. "Will liked crowds," one of his close friends said. "He liked to know he was their hub, but when the crowd was gone and he was himself, the showman slipped away, and he put on his Indian blanket. . . . He far from wore his heart on his sleeve; when something close and personal came up he said very little, became almost taciturn. Then, the crisis over, he would be back at prankin', as he called it. Often I found it hard to believe that the cut-up before me was the person who, a few minutes before, had twirled his eyeglasses in his hands and stared at the floor, saying nothing at all." A story of the quick transition of

Will's two selves is told by a person who was deep
in a serious conversation with him one day concerning a new picture, in the stable lot at his Santa
Monica ranch. Some strangers drove up, having
taken the wrong turn, arriving at the barn instead
of the house. Immediately Will became the clown.
"Say!" he drawled. "The depression ain't that bad.
We're still livin' in the house. Don't know how
much longer we'll be there, but we're still there!"

Will had a closeness, and a delight in a bargain,
that bespoke his "nine thirty-seconds" of Cherokee
blood. He never had an agent, for he did not need
one. After talking business matters over with his
wife, he came to grips with the problem himself,
coming off more advantageously than anyone else
could have done. More than wealth, he enjoyed the
thought that despite his lack of financial acumen at
home, he had managed to win through to success.
He was neither extravagant nor niggardly in regard to spending his wealth, but he dipped deep
into his pockets for charities and private benefac-
tions. Broken-down actors, friendless waifs, and in-
digent Oklahomans seemed to gravitate to him,
and he never failed to aid them. He had a special
fondness, too, for polo ponies, and maintained a
pension farm near La Crescenta, California, where
he sent many a worn-out polo favorite whose
former prowess had come to his ear. Here they

lived in peace and comfort to the end of their lives. About his numerous charities, however, Will Rogers never talked.

Seven times he worked to raise funds for the National Red Cross. In 1933–34 he donated some $20,000 to reinstate public-health nursing in places where it had been discontinued because of the depression. The year 1930 saw him tour the Midwest to aid the drought victims. For a considerable period half of what he earned on the air was divided equally between the Red Cross and the Salvation Army. But so quiet were Will Rogers' philanthropies that his left hand scarcely knew what his right hand did. "For God's sake, don't tell this!" he begged in embarrassment once when caught in a benefaction to an old woman who had been evicted from her home. "Folks will say it was just a publicity stunt. A fellow kain't do nothin' without somebody blabbin'."

A prolific writer, Will turned out many books, articles and short paragraphs of Rogerisms. At the time of his death he was writing a short column for the daily papers, with the caption, "Will Rogers Says." It was syndicated to hundreds of newspapers all over the land. How he found time for it all was a mystery, until it became known that his portable typewriter was a faithful companion on all his junketing. He worked hard grinding out his observa-

tions even between acts on the stage. Among col-
umnists of his level, he had scarcely a peer, and the
familiar line, "All I know is what I read in the
papers," was usually the introduction to some particularly keen insight into men and events. One of
his best-known books, *The Illiterate Digest,* began
as a movie "short." The title struck a member of the
Literary Digest firm as a bit flippant, and he wrote
Will Rogers about it. Back came the author-actor's
reply in record time, stating that he had never felt
so "swelled up" in all his life by their suggestion of
competition on his part. "But," he added, "I had already stopped the screen, 'cause the gent who was
putting it on got behind in his payments, and my
humor kinda waned. In fact, after a few weeks of
no pay, I couldn't think of a single joke."

Will Rogers was only twenty-one when he got
his first glimpse of Betty Blake, the young schoolteacher sister of the depot agent at Oolagah. She
was sitting on the porch, and Will's heart left him
instantly. Too shy to ask for an introduction, he fig-
ured out a more roundabout way of achieving his
objective. The bicycle was just becoming popular.
Will bought one, and practiced some of the stunts
he had seen done by cycle artists on the stage. Then
he went whizzing down the street in front of Betty's
house, all set to show off his newly learned tricks.
Something went wrong, however. The bicycle

turned turtle, and Will landed on his head. Betty rushed to his rescue, and the acquaintance so abruptly begun ripened into friendship. Will bought a rubber-tired buggy, and in later years he always stoutly maintained that he wore out a complete set of tires driving around the country while trying to persuade Betty to say "Yes." Finally he had to leave her and go trouping through the Southwest. His tour ended at Madison Square Garden in 1905, where his sudden success sent him back to try his luck again with Betty. They were married November 26, 1908, and spent a very happy life together. "I ain't no real movie star," declared Will not long before his death. "I got the same wife I started out with nearly twenty-seven years ago." He always had complete confidence in his wife's judgment. "Whatever I am or have done," he frequently said, "I owe to Betty. I ain't got no sense myself; but for her I'd still be ridin' the range."

Their ranch home at Santa Monica typified the simple comforts that both loved. Here Will had his polo-field, and a nine-hole golf course—though he never played golf. "A feller kain't learn two things as complicated as golf and polo in one life-time," he asserted staunchly, "so I guess I'll stick to polo. A pony can help you think, but I ain't never heard of a golf club thinkin' none."

The three Rogers children were adept pupils in their father's favorite game, and he delighted keenly in his "ideal family polo team." But he never mentioned this to his audiences, for regarding his family Will Rogers was very reticent. He did not want them exploited for purposes of publicity, and the world at large was not aware that he had any children until a few short months before his death. Then the young Rogerses left their home to make a name for themselves: Will, Jr., to enroll at Stanford University; Mary to win a place in a stock company and follow in her father's footsteps; and Jimmy to enter the Claremont School in California.

Will Rogers had one passion which meant more to him than acting or polo: flying. In the air he enjoyed complete relaxation. With no interruptions of any kind, it was the ideal way to rest and think. Crossing the United States by plane over twenty-five times, in addition to his frequent globe-trotting on foreign soil, brought his flying record up to more than 300,000 air miles. He was dubbed "the prime minister of aviation" and "the special No. 1 air passenger of the United States." In fact, he was said to be the first unofficial person to hold a permit to ride in the mail planes. Always he advocated the safety of flight in modern planes, with trained pilots flying over carefully charted paths.

All the famous flyers of his day counted Will

Rogers as a friend. He went aloft with Lindbergh many times. Frank Hawks, the speed king of the air, flew all over the Southwest with Will when the latter made his tour on behalf of the Mississippi Valley flood victims. But it was Wiley Post, the one-eyed fellow Oklahoman, who was closest to Will's heart. They made numerous flights together, and it was early in August, 1935, that the two completed plans for a vacation in the air. They meant to make a leisurely trip to the least known parts of the globe, with no particular destination in view.

Taking off from Seattle for Point Barrow, the northernmost outpost of civilization on the continent, they landed at Juneau, their first stop. Here Post observed lazily as he stepped from the plane, "We'll just float around here in Alaska till we get real ready to take off for somewhere!" In the light of subsequent events, the remark was prophetic. After Juneau, they appeared at Dawson, Aklavik, Fairbanks and Anchorage. Then their hybrid, much built over plane landed in the Matanuska Valley. "How do you feel, Mr. Rogers?" somebody shouted from the crowd which quickly gathered about the plane. "Why, uh, wait'll I get out, kain't you?" stuttered Will, with mingled delight and surprise. "I ain't up here to talk about my health! Say—any you fellers from Claremore?"

From Matanuska Valley Will Rogers and Wiley

Post took off once more on their course to Point Barrow, "the roof of the world." On August 15, in the dim half-light of the midsummer Alaskan night, a lone Eskimo seal hunter was startled to see a red, low-winged plane skim gracefully along the shallow river where he was hunting. Suddenly the great wings tilted uncertainly, and the big bird paused. In a burst of speed, it climbed some fifty feet higher into the air. Then it stopped, shuddered, and plunged swiftly downward, crashing into the river bank in a tangled heap of wreckage. The startled Eskimo heard the dull roar of an explosion, and saw a film of gasoline and oil spreading out over the water. When he investigated to see if he might help anyone in the wrecked plane, there was no sign of life.

Without delay, he set off over the desolate, lake-dotted land that stretched fifteen miles to the nearest post, where he gasped out breathlessly, "Airplane she all blow up!" Soon the whole world knew the unhappy news that Will Rogers and his companion had crashed to their death.

But the memory of Will Rogers remained alive. For his life had been one of worthy achievement which consisted, not in doing, but in being a candid and wise spectator of those who did. To the busy, workaday public, the man with the cracker-barrel wit who twirled his lariat and watched the world go by was the sympathetic critic of ideas and customs about which they lacked the time to philosophize. As such he enjoyed a special greatness: that of being a beloved man the world over.

Grant Wood

During the 1930's, when he was at the height of his fame, Grant Wood was often acclaimed as the founder of the American Scene movement in art, or pointed out as the foremost of America's regional artists. Grant Wood, himself, did not think very much of such pompous titles. His own credo was a simple one. He believed that an artist ought to paint honestly and faithfully the things he knew best. And the things that Grant Wood knew best were the gently rolling fields, the quiet farm houses, and the plain spoken people of his native Iowa.

For Grant Wood's roots lay deep in America. His ancestors had come to this country long generations ago, and had proved themselves, all the way down the line, to be men of vision and courage. His grandfather, a Quaker, had left a prosperous busi-

ness in Winchester, Virginia, and had gone West
as a pioneer because he could not tolerate the sight
of slavery.

Grant was born on his father's farm near Ana-
mosa, Iowa, on February 13, 1892, the second of
four children. For the small, tow-headed boy in
whom the artist was already stirring, life on the
farm was wonderful. There was an endless variety
of things to do. He went fishing in the Wapsipin-
icon River; he made a very grown up and careful
listing of all the birds he had seen in the neighborhood; and he tagged about after the farm animals
watching their bustling activity with a curious intensity. The reason for the interest became apparent, when one day he gave his mother a drawing,
telling her proudly that it was a chicken. His
mother, not at all convinced, smiled her assent and
went back to her baking. From then on, the youngster began to seek out quiet corners where he would
sometimes spend the whole day working away at
little charcoal sketches which he took very seriously.

Probably Francis Maryville Wood would not
have been pleased had he known that his son,
Grant, would turn out to be an artist. He was a
practical man and a good farmer. He dreamed of
providing his sons with a fine inheritance in the
form of rich farm land. He worked from early

CJ NAAR

morning until late at night. Eventually the long years of work took their toll; and in the winter of 1901, he died of what may well have been overwork. With characteristic courage, Mrs. Wood sold the farm, and, with a part of the proceeds, bought a small house in nearby Cedar Rapids. On the balance of the money, she managed, miraculously, to raise her four children.

Hattie Wood's father felt that he ought to do something for his daughter's orphaned children. When her son, Frank, was old enough, he set him up in the automobile business. He would have done as much for Grant had the boy displayed the slightest interest in any such venture. But Grant, although he was undemonstrative and seldom spoke of his ambitions, had definite ideas about his career. He meant to be an artist.

Because he had no teacher, Grant had to learn almost all the rudiments of his craft by himself. This was undoubtedly a good thing for him, for it turned him into a jack-of-all-trades who experimented tirelessly in every artistic medium. He worked in plaster, in metal, in oils, and in water color. In high school, his prescribed studies went by the board, while the young artist spent his time designing sets for the school plays and making sketches for the school paper. With money he earned doing odd jobs around the town, he subscribed to a mail order course in design and set himself up with a fine drawing board, a set of good brushes, and a supply of water colors.

On the night of his graduation from high school, Grant took a train up to Minneapolis. There he enrolled at the Handicraft Guild for courses under Ernest Batchelder; and, almost in the same breath, asked about a job to pay his expenses. Not in the least fazed, Grant took the first job offered him— that of a caretaker in a morgue. No instruction that Grant received in later years ever meant so much to him as this course with Batchelder. From him he learned technique, respect for fine craftsmanship, and an understanding of the value of accurate design.

During the next few years, people in Cedar Rapids did not know quite what to make of Grant Wood. Everyone liked him, but he seemed to be drifting so aimlessly that they had serious doubts that he would ever amount to much as an artist. Certainly the reports of him were not encouraging. In 1913, he went up to Chicago and worked as a silversmith at the Kalo Shop. He found that dull and soon left. He enrolled at the Chicago Institute, attended classes intermittently, but did not complete the term. The next year, he and Christopher Haga, a young Norwegian, started a craft shop of their own. The Wolund Shop produced some interesting designs, attracted a little attention in art circles, and before long closed its doors. In 1916, Grant came home with no money and no job.

If Grant had no money, he had wise and loyal friends who believed in him and were willing to share whatever they had with him. In this crisis, Paul Hanson provided Grant and his mother with a place to live and even gave them a part of his meager salary. The place to live was a shack in the woods which Grant weatherproofed, and fitted out with bunks. Life there was rugged and often bitterly uncomfortable, but Mrs. Wood did not complain and, for the first time in years, Grant was free to work as he chose. He spent much time working over sketches of his mother and of his sister, Nan, always one of his favorite models. In the town, he acquired quite a little reputation as an interior decorator, and people who were planning a redecorating job always consulted him about it first.

His freedom, however, was short-lived. World War I found him at Camp Dodge in the camouflage division of the U.S. Army. Grant liked the camouflage work—it fitted in with his practical ideas—but his army service nearly cost him his life. He came down with anthrax and almost died. In 1918, he went home, still rather weak and shaky.

Like that of many another veteran, Grant's postwar future looked bleak. Again he had no money

and no job. Again he had good friends. His immediate guardian angel was Miss Frances Prescott,
principal of Jackson Junior High School. It seemed
unlikely that shy Grant Wood, with his slow speech
and ponderous manner, would make a good
teacher. Yet Miss Prescott liked him and, somewhat
prayerfully, arranged to have him appointed as a
teacher of art. The young man's methods of teaching were unorthodox, and he completely ignored
the requirements of taking attendance and keeping
grades. But as the term went on, he became a favorite with his pupils and he instilled in them a gen-
uine liking for the subject he taught. As for Grant,
he was inordinately proud of his students' work.
No one ever unveiled a great monument with more
flourish and enthusiasm than Grant displayed
when he unrolled a frieze painted by his high
school boys.

Now that his teaching was bringing him a steady
income, Grant began to look hopefully toward
Europe, the mecca of most young American artists.
He saved every cent he could, and in the summer
of 1920, he and his friend, Marvin Cone, made a
quick sightseeing tour of France. Three years later,
Grant asked for a leave of absence from his school
and went off again to Paris. This time he remained
abroad fourteen months, studying under French
masters, and traveling on the Continent. The pre-

liminary results were not impressive. For, according to his own description, he came home sporting a
pink beard that did not match his face, and convinced that the Midwest was inhibited and barren.
Another year or so went by, and in 1926, Grant was
able to hold an exhibition of his own paintings at
the Galerie Carmine in Paris. On the whole, his
work was well received, although one or two cap-
tious critics remarked that he had no soul.

When Grant Wood came back from his last trip
to Paris, he had accomplished most of the things
that were then expected of a young American
painter. He had studied in Europe; he had held a
European exhibition; and he carried with him
a creditable number of paintings, all done in the
blurred manner of the French Impressionists and
bearing such titles as *Fountain of Voltaire, Italian
Farmyard* and *Blue Vase, Sorrento*. He had every
reason to be satisfied with himself. But the outward
appearances were deceiving. Inwardly, Grant was
seething in a ferment of new ideas. His European
experiences had broadened him and given him a
new perspective. Much of his time abroad had been
spent in poring over the old masterpieces. As Grant
thought of the stern, clear lines and the exquisite
craftsmanship of the old masters, he rebelled at the
shoddy, careless work that passed as modern art.
One thought crystallized in his mind. He realized

that, if he were to become an artist of any stature, he must give up all this imitative work which bore no relation to any life that he knew. And he must paint, as best he could, the things that were close to him and which he understood. His heart pounded with excitement as he thought of the richness of his artistic heritage.

At home, a piece of good luck awaited him. Dave Turner, Cedar Rapids' funeral director, was Grant's life long friend and his first patron. For years, many of Grant's paintings had hung in Turner's chapel, and Dave had gone up and down the state preaching Grant Wood to anyone who would listen. Now he came to Grant and suggested that he give up teaching and devote his time entirely to his painting. To make this possible, he offered Grant the use of a loft above his garage for a studio. Grant liked the idea and spent the next month or so converting the dreary loft into an attractive studio. In a few short years, Number 5 Turner Alley became one of the most famous addresses in America.

Free to concentrate on his painting, Grant now embarked upon a decade of work that was to change the whole character of American art. Ordinarily, he was a slow worker, sometimes mulling over a single idea for months, even years. Now he seemed filled with a surge of brilliant creative energy, and in quick succession he produced a series of memorable paintings. *John B. Turner—Pioneer* was a portrait of Dave's father, and in it Grant caught the quiet pride and the stern self-reliance of America's early settlers. *Woman with Plants* was a labor of love, a painting of Grant's mother, and in its dignity and strength it showed how deep was Grant's affection for her. *American Gothic* made its appearance at the Chicago Art Institute in 1930 and was awarded the Harris prize. Plain people looked at this painting of a tight-lipped farmer and his daughter standing before their unpretentious home, and they liked it for they saw themselves in it. Art critics looked at the painting and were startled. They rushed home to announce pontifically in their journals that in Grant Wood, America had a major new artist with a rich, original talent and a distinctively American style.

In 1932, Grant was able to carry out one of his most cherished ambitions, that of founding an art colony in Iowa. Early in the year, he combed the Midwest for a faculty, and that summer the Stone City Colony opened for a six weeks' course on the site of an abandoned quarry. The fees were nominal and the only requirement for admission was a desire to do some kind of creative work. The students bunked in old ice wagons, and thought it was all very gay and carefree and exciting. Grant, too, thoroughly enjoyed the summer, for he knew how much the opportunity to work in a sympathetic environment could mean to an aspiring artist. It was a great blow to him when the little colony floundered in its second year and did not open for a third term.

Stone City was always of special interest to Grant Wood, for it was the setting for one of his most famous landscapes. This painting and the group of stylized landscapes that followed it, *Young Corn, Spring Turning,* and the *Birthplace of Herbert Hoover,* did much to confuse the critics who attempted to evaluate Grant's work. They were powerful in design, curiously effective, apparently realistic, yet each had a strangely unreal quality. In despair, the critics took to calling Grant an "unreal realist."

Grant Wood was a man of broad sympathies and, like all sensitive persons, he was deeply affected by the depression which swept across America in the 1930's. Appalling poverty in the midst of plenty was something which he could not understand. He tried to find the reasons for this, and he began to take an interest in politics. Little by little, there crept into his work a note of caustic social comment. As an artist's protest against smug reaction, he painted his immortal *Daughters of Revolution.* There is mockery in every line of this painting. In the background is a powerful reproduction of Washington Crossing the Delaware. In the foreground are three rigid ladies, prissily discussing the latest gossip over a teacup. This brilliant satire brought down a torrent of wrath upon Grant's head. Some of the more vociferous patriotic societies demanded that it be withdrawn from exhibition. In other quarters, the artist was accused of being subversive and a radical. Grant took the criticism in his stride. He was not the first man to be called a radical because he hated hypocrisy and complacency.

During his artistic life, Grant went through a great many phases, but probably the painting most typical of him at his best is *Dinner for Threshers* which he completed in 1934. This large work shows a farmhouse kitchen with the hired hands at dinner and in the background a portion of the farmyard. The scene is one that recalls the farm of Grant's youth, and into it he put all his meticulous concern for detail, his passion for authenticity. It is a painting of the American Midwest as Grant Wood saw it, and that is as close to the truth as anyone could get.

In a way *Dinner for Threshers* marked the end of an epoch for Grant. His fame began to exact its price, and there were more and more distractions to keep him from his work. As the depression deepened across America, Federal Art Projects were set up in every state, and Grant was chosen to supervise twenty-four of the thirty-four Iowa projects. This entailed a wearying amount of traveling all over the state. That same year he was appointed as associate professor of art at the University of Iowa. His old love of teaching came back and he subordinated his own plans to those of his students. He envisioned a series of frescoes which were to be done for the university and he made designs for a new chapel on the campus. Suddenly in the spring of 1935, he married and moved with his wife to Iowa City to an old house which he had bought there. Characteristically, he tore the house apart, remodeling it from top to bottom to meet his exacting tastes.

Sometimes Grant used to complain that he was a dull fellow with nothing interesting about him. Yet an extraordinary number of people seemed to find in the Iowa artist a rare and rich personality. From all over the country, scores of noted people came to visit him at his home, not because he was famous, but because they liked his warmth and his casual friendliness. Grant was rarely too busy for his friends. He enjoyed good company and good talk, and he took a generous part in the merry tomfoolery that went on at the university under the guise of a Society to Prevent Cruelty to Speakers.

Always a down-to-earth kind of artist, Grant did not believe that art was a cloistered thing remote from the life of the people behind it. His own record was ample proof of that, for he had turned his talents to many a practical use. When one of his sketches was used as a decoration for a menu, he was rather more flattered than otherwise. In his student days, he had put some of his best effort into a mural for a local realtor. Asked to do a poster for an accident prevention campaign, he considered it an important assignment. In this period when his energies were being dissipated over a wide area, Grant came to emphasize the practical aspects of art even more than usual. He did a group of illustrations for a limited edition of Sinclair Lewis' *Main Street,* and he undertook a lithographing project designed to reproduce great paintings at very little cost.

Of course, all this was ammunition for Grant's critics. They began to speak slightingly of him as a gifted illustrator; they praised his draftsmanship, but ignored his creative talents. In part, because he wished to defend himself; and in part, because he believed that he could create a wider public understanding of the artist's problems, Grant made a lecture tour around the country. For years he had been tagged with all sorts of labels which he was now asked to explain. He told his audiences what he thought of all this. He had no patience with the so-called "schools of painting" or with rigid standards. "All I shall contend for," he said, "is the sincere use of native materials by the artist who is in command of them."

After a while, Grant managed to cut himself clear of all these activities which were consuming his time and energy. He went home to Cedar Rapids and began to paint again. With all his old brilliance and his gift for satire, he soon produced *Parson Weems' Fable*. This was a retelling of the legend of George Washington and the cherry tree. In the foreground, Grant depicted George, his father, and the cherry tree reduced to very unheroic proportions; while, in the background, big as life, stood Parson Weems, the instigator of this wopping tale, viewing the whole proceeding with a jaundiced eye. *Parsons Weems' Fable* was another of Grant's controversial paintings, but he got more fun out of it than of anything else he had ever done. In 1940, Grant took his first trip to Hollywood where he did a painting of one of the scenes from the motion picture, *The Long Voyage Home*. This picture, *Sentimental Ballad,* one of the last things he did, was in his best narrative vein and was very well received.

In the fall of 1941, Grant Wood could no longer hide the fact that he was a sick man. He entered the University Hospital, underwent an operation, and for a time put up a brave front for his friends, telling them of his plans for the future. But he understood that he would never leave the hospital alive. As he thought over his career he had few regrets; he had enjoyed life and had had the best kind of success a man can have—that of being able to spend a lifetime in the work he loved. He died on February 12, 1942.

Grant Wood's final place in American art is not yet determined. The controversy over his work still rages, and the critics can't make up their minds whether he was an inspired artist, an imaginative reporter, or merely a plodding craftsman. It may be that he was something of all three. It remains that few artists anywhere in the world have ever been able to interpret their native lands so sensitively, or to bring home to the plain people a greater awareness of the role that art plays in modern life.

As one looks at the record, one is struck by the number and variety of Grant Wood's paintings and by the care which he lavished on every one of them. Through every change of style and mood, Grant remained true to his own ideal. He painted the things he understood to the best of his ability.

A few of Grant Wood's paintings are to be found in galleries. Others are in the possession of wealthy owners. But by far the greater number are to be found in the homes of everyday people all over the country. That is the way Grant Wood wanted it to be.

Index

26622

.j920
BOL

Bolton, Sarah K.

Lives of poor boys
who became famous